HOW TO SCORE
IN **HOLLYWOOD**

HOW TO SCORE IN HOLLYWOOD

SECRETS TO SUCCESS IN THE MOVIE BUSINESS

KEVIN GOETZ
WITH BOB LEVIN

SIMON ELEMENT

NEW YORK AMSTERDAM/ANTWERP LONDON
TORONTO SYDNEY/MELBOURNE NEW DELHI

SIMON
ELEMENT

An Imprint of Simon & Schuster, LLC
1230 Avenue of the Americas
New York, NY 10020

For more than 100 years, Simon & Schuster has championed authors and the stories they create. By respecting the copyright of an author's intellectual property, you enable Simon & Schuster and the author to continue publishing exceptional books for years to come. We thank you for supporting the author's copyright by purchasing an authorized edition of this book.

No amount of this book may be reproduced or stored in any format, nor may it be uploaded to any website, database, language-learning model, or other repository, retrieval, or artificial intelligence system without express permission. All rights reserved. Inquiries may be directed to Simon & Schuster, 1230 Avenue of the Americas, New York, NY 10020 or permissions@simonandschuster.com.

Copyright © 2025 by Kevin Goetz

All rights reserved, including the right to reproduce this book or portions thereof in any form whatsoever. For information, address Simon Element Subsidiary Rights Department, 1230 Avenue of the Americas, New York, NY 10020.

First Simon Element hardcover edition November 2025

SIMON ELEMENT is a trademark of Simon & Schuster, LLC

Simon & Schuster strongly believes in freedom of expression and stands against censorship in all its forms. For more information, visit BooksBelong.com.

For information about special discounts for bulk purchases, please contact Simon & Schuster Special Sales at 1-866-506-1949 or business@simonandschuster.com.

The Simon & Schuster Speakers Bureau can bring authors to your live event. For more information or to book an event, contact the Simon & Schuster Speakers Bureau at 1-866-248-3049 or visit our website at www.simonspeakers.com.

Illustrations by Alexis Seabrook

Manufactured in the United States of America

10 9 8 7 6 5 4 3 2 1

Library of Congress Cataloging-in-Publication Data has been applied for.

ISBN 978-1-9821-8986-0
ISBN 978-1-9821-8987-7 (ebook)

The pathway to success is determined by the right decisions made along the way. To my husband, Neil, the best decision of my life.

CONTENTS

FOREWORD BY JIM GIANOPULOS   IX

INTRODUCTION   1

1. IF YOU WANT A BIG AUDIENCE, YOU NEED A BIG IDEA   5
2. DON'T MAKE A MOVIE FOR NOBODY!   43
3. GOOD ISN'T GOOD ENOUGH   69
4. FEATHERED FISH CAN NEITHER SWIM NOR FLY   99
5. FIX IT BEFORE YOU SHOOT IT   127
6. DANGER SIGNS ALONG THE ROAD TO COMPLETION   157
7. BALANCING THE ART AND THE AUDIENCE   183

EPILOGUE: EVERY MOVIE SHOULD MAKE MONEY   213

ACKNOWLEDGMENTS   243

NOTES   246

INDEX OF FILM TITLES   247

INDEX OF NAMES   253

FOREWORD

THOSE OF US WHO HAVE THE PRIVILEGE of working in the art and commerce of making movies recognize the enormous contributions of the wide variety of talent that it takes to make them successful. Success takes great writers, directors, producers, actors, editors, effects people, and composers. Yet there is another talent that people outside of Hollywood may not know about, a secret weapon that most of us have relied upon as we bring our movies to completion: Kevin Goetz. He and his team of research analysts and strategists truly understand the complete life cycle of a movie. Among the many things they do are putting audiences in seats nearly every night of the week, inviting them to watch movies before they are released to the public at large, and synthesizing the audiences' opinions into actionable next steps that filmmakers and studio executives take to heart as they put the final touches on their films. Kevin does that better than anyone I've ever met, and I've been doing this a long time.

That is not where Kevin's talent ends, however. He has been an important figure in the film industry for decades, knows everyone, hears the griping and frustrations on every side of the business, rejoices right alongside us when there are big wins, and stands with us when there are disappointments. He brings data. He brings perspective. Most important, he is an advocate for the ticket-buying audience, and he brings their voices into the room whenever we are trying to figure out what's working in a film, where there are opportunities to make it better, and when we need to admit that drastic changes are required.

FOREWORD

Over the years, Kevin and I have had many discussions about the films I've had a hand in green-lighting. He's asked probing questions about the validity of the ideas, the talent behind and in front of the camera, and the positioning of the films in the marketplace. We've talked about other movies that are comparable to the ones that I've agreed to make, how those pictures have fared at the box office, and who turned out to see them in theaters. We have debated about the use of research at the concept stage and how the industry can make better choices when gauging the level of investment against the size of the potential audience.

No one sets out to make a bad movie or one that will achieve less than its aspiration. Every film that gets made really does seem like a great idea at the time, and often it is. But along the journey of making that film, from its initial concept to the finished product, stuff just happens. And when those well-intentioned artists and the studio executives who back their visions have their first look at the initial film assembly, sometimes their expectations are met or even exceeded, but other times, well, not so much. And that's when Kevin and his team put their brilliant work into action.

The preview process informs both the final version of the film and the marketing strategy for its potential audience. It can be a celebratory event when the test audience laughs and cheers and applauds and scores it through the roof. When that happens, of course, everybody involved is happy and beaucoup marketing bucks start flowing. Other times the audience fidgets, there are awkward silences, there is unintended laughter, and the test scores come in looking pretty grim. This is when Kevin is truly the most important talent of them all. Where was the audience confused, bored, distracted, or out of the narrative flow of the movie? And why did all those people leave early, before the movie was even over? Understanding what's working, what isn't, what's holding back all or part of that audience sitting out there in the dark is an art form in and of itself. In that respect, Kevin is Picasso.

FOREWORD

Some of Kevin's talent lies in analyzing the data, but even studio executives like me could figure most of that out. Looking behind the numbers and interpreting the audience's message is another aspect of Kevin's brilliance. And there's more—the focus groups that are held after the screenings, which is when a smaller subset of moviegoers selected from the entire audience provide top-of-mind impressions about what they just saw. Managing the dynamic of that group, putting them at ease, drilling into their insights, filtering out their occasionally wacky, insane digressions, are all part of his unequaled skills.

Then there's perhaps the most important job of all, which is actually making the changes the film needs. Filmmakers, particularly directors, have spent many months, often years, making the film that is about to emerge into the world. They've toiled for endless hours to capture a certain scene or write a character arc or shoot that massive sequence or set piece. So it's often very painful for them to edit out what they've worked so hard to make, no matter what the test audience, the studio, or anyone else says. That is the case even when they're convinced it truly takes four hours to tell their story.

I once held a preview of a film by a very big director. As we walked out of the screening, he asked, "Well, what did you think?"

"You know what? It doesn't matter what I think. It actually doesn't matter what *you* think. It only matters what *they* think," I said as I gestured back to the crowd filling out the surveys in the theater. He was a little shocked, but he knew I was right.

Kevin is the way we find the answer to that important question "What did you think?" The first thing Kevin says when he welcomes an audience to a test screening is, "Look, I don't have anything to do with the making of this film, so feel free to be honest. It won't hurt my feelings." His ability to bring that objective insight and his enormous credibility as a preview maven serves to help convince even the most reluctant filmmakers when and how they need to make changes.

The Oscar-winning director of *The Revenant*, Alejandro Iñárritu, once said, "To make a film is easy. To make a good film is war. To make a great film is a miracle." Well, in that process, Kevin is a miracle worker. Thanks to Kevin, many good films have found their way to becoming great films, and many great movies have found the best path to their audience. Some not-so-great movies got better and others, well, maybe we had to admit they weren't such a great idea after all, and even the brilliance of Kevin Goetz couldn't save them.

Kevin and I have had a lot of adventures together over the years. He and his company, Screen Engine, were intimately involved in the testing and fine-tuning of *A Quiet Place*, *Mission: Impossible—Fallout*, *Rocketman*, and *Sonic the Hedgehog* (to name a few) during the years I served as chairman and CEO of Paramount Pictures. Our collaboration goes back decades, however, and during my tenure as chairman of Fox Filmed Entertainment, Kevin conducted research on nearly all our movies, including *Titanic*, *Planet of the Apes*, *Ice Age*, *Night at the Museum*, *Avatar*, *Kingsman: The Secret Service*, *The Martian*, and *Deadpool*.

Over the many years we worked together in finishing movies, Kevin was always an enormously helpful partner in the process for both the studio and the filmmakers. He continues to be a gracious and kind and honest voice during our journey, and he will forever be a treasured friend. I have relied on his input, and I trust him implicitly. If you are as fortunate as I have been to build a career in the movie industry, I know you will find the wisdom Kevin shares in *How to Score in Hollywood*, gleaned from his decades of experience working on movies, large and small, of great value.

—JIM GIANOPULOS

HOW TO SCORE
IN **HOLLYWOOD**

INTRODUCTION

How many times have you watched a seriously flawed movie, regretted wasting two hours of your time, and asked yourself, "How did this film get the green light? How did it make it past development? With all the power, money, and creative talent that Hollywood offers, how could such a disaster end up on the screen?"

Then there are those truly special films that generate buzz throughout the entertainment industry and stay on your mind for days; the ones you can't wait to discuss with colleagues and friends, to encourage others to see, and to root for when Oscar nominations are announced. You might wonder how Quentin Tarantino, Martin Scorsese, Christopher Nolan, Greta Gerwig, fill-in-the-blank greatest-of-all-time director pulled out all the stops to serve up such a delicious slice of movie magic.

Why are some movies so satisfying and memorable, while others go so terribly wrong? And what about those that fall somewhere in the murky middle, neither great nor awful, but with little chance of being financially successful? Wouldn't it be interesting to know how all these films were conceived, pitched, perhaps rejected, revised, pitched again, and finally green-lit?

I am the proverbial fly on the wall, someone who has been privy to some of the most intimate discussions about the films that Hollywood turns out, the decisions that are weighed in the process, and the risks that are ultimately taken. But I don't work for a studio. I am the founder and CEO of Screen Engine, one of the leading market research companies serving the entertainment industry. My colleagues and I test all things movie related, a process we describe as "from script to screen." We conduct studies on very basic concept descriptions (loglines), table reads, rough cuts, fully assembled movies before they are complete, or "locked," and the marketing materials—trailers, commercials, and one-sheet posters—that are used to promote the finished films to ticket-buying audiences and streaming service subscribers.

While I don't particularly like describing myself as an insect, I recognize the importance of being a fly on the wall, removed from the hubbub, and agnostic. I can assess a movie with enough distance, and usually accompanied by a boatload of data, to remain objective. That's a big advantage, because everyone associated with the production becomes myopic over the months and years that it takes to bring a major motion picture to completion. The studio people, writers, directors, producers, and editors have too much skin in the game to see things clearly all the time. I, on the other hand, represent the audience. I view every movie as if I am shelling out the money for a ticket, grabbing a bucket of popcorn, and settling in for an evening of entertainment.

In my line of work, I listen to what prospective moviegoers and focus group participants have to say when movies are still in the concept stage before a single frame is shot, and later, what test audiences think after they have watched an early cut of the film before its release. Let me tell you, those audiences don't hold back. Then I interpret and synthesize their collective opinions so the studio and filmmakers can make decisions moving forward, on either how to change or refine the film, lock it, or market it.

I've learned a lot during my tenure in the business and I've seen it all, from the frustrations, disappointments, and accompanying excuses to the biggest successes that have launched careers and made fortunes. I've been doing this for nearly four decades and have worked on over five thousand films. In these pages, I will share precepts gleaned from my years of observation, data collection, and analysis. My intent is to provide "tools, not

INTRODUCTION

hard-and-fast rules," an idiom I've heard bandied about by some of the most creative minds in the business. There will always be exceptions, but the guidance I'm providing applies to the vast majority of movies that seek to find big audiences.

Over the years, I have seen the industry evolve in many ways, perhaps most seismically through the changes sparked by the COVID-19 pandemic. Streaming is now the primary way audiences consume content, and going to a movie theater has become more of a special event. As a result, studios have shifted their measures of success. Box office is still important as the gold standard for *theatrical* releases. But other metrics, specifically for the streaming services, are now in place to track the length of engagement, how much buzz a film generates, whether it draws new subscribers and retains existing ones, and if it has the potential to launch or sustain a franchise. Marketing strategies have shifted as well, to social media and algorithm-driven targeting. For many content providers, new benchmarks such as viewership minutes and completion rates have become just as important as ticket sales. At the same time, the explosion of global markets producing their homegrown offerings across multiple platforms has opened new opportunities for stories that wouldn't have made it to a wide release a decade ago. All of this has altered how we gauge success and profitability, but it doesn't change the fact that good storytelling and smart strategy are just as important as ever.

I realize that not all films are made to make a profit. Some are passion projects that are financed by those who have deep pockets and a message to convey to the world. But those films are rare. Virtually all movies made by Hollywood's studios and production companies are capitalist endeavors, made with the intent to appeal to mass audiences and turn a profit. In the process, we hope they are also turning out art. The art and commercial sides of filmmaking are not mutually exclusive, and that is a basic premise I hope to demonstrate in these pages.

One of the biggest personal rewards of longevity as a motion picture strategist is that I've established close relationships with nearly all the top-tier studio executives and contemporary filmmakers. Most consider me an adviser, a confidant, even a partner. Many are personal friends. So the lessons that I outline in this book are brought to life by commentary and examples that these Hollywood insiders and friends have shared. Because I am still actively involved in the business and must protect my clients' and friends' confidences, I *personally* cannot tell tales out of school. But that hasn't prevented others from telling their stories, which they have graciously contributed to illustrate the key points made in each chapter. A word of caution: Some of these stories disclose surprises, twists, and endings in famous films, so consider this a blanket spoiler alert.

How to Score in Hollywood is a road map for making every movie the best version that it can possibly be and for the right price, avoiding the common mistakes that can derail a good idea, and knowing when to make corrections if necessary. It's not just about scoring; it's about scoring *well* and being invited into the inner sanctum of success in a tough business where the stakes are high and the rewards are higher still. If you currently work in the film industry—or aspire to—if you are a student of film, or if you simply love hearing stories about how movies get made, this is the book for you. Many of the lessons are also applicable to other industries, and the stories behind the movie examples are, well, just fun to read.

CHAPTER 1

If You Want a Big Audience, You Need a Big Idea

A GOOD STORY CAN BE THE UNDERPINNING OF A GOOD MOVIE, but not necessarily of one with broad appeal. Films that attract huge audiences and spark enthusiastic word of mouth almost always start with something more—a big idea that evokes a feeling, an *aha* realization that the concept will be transcendent. Every successful movie, even if there is a familiarity about it, stirs an emotional response. It sings to you, hits you in the solar plexus, inspires an urgency to see it. Some don't start out as big ideas but percolate over time and evolve to a rarified status where they resonate with large swaths of the movie-consuming population.

A movie about Barbie was not a big idea. The doll had been around for more than six decades, and while over a billion had been sold around the world, some of the luster had worn off the brand as social conventions changed in the late twentieth and early twenty-first centuries. Women felt Barbie represented an antiquated sense of femininity, and mothers worried about their daughters developing unrealistic ideas about body image.

Over the years, Mattel earnestly attempted to diversify the line of dolls, introducing professional versions and role models that were casually referred to as "sheroes." New body types, including "curvy" Barbie, were also added, as well as skin tones, eye colors, facial features, and hair textures representing different racial and ethnic groups. Yet the perception of Barbie as a blond Caucasian persisted, dating the brand and sparking criticism.

Several dozen animated Barbie films, most of them straight-to-video, and a handful of Barbie TV series had already been made. The notion of a live-action movie had been kicked around Hollywood for years, first with Anne Hathaway attached and then with Amy Schumer. (Okay, I admit the Amy Schumer idea was certainly intriguing, but would a large audience turn out to see an R-rated comedy star in what everyone perceived as G-rated material?) Yet even with such big-name talent attached, a Barbie feature film did not get off the ground.

Enter the two Robbies—Robbie Brenner, the newly hired executive at Mattel who was brought in to get their film division underway, and Margot Robbie, the enormously talented actor and producer whom most agree is as close to a human embodiment of the original Barbie as anyone could be.

The year was 2018 and Robbie Brenner, the former president of production at Relativity Media and the Academy Award–nominated producer of *Dallas Buyers Club*, had just joined Mattel, where she would oversee the development of their popular toy brands into movie franchises. I had known Brenner for years; my company, Screen Engine, had been commissioned by Relativity to test nearly all their movies—*Immortals*, *Safe Haven*, and *Mirror Mirror*, to name a few—and I had also tested several other films Brenner had produced outside of Relativity. On the weekends, she and I walked our dogs together, sharing our thoughts about life and the business, and I consider her a dear friend.

Brenner brought me in to conduct research on a long list of Mattel brands, the objective being to uncover which would inspire the greatest interest among moviegoers if they were used as the basis for theatrical films. When the results were in, Barbie landed at the bottom of the list. The brand was beloved by many, had tremendous awareness, and was nostalgic among adult women. But the data told us that outside of very young girls and some of their mothers, there was not much excitement for a Barbie movie. I told Brenner to run from it.

Other Mattel intellectual property (or IP) had fared much better in the research, and I suggested a more promising idea, a Magic 8 Ball movie in collaboration with Blumhouse. Jason Blum and his head of features, Couper Samuelson, could give it the horror imprimatur that would generate traction among genre fans, make it for a reasonable price, and Brenner would have her first win at Mattel—maybe not a home run, but certainly a strong double. She liked that idea but told me, "I have no choice. I have to make a Barbie movie. It's Mattel's biggest brand."

Meanwhile, Ynon Kreiz, the chairman and CEO of Mattel, struck a deal with Margot Robbie, who was interested not only in portraying the title role but in developing the idea. She and her husband, Tom Ackerley, have a production company, LuckyChap Entertainment, and they were all in. So Robbie Brenner and Tom Ackerley teamed up to gather script ideas.

"We met with about thirty different writers," Brenner recalled, "and heard thirty different Barbie movie takes. These were major writers. There was no shortage of people who were interested in trying to unlock this Barbie movie. But the ideas were sort of generic—she lives in Malibu, has her dreamboat, Ken—and it all seemed very familiar. You had seen it before. Nothing really stuck out."

Then Margot Robbie came up with the idea of bringing on writer/director Greta Gerwig. At that point, Gerwig had directed only two films, the critically acclaimed but very arthouse *Lady Bird* and the 2019 remake of *Little Women*, which had been commercially successful but was by no means a movie made for everyone. Gerwig was interested in the Barbie movie, and Brenner thought she might very well be the key to finding the solution they were looking for.

"We needed to do something very unexpected and very different, and with Greta, I felt we were going to get that secret sauce that most movies don't have," said Brenner. "From the very first frame of *Lady Bird*, when she [the title character, played by Saoirse Ronan] opens the car door and falls out, I was in. Greta is interesting and tells stories in such a dynamic way. So when I heard Greta Gerwig wanted to make *Barbie*, I was like, 'Sign me up!'"

Greta wanted her life partner, Noah Baumbach, to write the movie with her. So Margot Robbie, Robbie Brenner, and Tom Ackerley flew to New York for a meeting with Greta and Noah. They discussed broad ideas, and Brenner said, "Just sitting in the room with Greta was effervescent." Gerwig told the group that she envisioned the movie living somewhere between a high heel and a Birkenstock. That was a brilliant insight and a leaping-off point for the script. Brenner said, "As much as some people play with Barbie, love Barbie, identify with Barbie, others don't like her. She makes them feel bad about the way they look, makes them think they need to be perfect. What Greta and Noah did so brilliantly in the script is that they unpacked all of that. They talked about how it feels to look a certain way and *not* be perfect." With this talented team on board, and a deal already struck with Warner Bros., *Barbie* was underway.

David Heyman, the hugely successful and prolific producer, oversaw the entire project. Oh, did I mention that he also produced a few other hits like the *Harry Potter* and *Fantastic Beasts* franchises, the *Paddington* movies, *Once Upon a Time . . . in Hollywood*, *Gravity*, and *Wonka*? Talk about accomplishments (and with a posh British accent to boot!).

When *Barbie* was finished, my company conducted the first test screening in Arizona to a "blindly recruited" audience, where moviegoers only knew that they would be previewing a new comedy with a PG-13 rating, but did not know the title until they were seated in the theater. The studio was nervous about spoilers and word getting out, which was the reason for testing it away from Hollywood and to an unsuspecting audi-

IF YOU WANT A BIG AUDIENCE, YOU NEED A BIG IDEA

ence. Like all screenings that we conduct, attendees were required to sign nondisclosure agreements (NDAs), and we also took photos of everyone before they entered the theater and validated them against their IDs.

That first cut of *Barbie* played well enough, but when it was tested a second time in New Jersey with editorial changes made and an audience that knew beforehand what they would be seeing, the reception was mind-blowing. By now, the trailer had dropped, and as we arrived at the theater, a sea of pink extended for two blocks, foreshadowing what would occur at theaters across the world during the summer of 2023. Moviegoers of all genders and ages would arrive in delicious shades of pink and enter the Barbie Land world for an hour and fifty-four minutes of unadulterated fun.

Barbie may not have started with a big idea, but it certainly ended up as one. With Robbie Brenner's experience and exquisite taste, Margot Robbie and Tom Ackerley's determination to bring the project to life, David Heyman's oversight, and Greta Gerwig and Noah Baumbach's vision, it became a motion picture sensation. Where others had tried, this "dream team" cracked the code, changed the DNA of the Barbie brand, and elevated Mattel in the process, making it feel modern and cool. As Brenner says, "*Barbie* is the perfect intersection of art and commerce."

HOW DO YOU RECOGNIZE A BIG IDEA, especially if it develops over time, as *Barbie* did? Perhaps the best test is consensus. When everyone who hears about an idea feels that it is something special, it is probably a big idea. When it isn't a tough sell, either to the studio executives who are green-lighting it (giving it formal approval to move forward into production) or to the ticket-buying public, it's probably a big idea. Jason Blum, the horror impresario behind Blumhouse, says, "A big idea is one that can be described in a single sentence. If it takes five sentences, it's not really a big idea. The best ideas can be two words—*Wedding Crashers*. You know exactly what that movie is from the title!"

That brings me to another litmus test I use, which is the film's potential to elevate the genre into which it falls. By elevating the genre, I mean setting a higher standard that transcends the typical script conventions, clichés, and expectations associated with that genre. Additionally, films can be elevated through other means such as star power, stylized production values, and innovative cinematography and visuals. Films grounded in a big idea typically set a new bar for anything in the genre that follows it. It's what *Wedding Crashers* and *The 40-Year-Old Virgin* did for the R-rated comedy genre in 2005. *Despicable Me* raised the bar for animated family films in 2010. In 2018, *A Quiet Place* distinguished itself in the horror genre, while *Crazy Rich Asians* elevated the romantic comedy genre. In 2023, *Taylor Swift: The Eras Tour* set a new standard for concert films, and without a studio behind it. Big ideas all around.

From my perspective, big movie ideas tend to fall into three categories. The first is **something familiar told in a unique way or with a fresh spin**. *Barbie* is a perfect example of this. Baz Luhrmann's dazzling 2022 film *Elvis* also comes to mind. Most of us knew the basics of the life story of the King of Rock 'n' Roll. Luhrmann brought his signature magic touch to the film, using color and set design that transported us back in time to those iconic performances and moments in Elvis Presley's life that we'd previously only glimpsed in old photos and video clips. Aside from Austin Butler's stunning performance in the titular role, what also made that movie jump off the screen was Baz Luhrmann stylistically transforming what might have been another musical biopic in the hands of anyone else into a truly big idea. In my opinion, Luhrmann was every bit the star of *Elvis*. Watching that film, I felt like I was discovering something new about the rock-and-roll legend and getting a closer look than ever before at the larger-than-life artist.

IF YOU WANT A BIG AUDIENCE, YOU NEED A BIG IDEA

Remakes also fall into this "familiar but with a fresh spin" group, but only if they offer something that is entirely different from the original movie in some way. I think of another Baz Luhrmann movie, the highly stylized 1996 *Romeo + Juliet*, entirely different from Franco Zeffirelli's 1968 film, or the 2001 Steven Soderbergh version of *Ocean's Eleven*, a finely honed remake of the so-so 1960 Rat Pack movie of the same name.

The 2006 film *300* is another good example of familiar territory that was conceived with such groundbreaking style that it reinvented the genre and did huge business around the world. The project was led by producer Mark Canton, who before his involvement with this film had held top positions at Warner Bros., where he was executive vice president of production, and then at Sony as chairman of Columbia Pictures. At the time the idea of *300* was floated, Canton had his own independent production company.

300 is the story of King Leonidas of Sparta and his force of three hundred men who fought the Persians at Thermopylae in 480 BC. In Hollywood genre jargon, that's a historically based "sword-and-sandal" movie. Many similar stories had already been brought to the big screen, and it was going to be a steep uphill climb to get a studio behind this one, because a recent big-budget film in the genre, *Alexander*, had not done enough business to turn a profit.

I wouldn't fault you for wondering what even attracted Canton and his partners to spend any of their energy on such a project. The key to their interest, the sell, and the ultimate success of the movie was the source material, a historically inspired 1998 cult graphic novel written and illustrated by Frank Miller. Miller was already well known in Hollywood as the writer behind both *RoboCop 2* and *RoboCop 3*, and as cowriter and codirector of the *Sin City* film adaptation of another of his acclaimed graphic novels. The *300* series had a unique, original, bold, and dynamic illustrative look.

A friend of Canton's, producer Gianni Nunnari, had acquired the one-year option to try to sell the rights to make a movie based on the book series. When frustrated by not getting much interest, and with that year running out, Nunnari asked Canton to meet with him and Frank Miller to see if Canton had any ideas about what to do. The meeting was at Canton's home, and when his teenage son walked into the room where the three were meeting, he picked up the *300* book that was on the table. Paging through it, he said, "Dad, this is the greatest! This looks so cool; you have to do this one."

His son's enthusiasm captured Canton's attention. If his teenage son thought a movie about King Leonidas looked cool, there must be something special about this idea. Nunnari explained to Canton how he envisioned a film that would be just as exciting as the graphic novel. But it wasn't the story that would capture audience interest, it would be the unique visual style of the picture.

Nunnari had already brought on Zack Snyder to help realize that vision, having seen Snyder's movie *Dawn of the Dead* and believing that he was a director who could translate the look on the printed page into a successful major motion picture. Now convinced and without hesitation, Canton called his agent and told him to negotiate the $100,000 that would extend the option for another year.

Working over many months, the filmmakers put together a graphic presentation of what the *300* movie could look like and took it to Warner Bros. to see if they could persuade the studio to bankroll it. Picture them in the room: Canton and his team thought their presentation was spectacular and clearly demonstrated the potential of their big idea. With experience and success on their résumés and skin in the game (they'd already invested that initial $100K of their own money in the project), they made a confident pitch to the Warner Bros. executives, most of whom they had professional and social relationships with. On the other side of the table,

IF YOU WANT A BIG AUDIENCE, YOU NEED A BIG IDEA

the studio decision-makers were skeptical. The genre was challenging, and at its core, the story was a boring history lesson. The execution was unique, but would the film be commercial?

Undaunted and with complete conviction, the filmmakers kept the project alive, and the door was left open to further discussion with Warner Bros. But the big question remained: Could the movie be visually exciting and entertaining *enough* to overcome the typicality of the sword-and-sandal genre? Could the execution be the basis for a must-see film?

Curious enough to want to answer those and other questions, the studio finally paved the way to fund a proof of concept. With a million dollars and the use of a studio soundstage, the filmmakers were given the opportunity to deliver a two- to three-minute sequence. When the edited and completed result was shown in a studio screening room, it vividly displayed the compelling potential for *300* to be an entertaining, groundbreaking, worldwide box office success. The battle sequence that was created was so stylistically and visually stunning it overcame any concerns about a potential history lesson, completely captivating those in the screening room that day. The innovative, dramatic, and unexpected use of slow motion, the way the sequence used light and color, and the manipulation of dazzling imagery were all compelling. After follow-up meetings on casting and budgets, the movie got the green light.

I like this story because it says a lot about the process and the interaction between the studio and the filmmakers who had a definite vision of how and why the movie would be a big idea. They were persistent, focused, and diligently worked to overcome objections and see their vision through to the end. They were fortunate to be working with an open-minded studio that listened and supported them. The movie was made for the right reason at the right price, with the right talent both in front of and behind the camera. In 2007, *300* generated a global box office of $456 million on a $65 million production budget.

When I conducted the initial research screening of *300*, Mark Canton, as he often did, enthusiastically prepared me by letting me know that I was not going to believe what I was about to see. He was so right! I watched the film's first audience dine on its visual feast as they discovered something truly entertaining and original. *300*, of course, proved to be a big idea and one that would elevate the sword-and-sandal genre to new heights.

SELLING A BIG IDEA DOES NOT TYPICALLY REQUIRE a million-dollar proof of concept, like *300* did. Legendary producer David Permut is one of the best pitchmen I have ever known. If he believes in an idea, he will embrace it, pitch it, and *sell* it. He told me, "Look, regardless of the genre, all the films I've made over the years have one thing in common—a hook. The idea of needing the sizzle to sell the steak was instilled in me by a real mentor, Bill Sargent. This is a man who lived the highest of highs and the lowest of lows, consistently erratic. He took big risks that sometimes paid off but often didn't. He was filled with ideas."

In the 1960s and 1970s, Sargent produced several filmed productions of live performances, including *Hamlet* with Richard Burton, the stage musical *Stop the World: I Want to Get Off*, and *Give 'em Hell, Harry!*, starring James Whitmore as Harry S. Truman. Under Sargent's tutelage, David Permut received a producer credit on *Give 'em Hell, Harry!* Permut said, "It was videotaped in a single night and was so grainy it looked just terrible. No one wanted to distribute it, so we booked it into theaters ourselves. And then we got a call that it was nominated for a Best Actor Oscar. I was twenty-one or twenty-two years old and I'm at the Academy Awards! That was life with Bill."

Permut continues to reminisce about Bill Sargent. "He was never a small thinker. He decided that he was going to be responsible for getting the Beatles back together for a reunion. Bill and I met with George Harrison's lawyer and offered thirty million to get them back for a single concert that would be filmed and then distributed as a movie. In the meeting, our offer went from thirty million to forty million to fifty million. And then we were thrown out of the office. I remember Bill looking at me and saying, 'We got them; he's just playing hard to get.'" Sargent sent telegrams repeating his fifty-million offer, and the story landed on the cover of *People* magazine, with him as the man behind a Beatles reunion. "The only problem," said Permut, "was that we had just two million cash in the bank. When I asked Bill where we would get the other forty-eight million, he brushed it off as a mere technicality. If the Beatles had said yes, it would've been a technicality. Of course, they never did."

There is a big difference between selling the sizzle and selling the steak, and successful producers know how to pitch both. Case in point is a movie that Permut produced years ago that fits into the big-idea category under the heading of "something familiar told with a fresh spin." Permut was channel surfing one evening and came upon an old black-and-white police procedural, *Dragnet*, which he had enjoyed as a kid. "I remembered the show," he said, "and it made me laugh because after every dramatic moment, those four musical notes were played, *dum de-dum-dum*. I thought it was so funny. It was so over the top." Permut continued surfing, and the next thing he saw was Dan Aykroyd on an episode of *Saturday Night Live*. Something clicked and Permut said to himself, "I want to do the comedy version of *Dragnet*. And seeing Dan as the connection, I called his agent, Bernie Brillstein, and told him I had an idea to do something that had never been done before—take an old TV show, a heavy-handed drama, and make it into a feature film comedy. Brillstein wanted to know what the show was, and my answer was, *dum de-dum-dum*. He immediately called Dan, who loved the idea."

Permut, Aykroyd, and Brillstein set up a meeting with Frank Price, who was then heading up Universal Pictures. They did not tell Price's office what the meeting was about beforehand. Permut said, "We walked into Frank's office and Frank asked us what we had. In unison, all three of us responded, *dum de-dum-dum*. It was the shortest pitch in movie history! Within the year we were in production with Dan and Tom Hanks as his costar. *Dragnet* would go on to become one of the top hit films of 1987."

BEFORE MOVING ON TO OTHER EXAMPLES OF BIG-IDEA MOVIES, I'd like to comment on "comparables"—or "comps," as they are known in the industry—and how they are used to pitch a film idea and to size its potential. Those who are making the pitch will compare the idea with other titles that have been released and have a good track record, in the hope of convincing those who will finance it that it's worth the production spend required to make it. For example, *The Maze Runner* may have been comped to *The Hunger Games*. *Project X* might have been comped to *Superbad*. Those who green-light movies use comps, and not necessarily the same ones used by those who pitch it, to help decide whether to make it and how much to spend making it. More often than not, new ideas are compared to a number of previously released films to determine the best-, middle-, and worst-case scenarios.

Jokes have been made about the ridiculous comps that are used to describe a film idea. In the 2024 Netflix movie *A Family Affair*, a prima donna actor (played by Zac Efron) comically defends his choice to take the lead role in a movie that he describes as *Die Hard* meets *Miracle on 34th Street*. His long-suffering personal assistant (Joey King) argues that the script needs a rewrite. Obviously, the only aspect linking those titles together is that both stories take place during the Christmas season, and no one in the business would seriously consider using such disparate premises to project the potential of a new movie idea.

IF YOU WANT A BIG AUDIENCE, YOU NEED A BIG IDEA

During the green-light process, there are always debates about which comparisons to use, and many factors are weighed during an analysis. Reliable comps are based not only on the genre and similar story elements but also on the popularity of the cast and director, the anticipated production values (visual effects, set pieces, music, and sound design), and the seasonality of the release dates. Using the wrong comps can lead to dangerous territory, as I have witnessed. I adored and respected my clients at Relativity Media, but I was more than a little worried about them overhyping their 2014 film *Earth to Echo*. The story, about a group of kids who discover a cute alien and help it rebuild its spaceship to return home, was reminiscent of *E.T. the Extra-Terrestrial*. But *E.T.* was a once-in-a-generation phenomenon, and Relativity's president of marketing at the time, Russell Schwartz, knew they couldn't use it as a comp for the picture. He said, "We had to reach back in time, and comped it to *The Goonies* and *Stand by Me*. Like *E.T.*, those were much older movies from the mid-eighties, but we considered them the 'spiritual grandparents' of *Earth to Echo*. That's why we thought our movie was so unique—there had been nothing like it in many years."

I remember testing *Earth to Echo*, which is why I was worried. The film used "found-footage"–style camerawork to reflect the perspective of the kids, who recorded their adventures with the alien on their cell phones and camcorders. On the day of the first test preview, parents and kids settled into their seats in the theater for what they anticipated would be an early look at a fun new movie that was not yet released. But as the film played through the lens of its shaky camera, one kid in the front of the theater vomited, then a second, then another. It was like a chain reaction. Five or six children had to be taken from the theater because they got sick. Schwartz said, "That handheld style was a big thing at the time. We didn't realize how much of a concern it was going to be. Those kids throwing up in the movie theater during the screening would obviously hurt word of mouth." The talented producer Andrew Panay and his team went to work and recut the film.

Earth to Echo opened over July Fourth weekend 2015 in the sixth position, taking in just $8 million in the US, the equivalent of $10.5 million today, but hung on for 121 days (which would be miraculous by today's standards) and peaked at $39 million, which translates to more than $50 million today. That is a more than respectable multiple of five, meaning it made five times its opening weekend gross, enviable in the movie business and indicative that word of mouth was pretty damned good. Looking at Russell Schwartz's comps, *The Goonies* opened to $9 million back in 1985 and took in $64 million in the US, more than a seven-times multiple. (Of course, these are 1985 dollars, and if adjusted for inflation, today's equivalent would be an opening of more than $26 million and a total gross of roughly $190 million. The big point here is the "legs" of the movie, how long it stays in theaters and continues to build its box office take.)

Stand by Me had a different release strategy, opening on just sixteen screens, ostensibly to allow word of mouth to carry the movie. When distribution widened, on its first eight-hundred-plus-screen weekend, *Stand by Me* made $5 million at the US box office and eventually built to slightly more than a ten-times multiple of $52 million. So those two movies were, in fact, solid comps for *Earth to Echo*, opening in a similar range.

In a way, I always thought the best comp for *Earth to Echo* would have been another movie that coincidentally Russell Schwartz was responsible for marketing when he was president of marketing at New Line Cinema. It was *The Last Mimzy*, a 2007 film directed by Bob Shaye, who was New Line's founder and cochair. The premise has both philosophical and science fiction underpinnings and centers on a couple of young kids who discover a box of strange toys that give them super intelligence and other enhanced abilities. As the story progresses, it turns out that the items are high-tech devices disguised as toys and sent back from the future into the early twenty-first century to avert the ecological disaster that has destroyed that future world. The difficulty with positioning and marketing that movie was that the premise appealed to adult sci-fi enthusiasts, but two young children drive the narrative.

The Last Mimzy was a passion project for Bob Shaye, who had suffered a life-threatening illness in 2005 and was put into a medically induced coma so his body could rebound. For weeks, his colleagues at New Line wondered if he would make it. He did, but it took many months before he was able to return to work, and *The Last Mimzy* was the film he focused on once he was back. As Russell Schwartz reflected on the situation: "Bob had directed a movie early in his career and always wanted to direct another one. The combination of spirituality in *The Last Mimzy* and that it was about a rebirth appealed to him. He had survived this very serious infection and was rediscovering himself. He is an incredible person, and we supported him one hundred percent, but I knew at the time it was going to be a no-win."

Schwartz and his team conducted positioning research to inform a strategic marketing campaign, but they never could nail down good comps for *The Last Mimzy*. It had a worthy cast—Joely Richardson, Timothy Hutton, Rainn Wilson, Kathryn Hahn, and Michael Clarke Duncan—so they made the choice to appeal primarily to parents and position the film as one their kids should see. It was a tough sell, and Schwartz muses that if he had one "Get Out of Jail Free" card for his entire career that would absolve him of any blame for the failure of a movie, he would play it for *The Last Mimzy*. The film opened to $10 million in the US, landing in the fifth position on the weekend it opened in 2007. It eventually took in $21 million in the US, only slightly more than a two-times multiple.

Here are the similarities between *Earth to Echo* and *The Last Mimzy*, and the reason I think *Mimzy* would have been a good comp for *Echo*. Both featured stories with sci-fi and adventure aspects and had kids at the center. Both anticipated family appeal. Both were tough sells without any obvious comparable movies in recent decades. Both opened to a similar box office and rankings in the marketplace. Yet *Earth to Echo* played far better (despite all the puking at the initial test screening!) and earned stronger word of mouth, achieving five times its opening box office versus a much more meager two-times multiple for *The Last Mimzy*. The lesson here is that comps are only one part of the analysis and can be pretty good for gauging appeal out of the gate. What happens after that, in a real-world scenario where word of mouth takes over, is a different consideration entirely, and the reason we, as experts in the field, place so much emphasis on the intent to "definitely" recommend a film to family and friends, which we capture on the post-screening questionnaires. That strong endorsement represents the "legs" of a movie—in other words, how long it will remain playing in theaters. It's important to mention that beyond the top rating of "definite" recommendations, we also look at levels of intensity within that measure. Intensity signifies the passion and advocacy with which the audience will get behind a film.

MY COMPANY, IN PARTNERSHIP WITH COMSCORE, a global media measurement and analytics company, co-owns a product called PostTrak, which has become the industry-wide currency in audience exit polling. PostTrak gathers data from moviegoers around the country and in multiple international territories as they leave theaters each weekend. It helps to understand who actually showed up to see a particular title, what they thought of it, and whether they will endorse it to their family and friends. One of the many benefits of PostTrak is that it allows us to validate comps with empirical evidence. If a studio tells us that they expect a new film idea to attract certain demographics—say parents and kids seven to fourteen—we can mine PostTrak to support or refute the comps they are considering. If we find the comped titles attracted, for example, mostly parents and boys but few girls, or parents and kids nine to twelve but not younger kids or teens, we can warn them that they may be drinking their own Kool-Aid and need to adjust their projections to meet reality. I'd rather have one good, reliable comp than a dozen less reliable ones.

All studios, production companies, and streaming platforms—like Netflix, Amazon, and Disney+—use comps in one way or another. I was interested in Tendo Nagenda's perspective because he is a producer who previously held executive positions on both the theatrical and streaming sides of the business. He spent nearly nine years at Disney as executive vice president of production overseeing the contemporary remakes of *Cinderella*, *Beauty and the Beast*, *Dumbo*, and *Mulan*. From 2018 to 2022, he was vice president of original films at Netflix, handling their self-produced slate of movies, including *Glass Onion: A Knives Out Mystery*, *The Old Guard*, *Da 5 Bloods*, and *The Gray Man*. I was most interested in understanding how Netflix uses comps to determine which movies they should make and how much they should spend on producing them.

"Netflix is the most sophisticated company around valuing individual content within a streaming model because it has the most experience, in terms of both doing it for the longest period and the amount of programming it has streamed," said Nagenda. "It's been an evolution and will continue to be an evolution. At first it was pure viewing—how many Netflix subscribers watched this movie? How many viewed it completely? One of the measures we have publicized is viewing hours. If a viewer completes something, there will be more viewing hours than if it was started and stopped. Engagement, as determined by viewing hours, is the new model for measuring success."

We drilled down into *The Gray Man* as an example because it cost a reported $200 million to produce, and I wondered how Netflix measured success on an investment that large. Sure, *The Gray Man* had all the qualities of a big theatrical film. It was directed by the Russo Brothers (of *Avengers* and *Captain America* fame), stars Ryan Gosling and Chris Evans, features spectacular action sequences and special effects, and is based on a terrific *Bourne Identity* meets *Mission: Impossible* premise. (See what I just did? I comped it!) But how are those assets evaluated within the streaming model?

Nagenda continued. "Decisions are made based on experience—genre of the movie, star power, how it travels internationally, interest in the filmmakers, and how other similar movies on Netflix performed. We have comparative data. In the case of *The Gray Man*, we had *Extraction* [which the Russo Brothers produced], *Bird Box*, and *Red Notice*. We knew how those performed all over the world. We also knew the genre and how it typically plays within the territories. If an important area of growth is APAC [Asia-Pacific], and action films play well in that region across the board as dictated by the data from our comps, then we have an expectation around where *The Gray Man* will play well. Plus, we understand the importance of being able to provide that quality of content to that region." According to published data at the time of this writing, viewing hours generated by *The Gray Man* were substantially ahead of *Bird Box*, but lagged behind *Extraction* and further behind *Red Notice*. *The Gray Man* also paced ahead of *The Adam Project*, another successful Netflix film in the same vein although not a comparable at the time because it had not yet landed on their audience measurements. Even with mountains of internal data, comps are tough to gauge.

Nancy Utley, who was at Fox Searchlight (now Searchlight Pictures under the Disney umbrella) for more than twenty years and served as copresident for ten of those, has a very different perspective on comps. "It's a good indication if you *can't* compare a film to any other. Comps are death. What do you compare *Birdman* to? *The Shape of Water*? Some of these don't even make sense on paper. It's the filmmaker you believe in. You're betting on that person." Searchlight has always been a specialty studio, rallying behind smaller independently minded films that appeal to arthouse audiences and typically earn critical praise. I understand Nancy Utley's point for those very unique offerings, but most studio chiefs want some perspective on how a film might perform before ponying up tens of millions of dollars to produce it.

EARLIER, I WROTE THAT "BIG IDEAS" can be sorted into three categories. The second big-idea category is **a concept/story from other hugely successful source material that translates well to the big screen.** Usually these are movies based on books, but movies can also come from plays, video games, short stories, or articles that tap into subject matter that is broadly resonant. There are countless examples of these big-idea movies, and some of the very best have been shepherded by the incomparable Elizabeth Gabler, who ran Fox 2000 and now heads up 3000 Pictures at Sony. She has been responsible for films like *Hidden Figures*, *Marley & Me*, *The Devil Wears Prada*, and the *Diary of a Wimpy Kid* franchise. Gabler has one of the best noses in the business, is judicious, and is very into books. I consider her a hitmaker.

"I myself have to fall in love with the book—fall in love with the characters and be invested in the story," Gabler said. "It also must have a relatable concept that can be sold as a film. There are a lot of great books with wonderful stories, emotionally charged through lines, and characters that are amazing. But if you can't distill it into a concept that sounds compelling enough for people to actually go and see it, then it's usually a little independent movie."

Life of Pi was no such thing. It grossed more than $600 million worldwide, won four Oscars, and was nominated for seven others. Ang Lee's masterpiece was based on the 2001 Booker Prize–winning novel by Yann Martel. Gabler was passionate about the material, saying, "I thought it was the first truly international family film that is not animated. For me, it is the story of a boy who lost his family, which is often the theme in all these great Disney movies, and his only companion is a tiger. Because of the giant natural phenomenon, which is the backdrop to the story, all the things he goes through to survive are visual. The movie wouldn't need subtitles."

Gabler knew that there were only a handful of directors who were up to the task of directing such material, and her boss at Twentieth Century Fox at the time, chairman Tom Rothman, had a relationship with her top pick—Ang Lee. Rothman put Gabler in touch with Lee and a meeting was set up. Gabler pitched the idea, and Lee was fascinated but reticent. He wondered why a studio would be interested in making such a movie. He had to think about it. By the end of their first meeting, Gabler was never more convinced that Lee was the one who could tackle it and told him that she wouldn't make the film unless he directed it.

It was eight months before Lee agreed to take on the project, and only after Gabler suggested David Magee of *Finding Neverland* fame to pen the screenplay. Lee told Gabler that he and Magee had always wanted to work together, and *Life of Pi* seemed like a perfect opportunity for them to team up. Meanwhile, Tom Rothman was debating whether to even green-light the picture, especially given the anticipated production cost, which was well over $100 million. He questioned whether the story of a tiger and a kid in a boat could ever make back that kind of money. But Gabler knew *Life of Pi* was a big-idea movie. She marched into his office and with tears in her eyes, she begged him to make it. Rothman says, "I told her that I've made multiple movies with Ang. He's a genius. But I have stockholders." Gabler was insistent. "You have to help me," she said.

So Rothman went around and raised a lot of money. "There was no way I was going to take on the full burden of that film," he said. "We gave up a little but still made a very nice profit on it. Why does that movie exist? Because I believed in Elizabeth. I believed in Ang. I figured out a way to say yes."

In many ways, *Life of Pi* is a remarkable film. I remember testing an early version of it to a blindly recruited audience during the summer of 2012. Even with unfinished effects, moviegoers described it as visually stunning, which it is! Moreover, the story is so moving and thought-provoking that test audience participants described it as "a spiritual odyssey" that "speaks to the soul." I was blown away by it. It is a survival story told with such originality that there was little question in my mind that it was going to be a success.

SIX YEARS AND A DOZEN FILMS LATER, while still at Fox 2000, Gabler noticed that Reese Witherspoon, whom she was close to, had chosen *Where the Crawdads Sing* for her book club. Gabler knew the power of a Reese Witherspoon endorsement, plus she had once worked with and respected the book's author, Delia Owens. So she immediately purchased the book, and even before finishing it, she was on the phone to Reese's producing partner, Lauren Levy Neustadter, to express interest in making it into a movie. Neustadter encouraged her to finish the book before committing, so Gabler read another fifty pages, and still not finished, called back. She was most definitely interested.

The story of Kya, a young girl who is first abandoned by her family and then by the boy she loves, and subsequently survives on her own in the wild, struck Gabler as a strong premise. It is an overwhelmingly emotional story about being an outcast, living in solitude, and connecting with nature. Woven into the story is a murder mystery in which Kya is the suspect. It was easy for Gabler to fall in love with the book and its characters, and she felt the beauty of the North Carolina marshlands, a world that few people have seen, would also help to draw the audience in. "I just saw it," explained Gabler. "I thought it could be theatrical and cinematic."

What Gabler could not know was that Covid-19 would catapult sales of the book. Trapped inside their homes with nowhere to go during the pandemic, people across America were reading *Where the Crawdads Sing* and finding Kya's isolation relatable. The book stayed on the *New York Times* bestseller list for 150 weeks, and by July 2022, when the movie was released, it had sold fifteen million copies, which is huge in the publishing industry.

That was all good news as far as laying the groundwork for a feature film adaptation, but as development continued, Disney purchased Twentieth Century Fox and decided to shut down the Fox 2000 division. Gabler made her play, hoping she could take as many of her people and projects as possible and find a home somewhere else. Eventually, Disney let her take a handful of movies that she was working on developing, including *Crawdads*, as part of her exit package. She struck a deal with her former boss Tom Rothman, who by 2018 had become the head of Sony Pictures. Together they launched their new division at Sony, which they named 3000 Pictures.

Gabler's passion for the project moved it along, and she made the film for a good price. But a key challenge remained. With Covid still looming large, would people venture into theaters to see it? She credits *Top Gun: Maverick* for helping. It motivated a return to theaters over Memorial Day weekend 2022 that proved safe and fun and reminded people why they love going to the movies.

Where the Crawdads Sing opened in mid-July of that year and took in a profitable $144 million worldwide, impressive given that it was made for a modest $24 million. While it did not have the enormous box office draw of the other films discussed in this chapter, it is important to consider that *Crawdads* appealed primarily to females and was released when there was fear about the Covid-19 Omicron variant. As Tom Rothman summa-

IF YOU WANT A BIG AUDIENCE, YOU NEED A BIG IDEA

rizes: "Elizabeth believed in that movie like there was no tomorrow. She believed in it with every fiber of her being. And again, my job was to help her realize her vision."

I so admire Rothman for that passion and loyalty, which he has also shown to me over the years.

I'D LIKE TO SAY MORE ABOUT TOM ROTHMAN, who is a force of nature. He and I go way back, and I consider him not just a client but a mentor and a friend. He has always treated me like a member of his inner circle, and that makes me want to invest in his success. And successful he is. He has a wonderful track record and is one of the few studio chiefs of his generation who is still in his job. Tom credits his success with being creatively risky and fiscally prudent. But he also has the uncanny ability to recognize the commerciality of an idea, is a wonderful judge of talent, and has a deep understanding of the financial end of the movie business.

I love that when you walk into Tom's office at Sony Pictures Entertainment, you are greeted by a sign that reads BIG IDEAS. He says that while there are many choices that affect the success or failure of a movie, nothing is more important than the power of its idea. I couldn't agree more.

Tom likes to illustrate the far-reaching implications of an idea with the following comparison. "A great example of a big idea and a weak idea can be seen in the difference between 1994's *Speed* and 1997's *Speed 2: Cruise Control*," he said. "The big idea behind the original *Speed* is that there's a bomb on a bus in Los Angeles during rush hour, and if the bus drops below fifty miles per hour, the bomb explodes. The worst idea ever is *Speed 2*, where there's a bomb on a cruise ship, and if the ship stops, the bomb is going to go off and sink the ship."

Watching the first dailies of the sequel, Rothman turned to Kim Cooper, the physical production executive on the movie, and asked if the boat could go any faster given the title of the movie is, well, *Speed 2*. Rothman recalls Cooper's response: "Tom, it is going very fast . . . for a boat."

Reportedly, *Speed 2: Cruise Control* cost $160 million to produce and earned $165 million globally, a financial disaster in the world of movies given that there are big marketing and distribution costs, not to mention, as a rule of thumb, the studio only receives about 50 percent of the box office grosses. The other 50 percent goes to the exhibitors (theater chains). By comparison, the high-concept original *Speed* cost $30 million to make and earned close to $350 million at the box office, a whopping $185 million more than the second movie. Rotten Tomatoes critics gave the first movie a 95 percent Certified Fresh rating, versus a 4 percent Rotten score assigned to the second installment. That's the stark difference that Rothman so astutely points out.

THE THIRD BIG-IDEA CATEGORY is an entirely original story, usually tapping into themes that resonate within popular culture. These big-idea concepts might be the toughest to recognize because there is no track record from which to gauge appeal, such as a bestselling book, a top-selling toy brand, a superhero series, a video game, or any other known intellectual property. A case in point is *Get Out*, the surprising 2017 hit from Blumhouse and Universal Pictures. Jason Blum readily admitted to me that he did not know how big an idea it was right out of the gate.

The story in *Get Out* centers on an African American man, played by Daniel Kaluuya, who accompanies his white girlfriend, played by Allison Williams, to her parents' countryside estate. Kaluuya's character is on edge almost from the start, even before meeting the parents, and especially once he notices the strangely submissive behavior among their Black help. His discomfort intensifies as the story progresses, leveraging suspense and racial tension, and keeping the audience on the edge of their

IF YOU WANT A BIG AUDIENCE, YOU NEED A BIG IDEA

seats. The themes of prejudice are provocative, there is some well-placed humor to balance the tension, and there's an unexpected twist at the end.

Jordan Peele, of *Key & Peele* fame, had conceived the *Get Out* idea and written a speculative script, which he brought to Jason Blum. Blum said, "It sat around town for three years and was budgeted higher, and I didn't think it would turn into what it did. But I thought it was interesting and worth making." Blum told Peele that if he could bring it in for $4.5 million, they could get it green-lit. Peele figured out a way to make it for that price, and they moved ahead. "In my experience," Blum said, "showrunners, those who steer the vision for a TV series, like Jordan started out as, are the best fit for the Blumhouse system. They all write, they're able to shoot fast, and they can pivot on the fly. So even though Jordan hadn't done a movie, I wasn't worried about working with him. I've never had a bad experience with a proven showrunner directing one of our movies."

When the movie was finished, Blum took it to Sundance for a surprise midnight screening, where it received a glowing reception. But it wasn't until the second weekend after opening that Blum knew he had something special on his hands. The grosses dropped only 15 percent, which almost never happens with a wide release. It would eventually gross more than $255 million worldwide. Not bad for a little $4.5 million movie.

Of course, it's easy to see in retrospect that *Get Out* was a big idea. It was original, incorporated societal themes that resonated with moviegoers of all races and ethnicities, and delivered a perfect balance of humor, horror, and twists. It was also made for the right price and was written and directed by the truly talented Peele. I remember seeing it for the first time at a test screening and knowing immediately that it elevated the horror genre. In the subsequent films he has written and directed, *Us* and *Nope*, Peele has continued to come up with fresh, unique stories that lured big audiences and solidified his reputation as a big-idea generator and first-rate filmmaker.

Another big idea in the same genre, also from Blumhouse and Universal, is *The Purge*. "I didn't understand the scale of the idea until the film was done," Blum told me. "When we saw the marketing materials with the copy—'Crime is legal for twelve hours a year'—it was clear that it was a very sticky high-concept." Thinking about that, Blum saw an endless number of different scenarios that could be developed from the notion of a legal crime spree every single year, but only for a very limited number of hours. The crazy thing is that the first film, and the franchise that it would produce, almost didn't happen. Universal wanted to shelve the 2013 original film. It was finished, and they had a trailer and a release date. But in the aftermath of the tragic Sandy Hook Elementary School shooting, the studio had second thoughts and wanted to bury the entire thing. "It was such a sad time," said Blum, recalling the loss of lives.

Eventually, *The Purge* was released about six months later, in June 2013. "There was a fifty percent chance that the film would never be released," Blum said. "Now we've made six of them." Half a billion dollars and counting!

I REMEMBER SCREENING THE FIRST MOVIE in *The Purge* franchise, and it had one of the best recruit ratios for an unknown IP that I'd seen in recent memory. A recruit ratio is the number of invitations it takes to get a single moviegoer to show up at a test screening. The lower the number, the more compelling the premise. The recruit ratio is typically the earliest indication of how well the basic concept resonates with moviegoers. So I knew Blumhouse was onto something big. While the first movie was good, I think—and the audiences agreed—*The Purge* films have gotten better over time. Last year at Universal Studios Hollywood theme park, there was a live *The Purge* event at the Waterworld arena, which holds

IF YOU WANT A BIG AUDIENCE, YOU NEED A BIG IDEA

2,300 seats. The show ran every fifteen minutes, and it was the most popular event on Halloween Horror Night. That certainly speaks to the power of its idea.

NICK STOLLER IS A VERY FUNNY MAN. He's not the joke-telling type at a dinner party but rather a naturally funny guy who finds humor in everyday situations. He is one of a limited number of writer/directors in Hollywood who makes big-idea original comedies, the kind that draw huge crowds to the theater even in a postpandemic world where many people are content to watch these kinds of films in the comfort of their own homes.

Stoller was enamored with comedy at a very early age. Growing up in Miami, he got his hands on a Dave Barry book and thought it was the funniest thing in the world. It inspired him to write a letter to the humorist about a possible internship. Barry wrote back, politely declining the offer from the fourteen-year-old Stoller. In high school, Stoller started a satire magazine with a group of like-minded friends. His enthusiasm for comedy writing intensified as he entered Harvard, where he majored in English and worked on *The Harvard Lampoon*, the esteemed humor publication that dates back to 1876.

By the time he graduated from college, Stoller knew he wanted to write and direct movies, but he didn't have a pathway into the industry, so he moved to New York, got a job at the ad agency Young & Rubicam, and began applying to comedic TV shows based in the city. There were no takers. *Saturday Night Live*, the *Late Show with David Letterman*, and *Late Night with Conan O'Brien* turned him down. Rather than settle into a copywriting career at Y&R, Stoller made the move to Los Angeles, where he got his first lucky break as a staff writer on an animated series based on the Austin Powers character. The show was never picked up, but because of that job, Stoller was able to get representation at United Talent Agency (UTA).

That paved the way for his second lucky break. Judd Apatow, who was already beginning to set the world on fire as the comedic voice of a new generation, was developing the TV series *Undeclared*. It revolved around a group of college freshmen, so Apatow called UTA and asked to see their youngest comedy writers. Stoller was one of them. "I remember meeting Judd," he said. "I was obsessed with his tone and with his show *Freaks and Geeks*. He wanted us to pitch ideas, and I just wrote down a bunch of stuff that happened to me in college. When I presented them, I remember him laughing really hard." Stoller was hired and given an office that he would share with another young writer who also had an acting role in *Undeclared*, an eighteen-year-old named Seth Rogen.

Let me just pause here to reinforce the serendipity of life in Hollywood. Talent is the price of entry and is in no short supply. But everyone who is successful has a lucky break story. And as long as you work hard, continue to prove yourself, and don't burn bridges, the network one builds from that lucky break can pay major dividends. I've learned this in my own career by nurturing friendships, remaining loyal, and whenever possible, doing favors for others (especially those who are down on their luck). My friendships have been instrumental in building my own successful company, writing books that feature wonderful stories and lessons from some of the biggest names in the entertainment industry, and hosting my own podcast, *Don't Kill the Messenger*, in which I interview Hollywood luminaries. One relationship leads to a fortuitous introduction, which leads to an opportunity that just might be life-changing.

Back to Nick Stoller as a twenty-three-year-old: His network was sprouting tentacles. In addition to Rogen and Apatow, *Undeclared* also introduced him to Jason Segel, who played a character in eight of the episodes. The show lasted only a season, but it firmly launched Stoller's screenwriting career and solidified his relationship with Apatow. In the years that followed, they collaborated on a couple of screenplays, including one for 2005's *Fun with Dick and Jane*, a remake of the 1977 film. Stoller also remained friends with Segel, who by then had written *Forgetting Sarah Marshall* and asked Stoller to direct it. Apatow, whose star had risen to rarified heights in the wake of writing (with Steve Carell) and directing *The 40-Year-Old Virgin*, threw his support behind the duo. He agreed to produce *Forgetting Sarah Marshall* and their next film, *Get Him to the Greek*, which Stoller and Segel wrote together and Stoller directed. Those films were made for the right price and did well at the box office. They were based on fresh, original premises with relatable situations, and while they leveraged comedy, they included romantic and dramatic elements as well. This alchemy would become the essential element of the Nick Stoller brand.

Several years later, Seth Rogen and his friend and producing partner Evan Goldberg approached Stoller about directing a film they wanted to make. *Neighbors*, scripted by Andrew Cohen and Brendan O'Brien, is about a young couple with a newborn baby daughter whose lives are upended when a fraternity moves in next door. Stoller recognized the premise as a big idea, one that was very commercial and would be a great comedy vehicle for Rogen (who would play the young dad) and Zac Efron (who was on board as the head of the fraternity). Rose Byrne, whom Stoller praises as a gifted physical comedian who goes hard for the jokes, would be cast as the young mother. It was right in Stoller's wheelhouse—fresh and funny with a dramatic core, and deeply relatable. "That film spoke to me," he said. "I knew my emotional way into it. The two times I've had an existential crisis in my life were when I graduated college and when I had my first child. Both times, I felt that my life was in chaos, and I couldn't control anything."

Stoller knew what made the Rogen and Efron characters tick, and why they would relate to each other on some level. "There are a few emotional scenes that I added to the backbone of the movie," he said. "The emotion makes it funnier. The best comedies have that drama. In the movie, there's a scene where Zac's character is at a job fair. All his buddies have these job interviews, and he has nothing lined up. He's in free fall, which was exactly how I felt, and I think most people feel that way as they're graduating from college. That was a big touchstone for me in understanding who this guy was. For Seth's and Rose's characters, it was the conversation where they say, 'We can keep living the way we were living before we had a baby.'" In other words, they thought they could have their cake and eat it, too.

Seth Rogen and Evan Goldberg thought it would be very funny if the parents tried to be cool with the frat boys, adding a lot of those moments to the script. Again, all of that was relatable to Stoller. As a young father, the notion of settling into parenthood was still fresh in his mind. "I think that accepting you're a parent is a big part of having your first baby," he said. "I remember soon after we had our first child I went to some Hollywood party and ran into a friend of mine. When he saw me, he said, 'Why are you here?'" Stoller was jolted by the question and answered defensively, "I can still go to parties!" (By the time his next child was born, he was totally into parenthood and had no interest whatsoever in attending any of those Hollywood bashes.)

Many jokes in the *Neighbors* script resonated with Stoller, but others required work. There is a scene where the baby puts a used condom in her mouth. When he read that part, Stoller thought it absolutely needed to come out. As a young dad himself, he felt it crossed a line. But as the filmmakers worked on the screenplay, he came around. He thought, "This is so bad that if we keep it, that scene needs to change the way Seth's and Rose's characters behave." The filmmakers decided to make it an inciting incident, the breaking point at which the Rogen and Byrne characters say, "We've got to fight the frat."

Stoller concludes by giving credit all around. "Andrew and Brendan thought of the idea, but it was very much a collaboration. The five of us made that movie into something that was very funny. It's such a commercial premise. The poster says, 'Family vs. Frat.' That tells you everything about the movie. It's a generational battle. That's the big idea."

Neighbors was released just before Memorial Day 2014, drawing about six million moviegoers into theaters across the country on its opening weekend. It would eventually gross $270 million worldwide. Unquestionably, a very big audience.

IF THERE IS SUCH A THING AS A MODERN-DAY WALT DISNEY, his name is Chris Meledandri. As the head of Twentieth Century Fox Animation for nearly a decade, he shepherded the *Ice Age* movies, *Robots*, and *Horton Hears a Who!* In 2007, Meledandri left Fox to establish his own company, Illumination Entertainment, the production entity behind some of the most successful animated family franchises of all time: *Despicable Me*, *The Secret Life of Pets*, and *Sing*. These movies are big ideas born out of original concepts. I wondered about the inspiration for Illumination's first win right from the start, *Despicable Me*, and when Meledandri knew he had struck gold.

"I started the company and didn't know what the first film would be," he said. "I got a call from a Spanish animator named Sergio Pablos who was coming to Los Angeles and asked to meet with me. I remember agreeing to see him if I could be his first meeting." That was smart thinking on Meledandri's part, because he got a first look at something truly special. The two men met over breakfast, and Pablos presented three ideas, each one accompanied by imagery. The second of the three ideas was called "Evil Me," and the animator had about fifteen or twenty drawings that represented the premise of the storyline. It was about a villain who needs three little girls to help him commit a crime, so he goes to an orphanage, essentially to borrow them. While pulling off the crime, the little girls begin to see the goodness in the villain and get attached to him as a father figure. The Minions, as we would eventually know them, did not exist.

"I found the core idea emotionally compelling," said Meledandri. "I also responded to the idea of making a movie where the protagonist was a villain. I grew up on movies in the seventies with antiheroes, and even though it was unusual to think about an animated movie with an antihero as your protagonist, I loved the potential for a highly flawed character. In animation, when working on leading men, we found they tended to become flat very quickly. The villain characters were always more interesting because of their flaws." Meledandri felt the main character in "Evil Me" was not traditionally heroic but would come across as highly relatable nevertheless because he undergoes a dramatic change throughout the movie.

Illumination was still in its infancy with limited staff, but Meledandri had worked with two talented writers during his days at Fox, Cinco Paul and Ken Daurio. He brought them in, and based on Sergio Pablo's drawings and the essence of his characters, they went to work on the script. "Once I had the script development underway, I needed to build the team. I started with directors. I went to a collaborator of mine, Chris Renaud, who brought his skills to the project, having come up through storyboarding." Yet because Renaud would be a first-time director, Meledandri looked for someone from animation to partner with. He also needed to find a studio where he could assemble roughly three hundred people to make the film. As a startup, he was finding that he did not have access to the same level of world-class talent he had at Fox when he was overseeing *Ice Age*, *Robots*, and *Horton Hears a Who!* So he realized that he would have to look outside the US. This led him to a wonderful French animation studio called Mac Guff. They introduced him to an exceptionally talented animator named Pierre Coffin. Upon seeing some of Coffin's short-form animation, Meledandri immediately connected to the work

IF YOU WANT A BIG AUDIENCE, YOU NEED A BIG IDEA

and brought him aboard to work side by side with Renaud as directors. Meledandri and Universal would eventually buy Mac Guff, which is now Illumination Paris.

It wasn't until the team began to visually develop the movie that the Minions emerged. Coffin, Renaud, and a French art director named Eric Guillon began experimenting with a wildly imaginative approach to characters who had originally been conceived as human henchmen. Meledandri says, "They brought me what was a very early version of a minion and even in its earliest form, it had incredible charm." The minion's language added further specificity to the characters. Meledandri explained that this language has been almost entirely conceived by Coffin. More accurately, "It's like writing music, the way Pierre does it."

Explaining how these truly inventive characters and story ideas come to fruition, Meledandri said, "When you start making one of these films, it's a combination of the best-laid plans and the discoveries that occur along the way. At their best, these movies are made with the opportunity to locate those discoveries and then lean into what's working. We have freedom that allows the visual process of creation to influence the direction. That's because it is often the unexpected in these films that connects with the audience." The Minions were, quite obviously, one of those unexpected discoveries. But to my surprise, Meledandri told me that Scrat in *Ice Age* was very analogous. There was no Scrat character in the original script. See the pattern here? That endearing little squirrel-like creature would introduce *Ice Age* to the world, if you recall the original trailer for the movie where he struggles with an acorn. However, in both cases, the instinct to locate these characters was coming from the directors.

Interestingly, when Meledandri recounted the genesis of the big idea that was to become *Despicable Me*, he did not bring up the notion of stealing the moon. He focused on the emotional pull and the main character. "We recognized that an audience leaves the theater with their connection to character," he said. "That's what stays with them. We see our movies as character-first. Not to imply that story isn't important, but character is more important."

Two years before *Despicable Me* opened in theaters, Meledandri and his fledgling team, including executive Brett Hoffman, who is still with Illumination, came to my offices, then in Culver City. We had developed a friendship and innate trust in one another, and I believed in him. I vividly remember him showing me character renderings of a weird guy named Gru with a pointy nose and long skinny legs, and the three cute little girls, but no young male characters, which concerned me. I shared with him what I believe to this day are the five tenets of all successful animated movies:

1. It must have a *protagonist* the audience can get behind and truly care about.
2. It must be incredibly *funny*, with humor for both kids and parents, and a final hilarious beat.
3. It needs enough *action* to keep the kids engaged, especially boys.
4. It needs an *emotional* core at its center that pays off big at the end.
5. It must be an extraordinarily *fun*, entertaining, and satisfying ride.

I wasn't sure "Evil Me" had all those assets, but wow, Illumination delivered on every single one in the final film.

Perhaps you're wondering how the title of the movie changed to *Despicable Me*. When I asked Meledandri about it, he told me there was concern the word "evil" would be too severe in an animated film title. He explained: "In changing the title, my concern was losing the distinction that we had with 'Evil Me.' When we considered 'Despicable Me,' I felt it was going to be a challenge because it's a word way over the heads of our younger audience. But I liked the melodic quality of those two words, and eventually it became a real asset for us."

Universal Studios, which distributed *Despicable Me*, hired us to do research on the title, and I conducted focus groups with children. They not only didn't know the meaning of the word "despicable," they couldn't even pronounce it. "We were talking to you, Kevin, about everything back then," said Meledandri. "We found leading up to the film's release we were having trouble getting awareness levels to where they needed to be to have a successful opening. Based on your research, we realized the complexity of the word might be holding us back. Working with Universal, Illumination's head of marketing, Gail Harrison, began to experiment with creating marketing that played with the pronunciation of the word 'despicable'—our theory being if we could make it fun, we would get it to stick. Plus, we had Pharrell's song in our pocket."

Meledandri's son Nick is a music aficionado and had introduced Meledandri to Pharrell Williams's music years before. So when Kathy Nelson, who ran the music department at Universal, suggested a meeting with Pharrell, Meledandri jumped at the chance. "I told Kathy that I wanted to incorporate music into the movie as a song score as opposed to a traditional music score," explained Meledandri. "I used the analogy of *The Graduate* and how the Simon & Garfunkel songs were used to drive the narrative. I wanted to do the same thing with *Despicable Me*. Kathy said, 'There's someone I want you to meet,' and it was Pharrell." It turned out to be a perfect marriage of two hitmakers. Pharrell wrote the title song for the movie, which starts with the lyric, "I'm having a bad, bad day," and followed that with three more original songs. Three years later, he would write the companion song "Happy" as the theme for *Despicable Me 2*. It became the best-selling single of 2014 and catapulted Pharrell's fame to new heights.

I asked Meledandri when he knew *Despicable Me* would be such a big success, now with a fourth film that has taken in over $900 million and a franchise of seven titles, including the *Minions* movies, which have made well over $5 billion. He replied, "Listening to the audience is such an important part of charting our course. We have many opportunities to listen. With animation, the first opportunity comes from your crew. You can certainly tell what is engaging them as they're making the film. We had this amazing opportunity to then also bring the audiences in at early stages."

He continued: "Making *Despicable Me* was one of those rare films where you knew very early on that the enthusiasm the entire team was feeling was an indicator of what the larger world was going to feel. We believed that. But we had no idea of the scale of the impact. Through the making of it, there was an experience of joy and confidence that is remarkable, particularly given that it was our first film."

Not all of Illumination's films have been based on original ideas, but all have been big ideas. Meledandri developed a relationship with the Dr. Seuss (Theodor Seuss Geisel) estate when he was still at Fox and working on *Horton Hears a Who!* At Illumination, he brought *The Lorax* and the 2018 animated version of *The Grinch* to the big screen, both successful iterations of the Dr. Seuss IP. And speaking of developing a big idea from existing IP, in 2023, Illumination had a huge win with *The Super Mario Bros. Movie*, which took in nearly $1.4 billion worldwide.

As I reflect on Illumination's phenomenal track record, I would be remiss if I didn't mention *The Secret Life of Pets*, which was an entirely original idea, one that tapped into relatable human emotions and came directly from Chris Meledandri himself. "Like so many of us, I've been in love with pets, both the ones I had growing up and as an adult. My son James had a pet parakeet named Swizz when he was about seven years old, and the bird would sit on my shoulder in the morning as I shaved. I know a parakeet probably has a brain the size of a caraway seed, and yet we projected onto that parakeet all this emotion, personality, and intellect. Swizz is pecking on my ear! He's so happy this morning!"

Meledandri continued: "Pets occupy this central place in our lives because they provide us with unconditional love. It was an irresistible idea that had been knocking around in my head for a while, to think about what their lives are like when we're not around. How much are they missing us? Where are they napping? Are they hanging out with neighborhood friends? How do they feel when they're left behind? How excited are they when they sense we're getting close to returning home?"

This was the genesis of *The Secret Life of Pets*. Meledandri again brought his idea to writers Cinco Paul and Ken Daurio and director Chris Renaud, and along with Illumination's internal team, they started brainstorming about what the characters and story would be. Even with all this creative talent, it took nearly two years before they had a draft of the script. When it was released in 2016, *The Secret Life of Pets* was yet another big win for Illumination, taking in nearly $900 million worldwide. It spawned a successful sequel three years later, proving the idea had legs beyond a single installment. "Projecting an emotional life onto a pet is so satisfying and appealing, something that any of us who have ever owned a pet does. It is a universal fascination," said Meledandri.

I've worked on every movie Chris Meledandri has made. They all include an authentic emotional undercurrent and therein lies his genius. That's what makes for any great movie, animated or not.

CHAPTER 2

Don't Make a Movie for Nobody!

THERE'S A SINGLE QUESTION reverberating through the halls of every studio in Hollywood today: *Is it theater-worthy?*

Twenty years ago this wasn't a concern. Studios would roll out two or three major releases per week, confident that an audience would turn out like clockwork for the latest action blockbuster, buzzy indie comedy, or potential Oscar contender. Largely they were right. Moviegoing—the process of heading to a theater, buying popcorn, and plunking down in an air-conditioned auditorium with a hundred like-minded souls—was still one of America's favorite pastimes. And if you wanted to avoid spoilers and be part of the conversation at school or work on Monday, you had better be there opening weekend.

Then a new rival for America's attention emerged on the scene. In 2007, Netflix launched a streaming service, disrupting not only its own DVD-by-mail business but an entire content-distribution model controlled by the Hollywood studios. Suddenly consumers had endless entertainment options at their fingertips—in their own homes, on their own schedules, for the monthly price of a single movie ticket. Faster than you could say "ta-dum," a flood of streaming competitors entered the market, and the calculus for what could get audiences out of the house and into a theater changed—with studios still racing to catch up.

Anytime a few surefire hits miss and the box office slumps, I hear the same worries echo across the movie industry: "Theatrical is dead!" That cry is usually accompanied by other behind-closed-doors complaints about how "It's just gotten so hard," or "It's just not fun anymore." Then another blockbuster like *Deadpool & Wolverine*, *It Ends with Us*, or *Moana 2* comes along and wildly outperforms expectations, and everybody gets back to business as usual.

But make no mistake: the streaming revolution has fundamentally changed the nature of theatrical moviegoing. And to understand what makes it such a unique disruption, it's helpful first to understand all the other so-called extinction-level threats theaters have survived over the years.

THE FIRST POTENTIAL DISRUPTOR to theatrical moviegoing was the rise of television, a technology that was adopted by American households at record speed. In 1946, there were only about six thousand TV sets nationwide; by 1951, there were twelve million. Just four years later, half of all US homes had a television set.[1]

This wasn't the first time mass entertainment was available in the home. Audiences had been listening to radio programming like *Amos 'n' Andy*, *Fibber McGee and Molly*, and *The Fred Allen Show* every night for years when television came along. But bringing moving pictures right into people's homes? That was a game changer, one that left many wondering about the long-term commercial health of theatrical moviegoing.

"It was the first great threat to the movie business," Sony Pictures CEO Tom Rothman told me. "People were asking, 'Who's gonna go to the movie theater to watch Jack Benny when you can watch Jack Benny at home for free?'"

Turns out, plenty of people were still interested in watching Jack Benny on the silver screen. Television was an entertainment supplement—not a replacement—for theatrical films, with MGM musicals and the like continuing to draw big crowds.

Eventually, television became a whole new way to drive people into theaters. Network talk shows like *The Tonight Show* were eager to have the studios' stars on to discuss their newest projects. Television even became a new revenue stream for studios, as broadcast networks—and eventually cable networks and premium movie channels like HBO—paid big bucks to syndicate movies that could be aired for their own big ratings.

Television also helped usher in the era of the blockbuster when studios began running advertisements for movies on the big three networks—ABC, CBS, and NBC—in the 1970s. Studios had traditionally released films by region, rolling out movies in select markets over the course of several weeks and months. The 1975 release of Steven Spielberg's *Jaws* changed all that, opening nationally in 409 theaters.

This new release strategy required a new approach to marketing. In a 1975 interview with *The Hollywood Reporter*, Universal publicity director Clark Ramsay revealed that *Jaws* marked "the largest expenditure on advertising of a release in the history of the company." Television ads played a particularly pivotal role. "We attempted to buy thirty-second commercials on every prime-time show on June 18, 19, and 20—the three days leading up to the release. We got eighty-five percent of what we were looking for in prime-time spots with local buys."[2]

Audiences were unable to resist the television ads for *Jaws*, which featured John Williams's iconic score and Roy Scheider's instantly quotable line, "You're gonna need a bigger boat." The film banked $8.9 million in its first four days of release, on its way to becoming the highest-grossing movie of 1975. It went on to gross $477 million worldwide—about $2.8 billion today, adjusted for inflation.

The next potential disruptor to theatrical moviegoing came in the form of the VCR. Until this point, audiences still operated on Hollywood's schedule. If you wanted to see a film, you had to buy tickets for a theater's specific showtime, or remember to tune into a network broadcast, like *The ABC Sunday Night Movie*. The VCR—which, remember, stands for videocassette *recorder*—threatened all that. For the first time, viewers could watch entertainment on their own schedule, recording TV shows, sports, and movies when they aired, and playing them back whenever—and however often—they liked.

Studios, as you can probably guess, didn't love this. They argued that VCRs were breaking the law by allowing people to make unauthorized copies of their content. Motion Picture Association of America president Jack Valenti went so far as to testify in front of Congress that "the VCR is to the American film producer and the American public as the Boston Strangler is to the woman home alone."[3]

Universal Studios and the Walt Disney Company ended up suing Sony over their Betamax VCR in 1976. The case eventually made it all the way to the Supreme Court, where Fred Rogers himself—of *Mister Rogers' Neighborhood* fame—argued in favor of the new technology, saying the VCR gave families more control over how and when they watched television.[4] It was a decisive argument, one that was cited by the court when it ultimately ruled in 1984 that recording a television broadcast for personal viewing constituted fair use.

Did the VCR end up being the death knell for theatrical moviegoing that Jack Valenti and others thought it would be? Of course not. Movie theaters still allowed audiences to see first-run films months, if not years, before they would air on television. And studios were able to turn the VCRs popping up in homes across America into a valuable new content distribution system, with revenues climbing as they sold films on high-quality videocassettes to rental stores like Blockbuster and directly to consumers. They made even more money later on with the shift to other physical media types, like DVDs and Blu-rays.

Nobody ended up mastering the art of physical media better than

Disney. After losing the lawsuit against Sony, the studio went on to embrace home video for animated features like *Bambi* and *Dumbo*. But it did so with a unique twist: the movies would only be released from the "Disney Vault" for a limited time and in limited supply. If families wanted to "bring home the magic," they would need to move fast to snag a copy before the film was locked back in the vault, sometimes for years. This marketing gimmick drove huge demand, especially after a run of hits— *The Little Mermaid, Beauty and the Beast, Aladdin,* and *The Lion King*— left every little kid in America clamoring for a VHS clamshell case with their favorite movie inside.

That brings us to the age of streaming. At first glance, it may not appear that different from what came before, combining the syndication model of television with the on-demand nature of VCRs and other physical media players. Why wouldn't this be just another new revenue stream for studios to take advantage of while audiences continue flocking to theaters?

That's how Tom Rothman sees it. "Since the 1950s, we have competed with in-home entertainment that is available to audiences at a lower price point and with greater ease. We have always prevailed—and we will always prevail. Why? 'Cause it's fun to go to the movies."

Jeffrey Katzenberg, the former CEO of Disney, wrote something similar back in the 1990s.[5] "The more significant distinction between the big screen and the little screen isn't the screen at all. It's the audience. Television is an individual experience. The theater is a communal one. And there's something about seeing a film with several hundred strangers that makes a comedy funnier, a horror film scarier, and a tearjerker more heart-wrenching. The entire range of emotions registers with greater force in the theater. Home entertainment technology will not change this."

I'm not inclined to disagree with people like Tom Rothman or Jeffrey Katzenberg often. But I'm not as convinced that "fun" and "emotions" are enough to keep movie theaters afloat amid the streaming revolution.

Part of it, I fear, is generational. I, like many of my generation, am sentimental when it comes to movie theaters. Putting aside my test screenings entirely, they're the site of so many fond personal memories: first dates, birthday parties, nights out with friends. It's a nostalgia shared by many of my peers, evoked the second you get that first whiff of fresh popcorn walking through the door. For us, the movies were and are a *destination*.

Not so for the younger generations studios hope will create the blockbuster hits of today. They don't have the same affinity for theaters, and it shows in their attendance records. Research we've conducted indicates that more people than ever are watching movies—but they are only seeing a fraction of those movies in theaters. This is particularly true for Gen Z— the generation born between 1997 and 2012—who are digital *natives*, as opposed to digital *adopters*. They're likely to see fewer than *half* the movies per year in a theater as previous generations did at the same age. And while the data isn't in on Gen Alpha (born after 2012) yet, I'm expecting to see a similar downward trend. People young and old still love seeing movies, but they don't necessarily need to see every film together in a central place.

What makes this time so different? Why is the rise of digital entertainment consumption such an existential threat to theatrical moviegoing? To answer these questions, we must consider the three Cs: cost, choice, and convenience.

LET'S TALK COST FIRST. Going to the movies has always been an economical form of entertainment. America's first public movie theater—the Nickelodeon in Pittsburgh, Pennsylvania—charged a nickel to watch *The Great Train Robbery* in 1905, and thousands of people turned up every day to pay it.[6]

Prices rose over time, of course—first as movie palaces offered middle-class customers a more luxurious moviegoing experience, then as theaters became wired for sound to play the "talkies," through countless other innovations that kept people coming to theaters even as home entertainment became a reality—wide screens, stereo sound, even Smell-O-Vision. Still, moviegoing remained the best bang for your buck when it came to a night on the town.

It wasn't until the arrival of 3-D and premium large-format screens that price sensitivity from consumers started to have an impact on moviegoing habits. Theater owners and studios alike were successfully making the case for the added benefit they were offering: "See it on the largest screen possible!" "Feel like you're there!" But it came with a hefty cost. What was once a $40 or $50 night out for a family of four even a decade ago might now clock in at $60 or $70—and that's before concessions.

Premium large-format (PLF) screens succeeded in sending revenues through the roof, shattering box office records along the way. There's also been a steady rise in attendance at IMAX and other PLF theaters, proving that audiences will still turn out to see a Hollywood spectacle on the largest screen possible. But these facts hide a larger trend: people seeing far fewer movies per year in theaters. With higher prices, that same family of four might only see four movies in theaters per year instead of eight. In their minds, it's no big loss: there's plenty to watch at home.

That brings us to the next factor driving digital entertainment consumption: **choice**.

Before the advent of streaming, studios largely controlled when, where, and how the public saw movies. They decided when films would be released in theaters and how long they would play there. They controlled when films became available for pay-per-view, and when physical media like VHS, DVD, and Blu-ray copies would be sold. They brokered the licensing deals that would bring movies to premium cable channels and eventually the networks. Bottom line: if consumers wanted to see the latest and greatest in entertainment, they would have to do it on the studios' terms.

Today, the script has completely flipped. There aren't enough hours to keep up with the amount of content being rolled out on streaming services each day. And a lot of it is very high-quality content. Streaming services are paying big money to produce and distribute original films that look no different from what you would see in theaters—from Netflix's *The Irishman* and Amazon's *The Idea of You* to Apple's *Wolfs* and Pixar's *Luca* released directly on Disney+.

Streaming has also blurred the lines between watching films and just . . . watching. On streaming services like Max, movies sit alongside TV dramas and comedies, reality shows, stand-up specials, and even live sports, as just another option for consumption. And that's not even taking into account how many other video services like YouTube and TikTok are competing for attention on our phones—especially among young people.

For audiences, movies are just one of countless options available to entertain them at any given moment. And these choices have another thing going for them—**convenience**, the third factor transforming entertainment consumption.

While the advent of television and VCRs brought movies into people's homes for the first time, there really was no comparison to the theatrical experience. At home, you would typically be watching a movie on a screen a fraction of the size you'd experience in theaters, with tinny audio that couldn't compare to the booming speakers at the local multiplex.

Advancements in home entertainment have leveled the playing field in recent years. Massive TV screens and advanced home audio systems have become more accessible than ever to the average person. Dolby Vision and Dolby Atmos—high-definition video and surround sound technologies previously available only in theaters—have become readily available in consumer devices. This has made a theater-like experience as convenient as sitting down on the couch for many people.

It also can't be overstated just how much more convenient it is to decide to watch something at home versus going to a theater. Research that my company conducted in 2020 told us it takes an average of thirty-five minutes to decide to see a movie, leave the house, and drive to a theater. Even with all the options available on streaming services, it takes only an average of fourteen minutes to decide on something to watch at home.

When you put together the three Cs—cost, choice, and convenience—you get a perfect storm designed to keep audiences at home and out of theaters. I still vividly remember the first time I experienced the phenomenon for myself.

Back in 2017, my husband, Neil, and I were vacationing for half the summer in the Hamptons. It was a wonderfully relaxing trip. The weather was exceptional, and on this particular day, I'd already had a Scotch (or two) lounging by the pool. That was where Neil found me in the early evening, reminding me that it was time to get ready.

We'd bought tickets for that night to *The Beguiled*, a Sofia Coppola–directed Focus Features picture about an injured Union soldier who deserts the front lines and hides out at an all-female boarding school during the Civil War. As I begrudgingly went into the house to take a shower, I found myself thinking: Do I *really* want to go see this movie? The theater, a five-screen dive and the only option in town, was about ten minutes away as the crow flies. But it was a forty-minute trip when you factored in bumper-to-bumper traffic between East Hampton and our house in Amagansett.

I envisioned an alternate version of our evening. A friend who was staying with us had recently raved to me about a new Hulu series, *The Handmaid's Tale*. We could watch that from the comfort of our own home, Scotches still in hand.

I called up my friend and colleague Bob Levin (who, by the way, is the coauthor of this book). I knew he had seen *The Beguiled*, so I could get an informed opinion on its merits. Know what he told me? It was *good*. I responded: "You mean *very* good, or just *good*?" He said, "Just good."

That was all I needed to hear. Did I want to get showered, get dressed, get into the car, and drive forty minutes to see a movie that was just *good*? No f***ing way.

So Neil and I stayed in with our friend. We signed up for Hulu (a bargain at eight bucks a month) and watched an episode of *The Handmaid's Tale*—one of the best episodes of television I'd ever seen in my life, with production values as good as those of any feature film. Then we watched two more episodes. I never did end up seeing *The Beguiled* in a theater. (Though I did ultimately catch it at home, and I liked it far better than Bob did. But hey—that's the power of word of mouth.)

We all have a story like this—a time when we begged off going to the movies to watch something at home or decided to wait a few weeks for a film to hit a streaming service instead of making a special trip to the theater. And these small, individual choices are having a massive impact—not only on box office revenues but on what film studios consider to be worthy of a box office run.

"Streaming has changed the equation," said Josh Goldstine, former president of worldwide marketing at Warner Bros. Pictures. "If there's all this great stuff people can stream from their couch, why should they go to a movie theater? What might have been a theatrical release five years ago doesn't necessarily work today."

THIS WAS THE SITUATION Sony Pictures found itself in when it released the 2011 film *The Girl with the Dragon Tattoo*. The David Fincher-directed thriller was based on the internationally bestselling book, and the studio's testing set high expectations for its box office performance. But a good deal of time passed between this testing and the film's release—enough time for streaming to change how audiences perceived the project.

"Netflix had grown to just over twenty million subscribers, and with that growth came the start of calling into question what a theatrically worthy movie was," Sanford Panitch, president of Sony Pictures Motion Picture Group, told me. "By 2011, *The Girl with the Dragon Tattoo* looked more like a movie available on a streaming platform." And that was how audiences treated it; it debuted to just $12 million in the US on its opening weekend.

What does it take in this streaming era to be a movie worthy of being seen in theaters? We've already established that you need a big idea—but that's only half of the story. The other half is having a crystal-clear understanding of who your target audience is and how intensely your idea appeals to them.

IN THE EARLY DAYS OF HOLLYWOOD, just about every movie made became a movie for everybody by default. Moviegoing was such a novel, exciting form of entertainment that many people would plan a weekly trip to the theater with no specific film in mind to see. They just wanted to watch *something*, and studios were more than happy to meet that demand, rolling out a handful of new releases each week. By the mid-seventies, those weekly releases were being advertised on the big three networks most Americans were watching each night. It created a true monoculture, where people were generally talking about the same entertainment at the same time.

Today, the monoculture is nearly dead, another victim of digital media consumption. The singular conversation that used to be driven by major studios and networks has now splintered into thousands of different and concurrent conversations playing out online. As algorithms create perfectly curated walled gardens for every individual, it's next to impossible to reach everyone with a singular message. Massive cultural events like Barbenheimer can still occasionally break through, but it's rare. And when they do, they're most often "things that are less challenging, that are less threatening, that are more palatable, that have a homogenized feel," as Academy Award–winning filmmaker Ed Zwick said recently.[7]

The shift toward digital media consumption is so seismic that it has fundamentally altered not only the movie business but the TV and music industries as well. Unless you're the NFL, you're not getting more than ten million people tuning into a broadcast network. Unless you're Taylor Swift, you're not selling a million copies of an album in a week. And unless you're a Disney- or Marvel-branded movie, you're going to struggle to gross more than $100 million on an opening weekend.

In this environment, precise audience targeting has become more important than ever before. You need to know not only whom you're trying to reach but how and where you can find them.

Studios have traditionally thought of a movie's intended audience in demographic terms. This approach is a holdover from the days when television was the primary vehicle for raising awareness about an upcoming release, with networks selling ads based on the age and gender of the audience watching. This has allowed studios to target groups such as adults between eighteen and forty-nine or women between twenty-five and fifty-four, depending on the project. Even as the impact of TV advertising has weakened, this type of demographic categorization has persisted as one of the simplest ways to understand audience appeal.

Demographics can be broken into quadrants or octants, depending on the type of film you're making. For general-audience films, which are targeted to adults, studios consider four quadrants: younger men, younger women, older men, and older women (with studios often setting a specific age break based on what's most relevant to the movie being tested). Below is an example of a "topline," which is a single table exhibit that highlights the answers to the two most salient questions on the survey, the overall ratings and the intent to recommend the film to others.

EXAMPLE OF TOPLINE RESULTS BY QUADRANT

Ratings	Total Audience	Men <30	Men 30+	Women <30	Women 30+
Excellent	45%	40%	45%	45%	50%
Very Good	40%	36%	42%	38%	44%
Top 2 Boxes Combined	85%	76%	87%	83%	94%
Definite Recommendations	65%	58%	66%	64%	72%

Now let's say you're making an all-audience family film. Here studios want more granular detail on the groups they're targeting. This is when they will look at eight octants: boys under twelve; girls under twelve; teen boys between thirteen and seventeen; teen girls between thirteen and seventeen; moms; dads; nonparent men eighteen and over; and nonparent women eighteen and over.

EXAMPLE OF TOPLINE RESULTS BY OCTANT

Ratings	Total Audience	Boys <13	Girls <13	Moms	Dads	Teen Boys	Teen Girls	Non-Parent Men	Non-Parent Women
Excellent	52%	70%	60%	55%	60%	45%	40%	45%	40%
Very Good	27%	20%	25%	25%	20%	30%	30%	35%	30%
Top 2 Boxes Combined	79%	90%	85%	80%	80%	75%	70%	80%	70%
Definite Recommendations	60%	70%	60%	65%	70%	50%	45%	60%	55%

Studios and filmmakers need to be most honest with themselves when considering demographics. They need to know exactly what they're making and exactly who they're making it for, because any misalignment can result in the loss of millions of dollars. There's a choice to be made, demographically speaking: make a movie for everybody or make a movie for somebody, but don't make a movie for nobody (and yes, I know that's a double negative!).

The first option is to make a movie for everybody. These are movies that are typically made to be seen in theaters. They get whole families excited about a trip to the multiplex and inspire entire friend groups to prepurchase tickets for opening weekend. *Spider-Man*, *Barbie*, *Despicable Me*, *Deadpool & Wolverine*—these are all movies for everybody.

You want to see movies for everybody with a crowd because, as Katzenberg noted, you know the laughs will be bigger, the gasps will be louder, and the cheers will be wilder. Audience reactions to moments like Steve Rogers saying "Avengers . . . assemble" are still iconic years after the movie's release because they capture that inexplicable magic that happens when an entire roomful of people is immersed in a story together.

Movies for everybody deliver strong results in at least three out of four quadrants or at least six out of eight octants. This mass appeal, no surprise, often fuels massive box office—the top ten highest-grossing movies of all time are all movies for everybody. That's why these films can also carry the risk of a big budget.

THIS WAS CERTAINLY THE CASE for the 2009 Twentieth Century Fox film *Avatar*. We all know it now for the unprecedented hit it became—the highest-grossing movie of all time, more than $2.9 billion in revenues at the global box office, capable of spawning not only a $2.3 billion–grossing sequel but a wildly popular themed land at Walt Disney World.

But *Avatar* wasn't always such a sure bet. In fact, much of its pitch was downright risky. A nearly three-hour sci-fi epic with no preexisting IP, starring ten-foot-tall blue aliens in a world that would need to be almost entirely computer generated, using technology that hadn't even been fully developed yet? That is a tough—and *expensive*—sell.

I sat down with Jim Gianopulos, the former studio head of Twentieth Century Fox, to understand what went into green-lighting *Avatar*. "Of course it was a gamble—it cost a fucking fortune," he said. "But we were gambling on the vision of one of the greatest filmmakers of our time."

Avatar was the brainchild of A-list director and auteur James Cameron. It was his follow-up to *Titanic*, a big-budget epic plagued by delays and a ballooning budget that went on to become a global phenomenon—a four-quadrant smash. If Cameron's plans for *Avatar* were realized, it could be even bigger. *Avatar* had a story families could feel comfortable watching together, a sweeping romance, thrilling action sequences that would appeal to women and men alike, and the vivid, colorful world of Pandora that could transfix kids of all ages.

"Here's what it came down to," said Gianopulos. "Do you wanna be the guy who says no to the movie Jim Cameron passionately wants to make right after making the biggest movie of all time? Or do you wanna be the guy who says yes, and maybe it doesn't do as well as you hoped?"

For Gianopulos, the answer was a no-brainer. With *Avatar* having all the makings of a true eight-octant hit, Twentieth Century Fox committed to it and its reported $237 million budget (though Gianopulos admits the true cost ended up being higher), and a new franchise was born.

Of course, not every film can be a movie for everybody—even if studios wish they could be. This was the situation Disney found itself in with the 2013 film *The Lone Ranger*. Disney treated the film like a movie for everybody, attaching A-list talent and a reported $250 million production budget to the project. After all, *The Lone Ranger* had been a hit as a radio show in the 1930s and as a TV show in the 1950s—surely it would find an audience again!

But the 2010s were a very different time, and the Western-inspired adventures of Armie Hammer's Lone Ranger and Johnny Depp's Tonto struggled to find an audience. The film scraped together $260 million at the global box office, barely surpassing its production budget and causing Disney to lose a reported $190 million overall once marketing costs were factored in.

What went wrong? Believe it or not, the movie itself wasn't to blame. *The Lone Ranger* was never going to be a movie for everybody. Looking at it through an octant lens, it appealed primarily to boys and dads, along with some general-audience men. When Johnny Depp was cast as a lead, you picked up some interest from teen girls, moms, and general-audience women—but not enough to generate widespread interest within those octants. And offsetting that bump in interest, there was some backlash about Depp playing a Native American character.

Yet the studio treated it like it was going to be an eight-octant superhero movie, and they spent way too much money in the process. Had *The Lone Ranger* been made and marketed for what it was—a movie for *somebody*—things could have been very different. Movies for somebody can have their own lucrative runs in theaters if they strongly appeal to their target audiences. Returning to an earlier example, *Where the Crawdads Sing* worked in theaters because it had a large built-in fan base of primarily female readers who were eager to see the world they read about on the page realized on the big screen.

But making a movie for somebody—at the right price—comes with its own set of unique challenges. It requires a much deeper and more nuanced understanding of what resonates with a film's target audience(s). And you need to be able to pinpoint this from the beginning, not in hindsight.

Movies for somebody should appeal to at least two adjacent audience quadrants or deliver extremely strong results inside one quadrant. *The Fault in Our Stars* is a 2014 weeper about two teens who fall in love after meeting in a cancer support group. It made an impressive $307 million at the global box office largely on the strength of its appeal to younger females—driven by teen girls—while also generating some crossover interest in two adjacent quadrants: younger men and older women. Of course, it was also trading on a hugely popular book.

Movies for somebody can also find success targeting similar octants. *Pete's Dragon*—a family film from Disney about a young orphan and his dragon best friend—resonated with boys, girls, moms, and dads. And its $143 million worldwide box office gross was considered a respectable success against its "movie for somebody" budget of $65 million.

Trying to target nonadjacent quadrants or octants, however, rarely pays off. Consider *The Guilt Trip*, a 2012 comedy starring Barbra Streisand and Seth Rogen. The two stars appealed to wildly different audiences—older women and younger men, respectively. This could have effectively doubled the marketing budget, with two completely different campaigns targeting two completely different demographic segments with two completely different messages. This didn't happen, and the film eked out $5 million in the US on its opening weekend.

Here are some more examples of movies that were demographically for somebody. The 2024 film *Challengers*, starring Zendaya, made close to $95 million. Its appeal was primarily to women under thirty years old, but it appealed to men under thirty as well. *Napoleon*, the 2023 film starring Joaquin Phoenix, appealed primarily to males over thirty. While it did just okay in the US, posting $61 million in box office, it grossed another $160 million internationally.

The 2024 movie *Longlegs*, starring Nicolas Cage, appealed to the traditional horror audience of males and females under thirty, leading to its opening weekend of $22 million, a tremendous result for indie distributor Neon. Horror movies usually succeed because they are made for the right price for the known audience. Making a movie for the right price that appeals to men and women over thirty can make money, too. *Last*

Vegas (2013) had old friends played by Robert De Niro, Michael Douglas, Kevin Kline, and Morgan Freeman gathering in Las Vegas to relive their glory days.

"When I was pitched *Last Vegas*, I thought, wow, that's a very commercial idea—exploring longstanding friendships," says producer and former studio executive Amy Baer. "I hadn't felt like I had seen or read anything like that before. It wasn't just about four best friends going to Vegas to stop one of the three from marrying an inappropriate woman and burying old hatchets in the process. I mean, that's the plot. That's not the concept. The concept is, and the theme of it is, longstanding friendships. And that felt like something very relatable, but also the idea of older people juxtaposed with younger-skewing Vegas felt fun, too. I bought it and put it into development in 2009, when I was running CBS Films.

"When I left there, I went on to produce it, aiming to answer the important question of who the audience for the movie was, and what it would take to have that audience want to see four old people running around Vegas. It felt clear to me that the audience for it was older, because it very squarely spoke to things that were relevant to an older demographic: aging, friendship, loss, second chances, nostalgia, relevance. All those things felt honest. And that is, to me, how you must weigh material. What segments of the audience will it attract? You must know who you are making a movie for. With the casting of De Niro, Douglas, Kline, and Freeman, I knew that if I made it for the right price it should work." Even with that cast, it was produced for $29 million and went on to earn a global box office of $134 million.

Last Vegas succeeded because Baer went in knowing what she was making. The concept worked for the audience she was targeting, and the casting supported the concept. Importantly, she never made choices that could have sacrificed a single older audience member in an attempt to attract a younger one.

Baer pays keen attention to the makeup of the audience for a movie. She produced *Brian Banks* in 2018, which tells the story of a football player's shattered dreams, as he's wrongfully convicted of rape, sentenced to prison, and then takes up the fight to clear his name. It's not a movie for everybody. It's not even a movie for somebody, demographically speaking. But sometimes there are films that have a large enough *psychographic* appeal to make it a movie for somebody, and Baer knew there would be people with common behaviors and attitudes that would be drawn to the subject and quite interested in seeing it.

"We thought the audience would primarily be African American," Baer says. "That was the focus, African American males, both younger and older. Because many older and younger Black men could relate to the journey of that character—of being a Black man in our culture and being wrongfully accused of something. That's the audience we expected to see the movie. But its eventual success extended beyond, to sports fans and 'smarthouse' moviegoers [those who fall between strictly arthouse and sophisticated mainstream viewers] who related to the Greg Kinnear character being a social justice warrior. So many people loved the movie.

"However, those who were going to market the movie theatrically didn't have faith . . . that the intended audience would even show up, so the movie was minimally supported when released. The reality is that there was, as I expected, an audience for the film, as it has done very well on streaming and in the ancillary markets. The rights to the movie were sold before it was made, and its $10 million production cost was covered."

Brian Banks demonstrates that demographics aren't everything when it comes to making a movie for somebody. Psychographics—which define audiences by factors like personality and behavioral characteristics, lifestyle, social class, habits, cultural identity, and interests—can also be a powerful targeting tool, especially when marketing movies online.

HOW TO SCORE IN HOLLYWOOD

During 2023's summer of Barbenheimer, there was another massive box office story happening that far fewer people were paying attention to. On July 4, 2023, *Sound of Freedom* opened to a single-day gross of $14.2 million, almost eclipsing its $14.5 million production budget in one day on its way to earning a $184 million domestic gross. It was a smashing success story for Angel Studios, the company that distributed the film. And it was even more surprising given how small their marketing budget was: just $5 million.[8] How did they pull it off?

To find out, I sat down with Jordan Harmon, president of Angel Studios. Angel is a family business, one that Jordan cofounded with his brothers. "We were watching the entertainment space and how quickly it was evolving into something we didn't want in our homes," Harmon told me. But more faith-*friendly*, rather than strictly faith-*based*, options were few and far between. "A lot of values-based entertainment is cheesy and not actually entertaining."

Angel Studios was created to help fill this gap in the market. The company, which specializes in content that spreads positivity, inspiration, and goodness, chooses the movies they will produce and distribute in conjunction with a like-minded group of moviegoers called "the Angel Guild." More than 330,000 people pay twenty dollars per month to be part of the guild, which allows them to review potential film acquisitions and concept videos that have been submitted to Angel Studios for consideration. "Guild members are the gatekeepers. They decide what gets made at Angel," Harmon said. "For them, it's a statement that says, *I'd rather pay this than a Netflix subscription or a Disney+ subscription. This is going to represent me better; this is going to help create more content that is values based.*"

Sound of Freedom was one of the movies initially submitted to the Angel Guild for review. Starring Jim Caviezel, it tells the true story of a former federal agent who sets out on a mission to save children from sex traffickers. The film scored off the charts, receiving some of the highest ratings from the guild that Angel Studios had ever seen. "Because of the way we operate, we don't have any duds," Harmon said. "When we release something, we know exactly what the audience scores are going to be." That made *Sound of Freedom* an instant yes for the studio to acquire.

When it came time to distribute the movie, Angel Studios once again turned to the guild. They crowdfunded the money to market it, with about seven thousand investors contributing a total of five million dollars. If the movie succeeded at the box office, these investors would earn a return on their investment—effectively incentivizing them to become ambassadors for the film. This helped *Sound of Freedom* become a viral sensation, as word of mouth spread from the Angel Guild online and across the country. The film succeeded in theaters because it understood exactly who its target audience was—religious and conservative viewers who felt unseen and overlooked by traditional Hollywood studios. And those viewers turned out to theaters in droves—*Sound of Freedom* went on to become one of the ten highest-grossing movies of 2023.

But there's an exceptionally thin line between movies for somebody that can make it in theaters and those that would be more at home on a streaming service. *Theater Camp*, a 2023 comedy about the eccentric staff of a run-down—you guessed it—theater camp, grossed only $4.6 million in theaters after being acquired by Fox Searchlight for $8 million at Sundance. But the film went on to have a second life on streaming, becoming a popular pick on Hulu.

"Everything I work on, I want to be an event for someone—even if it's not demographically for that person," said the film's producer, Erik Feig. "When I was developing *Theater Camp*, I was confident three groups of people would love it: people who are really into theater camps, people who are really into musical theater, and people who are really into upcoming comedy talent. With that in mind, I can think how many people is that? What budget would that support?"

I can't underscore enough just how critical Erik's questions are to making a profitable movie for somebody. If you don't understand exactly who and how many people your movie appeals to and budget accordingly, you can fall victim to the biggest danger in Hollywood: making a movie for nobody, for way too much money.

Against all logic, it happens more often than you think. Movies for nobody are based on concepts that do not have enough appeal to inspire intense interest from at least one major demographic or one large psychographic segment. If that core group cannot be easily identified, sized, and counted on to turn out in big numbers to see the film, on what basis are you establishing a budget to produce and market it? Examples like *Pushing Tin*, a dramedy about air traffic controllers; *The Big Year*, a bird-watching film starring Owen Wilson and Jack Black; and *Ravenous*, a horror movie about cannibals set during the Mexican-American War were all movies for nobody, because there wasn't a single demographic quadrant or psychographic segment with enough interested viewers to justify spending marketing dollars chasing after them, let alone the production spend to get them made in the first place.

Movies about Hollywood, maybe surprisingly, often end up being movies for nobody. *Ed Wood*, *Gods and Monsters*, *Hollywoodland*, *The Disaster Artist*, and *The Unbearable Weight of Massive Talent* were films with movie industry themes that struggled to find audiences large enough to cover even their production budgets. So it went with *Babylon*, director Damien Chazelle's 2022 film about decadence and depravity in the early days of Hollywood. The movie was green-lit by Paramount CEO Jim Gianopulos, who envisioned it as an elevated drama that would appeal primarily to older audiences. "We had a great director, fresh off his Oscar win for *La La Land*, and we had two of the biggest movie stars in the world—Brad Pitt and Margot Robbie—playing characters I thought audiences could invest in," Gianopulos said. But what started out as a movie for somebody ultimately became a movie for nobody. As the project moved through production, the three-hour epic lost sight of its characters' motivations and instead focused on the underbelly of Tinseltown during the transition from silents to talkies. The movie was dead on arrival with audiences, making just $63 million worldwide against its reported $110 million budget. Chazelle later said, "Certainly, in financial terms, *Babylon* didn't work at all. You try to not have that affect what you're doing creatively, but at some level, it can't help but affect it."[9]

I, for one, really enjoyed *Babylon*. But then again, I was part of its very tiny psychographic audience—Hollywood insiders who love the messiness that often goes on behind the scenes in Tinseltown. For just about everyone else, *Babylon* was too long, too dramatic, and too "inside baseball." There's a lesson to be learned here: movies about Hollywood are seldom as interesting as people in Hollywood think they are.

Even movies with strong existing intellectual properties can end up being movies for nobody. The 2018 film adaptation of *A Wrinkle in Time*, a classic young adult fantasy novel from 1962, failed to resonate with modern audiences because they couldn't figure out who the movie was for. The story was ostensibly for kids, but its stars—Oprah Winfrey, Reese Witherspoon, and Mindy Kaling—primarily appealed to older audiences. It was directed by the extremely talented Ava DuVernay, more known for her serious adult projects like *Selma* and *13th*. Although visually stunning, it ended up being the worst of all worlds—a movie that didn't look exciting enough for kids and that looked too juvenile for adults. It only grossed $132 million worldwide against its reported $103 million budget.

But perhaps my favorite story about a movie for nobody involves a bunch of penguins. Seriously.

"It all started with a phone call from Bob Saget, asking if I'd seen *March of the Penguins*," producer David Permut says. He had seen the documentary about penguins living in Antarctica—it was the talk of the

2005 Sundance Film Festival he had recently attended. "So Bob just starts riffing with his very blue humor about the mating rituals of penguins. I was laughing my ass off. And I couldn't get it out of my head. So the next day I told him, 'We need to make the sexploitation version of *March of the Penguins*.'"

Permut's initial idea was to put a new, R-rated audio track over the existing *March of the Penguins* film. But that was a no-go with Warner Bros., which knew its project had a good shot at an Oscar (rightly so—it eventually won the Academy Award for Best Documentary Feature). But Permut and Saget wouldn't be deterred. "I realized plenty of other people had filmed penguins over the years, so we could make our own movie using stock footage," Permut said.

Permut and Saget assembled a truly impressive lineup of comedic talent to participate in the project, which they dubbed *Farce of the Penguins*: Samuel L. Jackson narrated, while stars like Whoopi Goldberg, Jim Belushi, Damon Wayans, Brie Larson, and Jason Alexander signed on to voice various penguins. Once it was finished, Permut thought the best release strategy was straight to DVD. Saget, however, was convinced that the movie could have a lucrative theatrical run. They called Screen Engine to help settle the matter, and we scheduled a test screening at the Landmark Westwood in Los Angeles.

"My sister came to this screening—the first and only time she ever showed up to one of my tests," Permut said. "It's a packed house, the audience is pumped, the vibe is over the moon." That lasted for about the first ten minutes of the screening. "A few people start leaving, then a couple more. Bob Saget is sitting next to me, gripping my arm. Then entire rows start to exit en masse, and he's squeezing even tighter. It was like somebody fucking yelled 'Fire!' in the theater. And I watch as my sister, who's sitting in front of me, just sinks lower and lower into her seat."

Permut's sister was one of the few who stuck around. By the time the movie ended, only about a third of the original audience remained. We dutifully handed out the comment cards, but once I glanced at them and saw that most of the moviegoers were rating the film "fair" or "poor," I told Permut it wouldn't be productive to hold a focus group. Scores that low are rarely accompanied by comments that are constructive, and it would be painful for the filmmakers to sit through what would undoubtedly be an onslaught of negativity. The writing was already on the wall: dire, dismal, *disaster*.

There would never be a theatrical release for *Farce of the Penguins*. Our test screening revealed that it was a one-joke movie that most people felt overstayed its welcome. But that one joke did end up finding a small but dedicated fan base once it was released straight to DVD: stoned college kids.

About ten years later, Permut himself found redemption when we reunited to test *Hacksaw Ridge*, a film he produced that was directed by Mel Gibson and starred Andrew Garfield as a pacifist combat medic serving in World War II. Our test audience was enthralled by the movie—they absolutely loved it. I had to laugh when I told Permut later, "You now have the honor of producing one of the lowest-testing movies in my company's history *and* one of the highest."

CHAPTER 3

Good Isn't Good Enough

STUDIOS HAVE BEEN USING SLEIGHT OF HAND to protect mediocre movies for decades. In the early days of Hollywood, a lack of other entertainment options meant even bad films had a chance to find an audience. Later, slick trailers, exciting TV ads, and carefully chosen "pull quotes" from reviewers could make a lackluster movie look good enough to get people into theaters on opening weekend—even if poor word of mouth spread after that.

Today the accessibility of entertainment news sites and social media have fundamentally changed the power dynamics between studios and audiences. The internet has made it possible for any moviegoer to feel like a Hollywood insider—following casting rumors with *Variety* and *The Hollywood Reporter*, debating box office tracking numbers on Reddit, and watching reviews from around the world roll in on Rotten Tomatoes. In this hyperaware environment, it's increasingly difficult to hide a bad or mediocre movie.

Audiences are savvier than ever, and much like the titular shark in *Jaws*, they can easily smell blood in the water. When rumors of a movie misfire take hold, the internet-enabled entertainment ecosystem kicks into overdrive, with negative momentum that can doom a film long before it ever opens in theaters. *The Flash*, the 2023 Warner Bros. movie about a popular DC Comics character, is a recent notable victim. The film was dogged by multiple issues during production, including director changes, pandemic-related delays, and controversies surrounding star Ezra Miller. While Warner Bros. Discovery CEO David Zaslav tried to generate buzz for the project at CinemaCon by calling it "the best superhero movie I've ever seen,"[1] early fan screenings were met with a decidedly mixed response. These screenings also ended up spoiling many of the movie's surprises well in advance of its official release.

When *The Flash* finally opened in theaters, any excitement for the film had vanished. In late April 2023, the movie was predicted to open to more than $100 million in the US over the four-day Juneteenth holiday weekend. By the time it finally opened on Friday, June 16, these estimates were revised down to $70 million. As negative word of mouth spread rapidly throughout the weekend, the numbers got even worse: *The Flash* earned $61.2 million in the US over its first four days, which seems like a lot of money but is only a drop in the bucket against its reported $200 million production budget, which didn't even factor in worldwide marketing costs that probably topped $100 million. There are tried-and-true models used in Hollywood to forecast total gross using opening weekend box office and the positive word of mouth captured in exit polling over that first weekend. *The Flash* took in $24 million on its opening Friday, followed by $16 million on Saturday (a 35 percent drop), and $15 million on Sunday. On Juneteenth Monday, the gross was down to $6 million. The trajectory over its opening weekend was just the beginning of things to come. The following weekend was down a whopping 72 percent, with the movie earning just $15 million over the entire three days. In short, it was an unmitigated disaster.

Would Warner Bros. have been better off if it had shielded its less-than-perfect product for as long as it could? It's unlikely. Limiting sneak peeks or lifting review embargoes as close to a movie's opening day as possible come with their own risks. Audiences are wise to these tactics, and the use of them is its own signal of an impending dud. And there's no hiding once a movie opens to the public. As we saw with *The Flash*, word of mouth blazes fast—and Thursday-night previews can leave a movie dead in the water by Friday afternoon.

People fundamentally do not want to have their time wasted. If they're making a trip to the theater, what they're seeing had better deliver the goods. Studio head Tom Rothman says it best: "There was a time where the range of what you could make, and how well you could make it, was much wider. The range of what was good enough to justify investing in a movie, and what was good enough to get people to go see a movie, was much wider. Today that is not the case. Today 'good' is not good enough."

Robbie Brenner of Mattel Films agrees: "There's so much noise, so many distractions, so much television, social media, and gaming. The movies that really work in that world are the ones that resonate, feel sticky and singular and different. Those are the movies that drive people to the box office."

I couldn't agree with Tom and Robbie more. Success in theaters today is only possible when all the stars align—when an elevated idea and elevated execution come together to create something truly special. Because to get people to turn off their favorite streaming service and get out of the house, a movie can't just be *good*. In many cases, it can't even just be *great*. It must be *exceptional*.

Let's look at some examples of what's working across a few different genres.

ACTION-ADVENTURE MOVIES have always been staples of the big screen. Many promise jaw-dropping special effects, pulse-pounding sound, and thrilling action scenes that leave you on the edge of your seat. But certain films have become legend in their failure to deliver—from 1980's *Heaven's Gate*, which was such a monumental and public disaster that it brought down an entire studio, to more modern flops like *John Carter*, *The Lone Ranger*, *Cutthroat Island*, and *Battleship*. What sets the successes apart from the failures?

Some blockbusters push the boundaries of what's possible with their action sequences. The *Mission: Impossible* franchise has stayed relevant for almost three decades in large part due to the willingness of star Tom Cruise to perform his own increasingly outrageous stunts. Moviegoers have turned out in droves over the years to watch Cruise scale the world's tallest building (*Ghost Protocol*), hold on to the outside of a flying plane (*Rogue Nation*), and "speed-fly" off a mountain (*Dead Reckoning*)—all the while wondering *How the hell did he do that?* In fact, Cruise's stunts were so critical to the promotion of *Mission: Impossible—Dead Reckoning* that Paramount Pictures ran a behind-the-scenes featurette for the speed-fly scene in front of IMAX screenings of *Avatar: The Way of Water*.[2]

Other films—like *300*, one of the projects we discussed earlier in the book—have found success by finding a unique visual identity. Director Denis Villeneuve has built an entire career out of making visually striking movies, including *Arrival*, *Blade Runner 2049*, and, of course, *Dune* and *Dune: Part Two*.

A distinctive visual style was part of what Cale Boyter, the producer on *Dune*, was looking for from a director. "I always thought that Frank Herbert was the Tolkien of sci-fi," Boyter said. "So I wondered: If you could do an elevated version of *Dune*, could you turn it into a *Lord of the Rings*–type of experience?" After watching *Arrival*, he was convinced Villeneuve could pull it off.

For Villeneuve, it was a childhood dream to turn Frank Herbert's science fiction epic into a movie—and he knew how he depicted the desert planet of Arrakis would make or break the project. He turned to Jordan's Wadi Rum Desert—otherwise known as the Valley of the Moon in Arabic, and famously the filming location for *Lawrence of Arabia*.

"The rock formations are so strange and beautiful, exactly as I imagined them when I read *Dune* as a teenager," Villeneuve told *The Hollywood Reporter* in 2021. "The quality of the light and the enormous scale of everything—you have an encounter with nature there that fills you with humility."[3]

Villeneuve used the massive landscape to create tension for audiences, filming objects just at the edge of the screen to evoke "that feeling of a nightmare, where your eyes see part of something coming into your field of vision and you feel its presence, but you never completely see it." His goal was to inspire awe: "We really worked on this idea that the world was bigger than our lenses, like the camera is struggling to capture what's there." Boy, did he succeed. *Dune*—and its sequel, *Dune: Part Two*—are visual jaw-droppers that were unlike anything ever seen before, stunning audiences around the globe.

But it wasn't just visuals that attracted audiences to the *Dune* film series. "How do we make the movie emotional? That was a big question we wrestled with," Boyter says. His attention soon turned to the relationship between the characters of Paul Atreides and Chani, who would eventually be played by Timothée Chalamet and Zendaya. "There's a love story that is inside the book, but it's certainly not front and center. So we said, 'Let's make a movie that breaks people's hearts.' That became our guiding light."

Boyter's instincts remind us that sometimes it's the most basic principles of good storytelling that turn an action movie into a must-see. "The cheapest and best thing you can do is have characters that people care about. If you have that, the rest is gravy," producer Neal Moritz said. "What made *The Fast and the Furious* movies such a success were the group of personalities we had. Everybody could somehow relate to one of them. They wanted to be part of that family."

Did they ever. Spanning more than two decades, *The Fast and the Furious* franchise has grossed more than $7.3 billion worldwide across ten films and one spin-off feature by combining the thrills of a classic car racing movie with a sprawling cast of memorable heroes and villains. Don't get me wrong, the action in these films is top-notch, especially when you consider how much is achieved through practical effects and stunt coordination. But the ever-expanding mythology of the films' universe and the chemistry of the cast—which began with Paul Walker, Vin Diesel, and Michelle Rodriguez and later added the likes of Dwayne Johnson, Charlize Theron, and Jason Momoa—are the biggest reasons fans have kept coming back year after year.

Fan loyalty to the franchise and its characters was clearly displayed when series star Paul Walker passed away in a tragic car accident while he was away from set during production on the franchise's seventh installment, *Furious 7*. "I got the news, and I just couldn't believe it," Moritz said. "Everybody's initial thought was that we were just going to stop. We're not going to finish the movie."

Then Chris Morgan, the film's writer, came up with an idea for how to complete the project while honoring Walker. With the actor's younger brothers serving as stand-ins, they could use CGI and archived footage of Walker to complete a final scene that gave his character, Brian O'Conner, a happy ending. After pitching the idea to the studio and the cast, they collectively agreed to move forward.

"At the first test screening, I was very nervous about how the audience was going to react," Moritz said. "We see Paul and Vin driving down the road, and the road separates. Paul goes one way, Vin goes the other. Then the movie ends, and there's silence. I could only hear some crying. And I'm like, 'Oh my God, did it work? Did it not work?' It felt like it worked, but I wasn't sure."

Then Moritz made his way to the theater lobby to wait for the screening's test results, where he was stopped by several members of the audience. "They thanked me for making the movie. As close as Paul was to me and to our cast and crew, and how much we cared about him . . . I had forgotten how much he meant to the audience. They needed closure as much as we did. It was truly one of the most fulfilling things I've ever done in my life."

Furious 7, dedicated to the memory of Paul Walker, went on to deliver a franchise-best $147 million opening weekend in the US, and it remains the highest-grossing *Fast and Furious* film with $1.5 billion at the global box office.

THERE'S PERHAPS NO GENRE more reliant on elevation than dramas. Between streaming services and the rise of prestige television shows like *Mad Men*, *Breaking Bad*, and *Succession*, studios have to offer something ever more compelling to get people—primarily adults—into theaters for a two- or three-hour drama.

This is something with which producer Mark Gordon is all too familiar. He's one of the brains behind *Saving Private Ryan*, one of the most acclaimed and successful dramas of all time . . . that almost never saw the light of day.

Gordon sat down with me to talk about how the project was first conceived. "I met with a screenwriter named Bob Rodat, and we really liked each other. We decided to keep meeting until we came up with a story we wanted to work on together. This went on for a couple of months, neither of us particularly excited about anything we talked about. Then, in something like our fourth meeting, Bob said, 'You know, I just read this story about a soldier trapped behind enemy lines right after D-Day. Three of his brothers had already been killed in the war, and the army decided they needed to get him out before he was killed as well. What do you think?' I told him, 'That's the best story I've ever heard in my life.' He asked if I thought we could sell it, and I confidently replied, 'Of course we can sell it.'"

But the journey to a green light ended up being more complicated than Gordon had hoped. "We took it to Fox, where I had a deal after producing *Speed* there. They passed. We took it to Warner Bros. They passed. TriStar—passed. Everybody passed."

A bit of good news finally came when Paramount agreed to give Gordon and Rodat the money to develop a full script. "Bob and I made a deal with ourselves that the draft we would give to Paramount had to be perfect. Nobody would get to see it until we were both a hundred percent happy with it. We worked through so many different variations—we must have done twenty drafts."

Even after producing a script that both men thought was the best they had ever been involved with, the reaction at Paramount wasn't what they had hoped. The studio was developing two other war movies, and they weren't sure which project they wanted to move forward with.

But Gordon refused to stop advocating for their script. "I had a meeting with Tom Hanks to see if he might be interested in the movie. He was—and without me knowing, he spoke to Steven Spielberg about it, who also eventually decided he wanted to do it. I had the great pleasure of calling up Paramount and saying, 'Well, would you like to make the movie now that Tom Hanks and Steven Spielberg are attached?' That's how it ultimately came together."

Saving Private Ryan went on to become a box office, critical, and award-winning success, eventually taking home five Academy Awards. But its winding road to a green light illustrates just how important it is to have the full package when you're creating a drama for theaters. You truly need it all—a great story, a top-notch script, and major talent both behind and in front of the camera.

The success of a theatrical drama can also come down to impressive technical achievements that demand to be seen on the biggest screens possible. This is the path that director Christopher Nolan has mastered.

The Dark Knight, the second movie in Nolan's Batman trilogy, was the first feature film to include multiple scenes shot using IMAX cameras.[4] He continued to experiment with the ultra-high-resolution cameras in 2017's *Dunkirk*. About 70 percent of the footage used in the World War II movie was shot on IMAX, creating an experience Nolan himself likened to "virtual reality without the goggles."[5] He later said, "This is something that nobody will ever be able to see in their living room. It's the best argument that cinema has against the competition represented by improvement to home video systems."[6]

Nolan's statement was proven true just a few short years later with the release of 2023's *Oppenheimer*. The film, about the father of the atomic bomb, was a critical smash—eventually winning seven Academy Awards, including Best Picture. But perhaps even more impressive were its box office accomplishments. As moviegoers poured into theaters around the globe, it raked in a stunning $975 million worldwide—pretty much unheard of for a three-hour, R-rated drama.

Bohemian Rhapsody, the 2018 film about Freddie Mercury and his band, Queen, achieved a similarly impressive milestone—earning more than $900 million worldwide, the highest-grossing music biopic ever. It's hard to overstate what an accomplishment this is. Other dramas about iconic music acts have failed to get anywhere close to this level of success: *Whitney Houston: I Wanna Dance with Somebody* ($59 million worldwide); the Amy Winehouse biopic *Back to Black* ($50 million worldwide); the James Brown movie *Get On Up* ($33 million worldwide); the Aretha Franklin film *Respect* ($32 million worldwide); and the Cole Porter biopic *De-Lovely* ($18 million worldwide), to name just a few.

So what makes a musical biopic that's worthy of being seen in theaters? Graham King, producer and the driving force behind *Bohemian Rhapsody*, shared the framework he uses when deciding what films to make. "There are two rules for me. One, do they have a cinematic story to tell? And two, can you really give fresh information to the public through a cinematic experience?" King said. "A lot of my job is talking about the difference between making a documentary and making a cinematic experience."

In the case of *Bohemian Rhapsody*, there was no question in King's mind that the story of Queen and Freddie Mercury needed to be seen on the big screen. "A streaming company originally wanted to make this movie," King said. "Financially, it was a wonderful deal for me. But as a producer, you live and die by the decisions you make. And eventually I went back to them and said, 'Freddie Mercury really invented playing for the masses. If you ever went to a Queen concert and were lucky enough to see Freddie with one hundred fifty thousand people, you were holding the hand of the person next to you, swaying to "We Are the Champions." You were dancing with them to "We Will Rock You." He created that. And I have to create that in a movie theater—because if I don't, I've failed Freddie and the band. So I cannot put this on streaming.'"

It was the right move in every respect. The final film had high stakes, a lead character overcoming extraordinary odds, thrilling musical sequences, and an electric performance from Rami Malek that would eventually secure him an Academy Award for Best Actor. "Truly, I knew we had something special. I just didn't realize the size and the scope of it," King said. "I've never had a film score higher in a preview than *Bohemian Rhapsody*."

In fact, *Bohemian Rhapsody* was one of the top movies tested *in the history of testing*. That's how much audiences loved it.

THERE'S NO SHORTAGE OF LAUGHS to be found in entertainment. Network television runs a steady stream of thirty-minute comedies each season. Streaming services regularly run stand-up specials from the hottest comics. And anyone with a cell phone has a shot at promoting their unique brand of hilarity on YouTube or TikTok. With all that competition, what makes a comedy that's worthy of being seen in theaters?

Sony Pictures executive Sanford Panitch takes many of his cues from audiences. "*Ghostbusters: Afterlife* was a movie driven into production by audience interest," he said. Another Sony executive, Jeffrey Godsick, had shown him how strong the *Ghostbusters* franchise still was, with ongoing demand for everything from clothing to collectibles.

"When I understood the audience-driven opportunity, I went to Jason Reitman to talk about what a new *Ghostbusters* movie could look like," Panitch said. "Jason, of course, had his own deep affinity for the property. He was seven years old when his dad, Ivan, directed the original movie. He had dressed up as a ghostbuster, played as a ghostbuster. And the more we talked, we realized that seeing *Ghostbusters* through the eyes of young kids was our entry point."

Reitman penned the script, eventually crafting a story that featured two kids moving to a small town with their mother, only to discover the original 1959 Cadillac Ectomobile and a familial connection to one of the original Ghostbusters. It was a love letter to the franchise audiences had adored in the 1980s, even featuring cameos from key members of the original cast like Bill Murray, Dan Aykroyd, and Ernie Hudson. "I gave the script to my boss, Tom Rothman, without letting him know who wrote the screenplay or how long I'd been secretly working on it," Panitch said. "It was a go from that moment on."

Nostalgia was enough to get Sony Pictures interested in expanding and reinvigorating the *Ghostbusters* franchise. But it's often not enough on its own. When producer and copresident of Imagine Entertainment Brian Grazer wanted to remake *The Nutty Professor*, a 1963 comedy starring Jerry Lewis, he knew he had to pull out all the stops. He saw the potential for the movie to be a big hit with a new generation, if Eddie Murphy was cast as the lead. But Murphy's career had cooled down from his prime *Beverly Hills Cop* days, and Universal Studios was reluctant to sign off on the project with him attached.

Just as Mark Canton had Zack Snyder film a sequence of what *300* would look like to get a green light, Grazer set out to show the studio just how perfect Murphy was for the titular role of *The Nutty Professor*. "Eddie wasn't going to agree to do a screen test to get a part," Grazer recalled. "But I could get him to agree to have Academy Award–winning special makeup director Rick Baker turn him into several of the characters." When Universal executives saw the footage Grazer and Baker had captured of Murphy transforming into everyone from the enormous Papa Klump to elderly Granny Klump, they got the vision for what the movie could be and eagerly signed off on Murphy's casting. *The Nutty Professor* went on to gross $274 million worldwide and spawned a sequel, *Nutty Professor II: The Klumps*.

It's worth detouring here to talk about one of the most unjustly maligned subgenres of the comedy world: the romantic comedy. The trades regularly declare the entire genre dead at the box office, something better relegated to books or the small screen. Then a movie like *Anyone But You* hits big, and studios remember that women like going to the movies, too.

For romantic comedies, casting is everything. It's not enough just to find two actors that audiences want to see bounce off each other. They also need to have that certain something—a magnetic chemistry that leaps off the screen. It's a tough recipe to get right. But when it hits—like with Tom Hanks and Meg Ryan, Emma Stone and Ryan Gosling, Drew Barrymore and Adam Sandler, or Jennifer Lawrence and Bradley Cooper—it can hit big.

For Universal Pictures executive Dwight Caines, his vote in favor of making 2022's *Ticket to Paradise* all came down to the movie's two attached stars, Julia Roberts and George Clooney. "At the green-light meeting, I was asking two questions: Are these two movie stars meaningful today? And are they meaningful to this specific movie? The easy answer to both questions was yes," Caines said. Even with plenty of comedy-romances being released on streamers, Caines knew Clooney and Roberts could get people out of the house—especially given the success of their pairing in the popular *Ocean's Eleven* franchise. "This particular movie, with this talent, was completely worthy of a theatrical release. People have longed to see these two stars do a movie like this." He was right—*Ticket to Paradise* went on to earn almost $170 million worldwide.

Casting was also critical to the success of *Anyone But You*, which paired two up-and-coming actors popular with millennial and Gen Z audiences—Sydney Sweeney, who gained recognition on the hit HBO shows *Euphoria* and *The White Lotus*; and Glen Powell, at a new level of fame after mega-blockbuster *Top Gun: Maverick*. But the film also elevated itself through its setting. Much like *Ticket to Paradise*, which set most of the movie's action in picturesque Bali, *Anyone But You* filmed in Australia, with several key scenes taking place in and around the iconic Sydney Harbor. When the movie opened the weekend before Christmas in 2023, the combination of beautiful people falling in love in a beautiful place kept audiences turning out deep into the winter months. It ended up grossing $220 million worldwide on a reported budget of $25 million.

PEOPLE LOVE A GOOD SCARE—and nothing delivers better than a great horror movie. But part of what makes for a good scare is the element of surprise. After all, where's the fun if you already know what's coming?

Staying one step ahead of audience expectations is what separates a good horror movie from a great one. Filmmakers in the genre know this, and they're constantly pushing the boundaries to elevate their projects above what's been done before.

No series captures the elevation ethos better than the *Scream* franchise. The first film, released in 1996, set out to deconstruct the entire genre with a plot that twisted and remade standard horror movie tropes for a new generation. Who can forget the iconic opening scene, which saw Drew Barrymore (the presumed star of the film based on an intentionally misleading marketing campaign) get brutally murdered after being quizzed on her favorite scary movie?

Scream and its subsequent sequels set themselves apart because they featured characters who closely resemble the very audience they hoped to attract—horror movie fans who had seen it all. "Elevated horror puts real characters in extraordinary circumstances. The more real they feel, the more you can care about and identify with them. How would *you* react if you were put in the most insane situation ever? That's what we've done really well with *Scream*," said William Sherak, my longtime friend and one of the franchise's producers.

Across four films, Neve Campbell's Sidney Prescott, Courteney Cox's Gale Weathers, and David Arquette's Deputy Dewey became the heart of the series. And when it came time to reboot the franchise in its fifth entry, 2022's *Scream*, these original characters were central to the filmmakers' plans. "We knew we wanted to do a handoff story to help bring these new kids into the franchise," Sherak said. "The only way to do that was to bring back Neve, Courteney, and David—our survivors. I don't think that movie works without them."

The *Scream* reboot definitely worked for audiences, grossing $30 million on its opening weekend in the US by bringing together fans of the original films and new Gen Z audiences. Paramount quickly approved a sequel. But when Neve Campbell refused to reprise her role again after a salary dispute, the producers of *Scream VI* were forced to stare down a thorny question: Would audiences turn out to a *Scream* movie without her?

"Sidney Prescott is one of the greatest female horror leads of all time. Of course we were nervous to do it without her," Sherak said. But the filmmakers had other tricks up their sleeves to elevate the concept of *Scream VI* in the eyes of audiences.

"We thought of it like the B-side of an album. It had to be a different movie," Sherak said. "We let Ghostface hold a gun for the first time. We moved the action to New York City, which added a new energy that our original small-town setting didn't have. It became this action movie hidden inside a horror movie—a bigger movie all around." Thanks to the film's new setting and the rising profiles of its Gen Z stars, Melissa Barrera and Jenna Ortega, *Scream VI* cruised to a $44 million debut in the US—the franchise's all-time best opening weekend.

Scream VI proved that audiences would turn up for a *Scream* movie without Sidney Prescott (though I'd be remiss if I didn't mention how thrilled Sherak was to get Neve Campbell back for *Scream 7*). But not every project can sustain the loss of its star.

When Universal Pictures was considering a reboot of the famed *Halloween* franchise, I was called in to test the concept by Bill Block—who ran Miramax and held the rights to the property—and Jason Blum of Blumhouse Productions, the lead producer on the film. They were in talks with the film's original star, Jamie Lee Curtis, to reprise her role as Laurie Strode. But she was asking for a big paycheck, and the producers wanted to understand how essential her participation would be to the overall success of the project. So I tested their concept: first with Jamie Lee Curtis to star, then without. The results were crystal clear. "Pay the woman!" I told them. "You can't make this movie without her." Luckily, the studio listened. *Halloween* (2018), starring Jamie Lee Curtis, opened to a whopping $76 million in the US, on its way to a $255 million global haul and two additional sequels.

That, my friends, demonstrates the power of what I like to call "Capability Testing."

TO GIVE CREDIT WHERE CREDIT IS DUE, my coauthor Bob Levin was the first to come up with the term **Capability** as it relates to assessing the value of a movie. It was in the early days of Screen Engine, and we were looking for a way to describe our philosophy and research methods that touched the entire life cycle of a film. We conducted research screenings that gave insight into the **Playability** of a movie and how strong its word of mouth would likely be. We tested creative advertising materials, which revealed the **Marketability** of a project. We used awareness tracking and press and critics' screenings to get a sense of the **Buzzability** around a movie.

But it was our earliest—and I would argue most critical—research tool that was the hardest to name. We held early-stage concept tests that measured the strength of a movie's core idea with its intended audience. We wanted another "-ability" word to describe it, but "conceptability" was a nonstarter. It was Bob's stroke of genius to land on the word "capable," which suggests the ability to achieve a goal. That's exactly what our concept tests were doing—measuring the ability of a movie's core elements to achieve its goal of connecting with audiences. Thus "Capability Testing" was born.

Here's the simplest definition of a Capability Test: it measures all the elements of a film that might affect initial audience interest. And when it comes to figuring out if a movie's idea is elevated enough to succeed in theaters, it is one of the most powerful gadgets in the toolbox.

Testing movie concepts is nothing new. The practice has been around since the 1930s, when famous public opinion pollster George Gallup first brought his skills to Hollywood. Gallup conducted "story testing" for more than a dozen studios and independent producers, working on everything from Disney animated features to *Gone with the Wind* (still the highest-grossing film of all time, when adjusted for inflation).[7]

Before Gallup, the potential popularity of a movie was measured by no more than the gut reaction of the studio chief in charge of choosing what movies to make. Gallup's approach was far more scientific. He was the first to construct a cross section of the American moviegoing population, allowing him to collect data on why some movies became popular and why others failed.

The bulk of Gallup's research revolved around story tests that zeroed in on the narrative elements of a film that were most likely to appeal to a mass audience. He did this by testing variations on plot, settings, and characters, allowing studio executives to get new insights into the narrative features their movies needed to succeed.

Capability Testing uses the best of story testing but also offers an early blueprint for marketing strategies and, even more important, an overall risk assessment for a project. It seeks to measure the audience appeal of everything about a film—from its title and story beats to its casting, director, setting, even its source material (article, book, play, video game) if any exists. These insights help create what I call the "success equation" for a project, a critically important metric for studio executives who are tasked with making multimillion-dollar decisions on which movies get made and which don't.

A Capability Test begins with usually no more than a three-hundred-word description of an idea. This should be a bare-bones elevator pitch, free of any sort of hyperbole like "the laughs keep coming," or "intense action unlike any you've ever seen," or "Oscar-worthy performances from . . ." These yet-to-be-substantiated claims are best left to the marketing department, because ultimately, these claims may not be fulfilled.

Remember, Capability Tests are about measuring the *essence* of a project, not its execution. Accuracy and clarity are a must. Having conducted hundreds of these tests, I can tell you that most of the time, if it looks like a pig, snorts like a pig, and lives in a sty . . . it's a pig. Putting lipstick on it doesn't make it any less of a pig—it just looks like you're trying to cover something up. The whole point of this exercise is to test the idea behind a movie and understand the true risk of making it.

With a clear description of the idea in hand, it's time to test it with moviegoers who broadly represent the audience expected to watch the film. The test participants are asked to go through the description carefully, highlighting the bits that resonate with them. After the description is presented, any additional details that might positively or negatively affect interest are sequentially introduced, such as cast, director, title, whether it's based on a known piece of IP, whether it's based on a true story, etc.

The data received from these tests help to identify a project's strengths and weaknesses. Parts of a plot that aren't resonating can be scuttled, while elements that are popular—like how a character overcomes a challenge, or how the story balances drama and humor—can be amplified even more. Testing can also preview audience expectations for a project. If respondents say a concept sounds like it will be "scary to watch" or "outrageous in a good way," the movie itself should strive to deliver on those expectations.

Capability Tests can uncover a movie's fatal flaws long before a single frame of film is shot. Consider what happened with *Kingdom of Heaven*, a 2005 historical epic directed by Ridley Scott. It should have been a slam dunk for the director, who had scored with the sword-and-sandal hit *Gladiator* just five years before. But *Kingdom of Heaven* was a very different film—a fictionalized retelling of the events leading up to the Third Crusade—with complicated politics. The film, which portrayed

Muslim characters as decent and merciful while Christian characters acted as villains, was released only four short years after the horrors of September 11. Xenophobia toward Muslims was still at an all-time high, with one professor even calling the film "Osama bin Laden's version of history."[8] The movie didn't stand a chance of attracting its primarily male-targeted audience in that environment, opening to less than $20 million in the US.

Another good example is the 2015 film *Ricki and the Flash*. The project had many things working in its favor—an A-list star in Meryl Streep, a script by *Juno* writer Diablo Cody, and an Oscar-winning director in Jonathan Demme. But all that talent in front of and behind the camera couldn't overcome an inherent flaw in its DNA—the story is about a mother who abandons her three children to pursue her dreams of becoming a rock star. The setup for the entire film ended up being outright rejected by the audience—primarily, well, moms—who couldn't relate to or root for a protagonist who could leave her family behind for such selfish reasons. The movie went on to gross only $41 million worldwide.

Delivery Man, the 2013 film starring Vince Vaughn, similarly couldn't escape an icky premise. Vaughn played a man who learned his sperm bank donations had resulted in the births of 533 children—creeping out audiences who couldn't help but wonder: *Could someone have inadvertently dated—or even married—their brother or sister? Eww.* The ick factor only got worse at the end of the film, when the entire clan reunited. It was no laughing matter—the comedy earned only $53 million worldwide against a reported budget of $26 million before marketing costs.

Kingdom of Heaven, *Ricki and the Flash*, and *Delivery Man* are perfect examples of movies with fatal plot defects that would likely have been uncovered if they had gone through the pre-greenlight Capability Testing process. But Capability Tests are also useful when it comes to ideas that fall into what I call the "murky middle."

Ideas in the murky middle are neither obviously strong nor obviously weak. In poker terms, we all pretty much know to fold when we're dealt an unsuited seven and two, and to bet big when we get pocket kings. But an unsuited ace and six? That's a trickier decision. You might win, but the odds of losing are greater. And so it goes with moviemaking.

Most projects start their lives in this middle ground. For example, a project might have a kernel of an interesting idea, but it feels too similar to something that's come before it. When a movie concept we're testing comes back in the murky middle, it usually means one thing: more work needs to be done. Capability Tests can be used to identify and fix whatever's not working and elevate and enhance whatever is working.

"Why be afraid to die now if you're going to die an even uglier death later on?" said Nicole Brown, president of TriStar Pictures. "It's never about giving up—we'd never throw in the towel, but a Capability Test helps you find out what your challenges are so you can solve them when you still have time to—and before it's expensive to do so. That information from an audience is unbiased and important in discussions with filmmakers—it helps take egos out of the discussion."

Bill Block—veteran agent, producer, studio head, and film financier—agrees. A believer in making movies for the right price, he's never shied away from having me read a script and perform a Capability Test. On his 2014 movie *Fury*, an early Capability Test showed extraordinarily strong interest among both young and old men, a strong two-quadrant movie. If budgeted appropriately at $80 million, the research—when combined with the comps—said the project should make money.

The enthusiasm of the male audience gave Block the confidence to unconditionally commit to Brad Pitt starring in the movie. When Brad's agent, Bryan Lourd, told him, "Brad will do it. Can you start in eight weeks?" Block didn't hesitate. "Without consulting anyone, I agreed that production would start in eight weeks," he says. "I didn't even call the director. I said, 'Yes, we can.' Then I called *Fury*'s producer/writer/director, David Ayer, and told him he got the green light to make his movie with Brad Pitt as its star." *Fury* went on to gross just shy of $212 million globally—a solid moneymaker.

Yet even with all their benefits, Capability Tests still have their detractors—and they're still not part of every green-lighting process. Some companies will pursue murky middle ideas based on little more than gut instinct.

For some, I think fear gets in the way. After spending months—if not years—developing a project, some executives and producers can find it hard to face the possibility that audiences won't be equally enamored of their baby. There's also an element of confirmation bias at play, where it becomes easier to ignore or discount opinions that don't match your own.

Others, like accomplished film producer Amy Pascal, disagree with the entire idea that audiences can provide valuable insight on a movie before it's made: "How can an audience know what a movie will look like in advance? How would they know if they'd want to see it? Filmmakers can see and hear things we can't, and I believe in them."

Producer Sean Bailey, former president of Walt Disney Pictures, has a similar—but slightly more balanced—perspective. "I want to know a lot about the audience. You need huge respect and huge affection for them, and you want to learn as much as you can about them before making a decision. But the movies that truly surprise and electrify, I don't think the audience would necessarily have said, 'I want specifically that,'" Bailey said. "Ultimately, I fall more into the Steve Jobs camp: 'It's not the customer's job to know what they want.'"

Jobs is often quoted when someone wants to dismiss the value of early market research. I would posit that people may not be able to tell you what they *want*—like a little rectangular device that could serve as a computer, telephone, and camera all in one—but when presented with an idea, they can absolutely tell you what they do and don't *like*. (*A mobile device that can do all that? Holy shit . . . sign me up!*) It would be naive to think that Apple products haven't been informed by reams of data on why consumers buy Apple devices and how they use them.

I want to be clear: I'm not saying that moviegoers should be the primary decision-makers on what films get made. There are plenty of tremendously successful movies—*Juno*, *Slumdog Millionaire*, *Black Swan*, *Life of Pi*, *Everything Everywhere All at Once*, and hundreds more—that most likely wouldn't have fared well in a Capability Test. Should they have been killed at the concept stage? No way! The point of this research isn't to prevent the production of movies that don't test particularly well. Instead, it's to bring clarity to what an uphill battle it will be to make the movie work, so everyone can go into the project with eyes wide open and budget appropriately based on the risk.

Because the marketing of a lukewarm-testing movie will be a challenge, the execution of its concept must be top-notch. It must be so good, in fact, that critics and early audiences can't help but talk up the movie for you and become evangelists for it. And even with great reviews and word of mouth, you must still accept the risk that the movie might not find a big enough audience, and budget accordingly.

The entertainment company A24 is run by executives who have damned good instincts about what is and isn't going to work in theaters. Their success with films like *Everything Everywhere All at Once*, *Room*, *Midsommar*, *Civil War*, *Uncut Gems*, *Lady Bird*, and *Hereditary* have earned them the right to take on higher levels of risk and to roll the dice on projects they love. But not every decision they make proves to be commercially successful; films like *Tusk* and *Dark Places* come to mind. Those snake-eyes rolls need to be taken into consideration when determining the right price to make and market movies.

GOOD ISN'T GOOD ENOUGH

Over the years, I have listened to opinions that concept tests in the movie business tend to be idea killers. Some think that a two-hundred- to three-hundred-word description cannot do justice to the idea that will come alive on the screen in finished form. The settings, visual effects, music, and talents of a great director and cast cannot possibly be captured in a written paragraph. Even an unfortunate choice of words in the description can derail what would otherwise be a great concept. But I strongly disagree. Capability Tests measure the intrinsic value of the core idea against normative data that we have gathered over hundreds of concepts that we have measured. If there is little interest in the underlying concept, all the dressing in the world is unlikely to produce the result needed to make it commercially successful. On the other hand, if there is quantifiable, above-average interest, all those other elements will often become additive.

Results from a Capability Test will raise a yellow flag on a mediocre (murky middle) idea, yet this type of research is also the first step in validating a great one. It can provide the confidence to move forward and spend money to take the idea to the next step. Case in point is the 2024 postsummer runaway hit *Beetlejuice Beetlejuice*. Fully seven years earlier, Toby Emmerich, who was then chairman of Warner Bros. Pictures Group, commissioned Capability Testing to get a beat on moviegoer interest on several Warner Bros. projects, including a sequel to the 1988 Tim Burton film *Beetlejuice*. The original—which starred Michael Keaton in the title role, along with Alec Baldwin, Geena Davis, Jeffrey Jones, Catherine O'Hara, and a seventeen-year-old Winona Ryder—had been both a critical and commercial success for the studio, even winning an Oscar for Best Makeup. The *Beetlejuice* franchise was expanded with an animated TV series, a few video games, and much later, a Broadway musical. As early as 1990, the idea for a sequel was being considered, but attempts at a script were eventually shelved. It wasn't until 2017 that Screen Engine was brought in to put some data behind potential interest in a second theatrical endeavor.

The *Beetlejuice 2* concept that we tested was based on Winona Ryder's character returning to her father's home as an adult with her thirteen-year-old daughter in tow for another encounter with Beetlejuice. The written description referenced members of the original cast reprising their roles and Tim Burton directing. Response to the idea was off the charts, transcending gender and age, and landing in the top 10 percent of all concepts that my company has tested . . . ever. Participants in the study were drawn to the blend of comedy and supernatural elements, and they loved that the characters and stars from the original movie, particularly Michael Keaton, would be back for a sequel.

Interest was so widespread that a second round of Capability research was conducted the following year in several international territories. The results were consistently strong, especially in the United States, and also in Brazil, which is typically a window into potential for all of Latin America. Armed with data and insights from the tests, Warner Bros. moved forward. It takes years for a project of this scope to come together, and eventually Warner Bros. partnered with Brad Pitt's company, Plan B, to produce the movie. With Burton, Keaton, Ryder, and O'Hara lined up, principal photography was completed during the summer of 2023.

Beetlejuice Beetlejuice was released on September 6, 2024, taking in $111 million over its opening weekend, outstanding under any circumstances and especially on the weekend immediately following Labor Day. It remained the number one theatrical release for three straight weeks and has taken in well over $400 million to date worldwide. The sequel's success was evident not only in the US but also in the UK, Europe, Australia, and Latin America, including a big opening in Brazil as the research had suggested. What's more, the opening weekend results were in line with what we discovered when the concept was first tested—the percentage of moviegoers who thought *Beetlejuice Beetlejuice* was "excellent" in exit polling was virtually identical to the percentage of respondents who were "definitely interested" in seeing it when we conducted the Capability Test in 2017. Early testing provided the validation that these characters, even thirty-six years later, were beloved by those who remembered the original film, were intriguing to new generations of moviegoers, and could shine once again in a contemporary continuation of their story.

A strong Capability Test is also by no means a guarantee of success. There are countless ways things can go awry between preproduction and the release of a film that can ultimately lead to disappointing box office results.

I was once confronted by a studio executive who was livid about a specific film's poor box office performance. He said the strength of the Capability Test my company had run was a big reason why they decided to make the movie. After the exec exhausted himself with a tirade, I reminded him of a crucial finding we had presented with our results: the single strongest element driving consumer interest in the film's concept was the A-list talent attached to star in it. But before the movie went into production, that star dropped out—and was replaced by another, somewhat polarizing figure. When this happened, I had suggested running another Capability Test with the new actor factored in, so we could determine if there were any changes in enthusiasm compared with the first test. The studio chose not to do it—and they lost a lot of money because of it.

Terry Press, a veteran studio executive currently in a top post at Steven Spielberg's Amblin Entertainment, captured the risks well when she said, "Making a movie isn't like assembling a car. There are so many variables at play that can go out of whack, and suddenly the movie doesn't work anymore. You have to be able to walk away when the elements no longer make sense. If you don't, you're headed toward failure."

HOW TO SCORE IN HOLLYWOOD

TO UNDERSTAND CAPABILITY TESTING IN PRACTICE, let's put ourselves in the shoes of a studio executive. That's right, we're the head honcho now, and we're thinking about green-lighting a movie called *Critical Conditions*. Here's the fictional concept we want to test:

> New York City is destroyed, as climate change raises sea levels and unleashes massive floods. It's a cataclysmic event so devastating that skyscrapers tumble like dominoes and tsunamis the size of mountains swallow up most of the East Coast. Civilization as we know it breaks down.
>
> As floods move into the interior of the country, the city of Pittsburgh becomes a fragile island. But with waters rising, buildings begin to crumble—including the high-rise apartment building where Joe Fernandez, an ex–Navy SEAL, and his wife and nine-year-old daughter live.
>
> But saving his family from their disintegrating home is only the start of Joe's harrowing adventure. As he tries to get his family out of Pittsburgh and into Canada, Joe must use every aspect of his special training to save their lives from a level of natural wrath not yet seen in modern times.

The first step in Capability Testing is defining your audience. Who is this movie supposed to appeal to? These are the same people with whom you want to test your concept. In the case of *Critical Conditions*, we have an action movie designed to run in theaters and appeal to a broad general audience. This means we would test the concept with a representative sample of the US moviegoing public: say, for example, a thousand people, male and female, between fifteen and sixty-four years old, who have seen at least two movies in theaters within the last six months. The opinions of these people—the prime prospects we are most hoping will buy tickets to see *Critical Conditions*—are worth their weight in gold.

How do we find these people with the golden opinions? Believe it or not, there are many companies that specialize in customer acquisition. Known as sample providers, they assemble large, curated panels of people. Individuals who are willing to be surveyed have previously signed up with one or more of these providers and share general information about who they are, what they do, where they live, and what they like. We then set quotas that define how many people of each gender, ethnicity, race, and age range we want to survey. We can even establish more specific qualifiers that ask respondents to share information like their geographic location, if they're a parent, the types of movies they usually see, and even whether they consider themselves to be fans of a particular movie genre. At every step of the process, there's tremendous "research hygiene" put in place to make sure we're surveying a legitimate, random, and representative sample of the population we're trying to reach.

We conduct the Capability Test online, presenting our selected pool of respondents with the *Critical Conditions* concept and asking them to rate their level of interest in seeing it in theaters. Their choices: "definitely" interested, "probably" interested, "probably not" interested, and "definitely not" interested. We've already established that a lot of resistance needs to be overcome to get someone out of the house and into a theater, so we're only really looking at how many people say they are "definitely" interested in the concept. We also ask people if this movie would need to be seen in a theater, or if it could just as satisfactorily and easily be seen at home.

After reading the elevator pitch for *Critical Conditions*, 47 percent of respondents express "definite" interest in seeing the film. Based on other concepts we've tested, we know this is firmly in the murky middle—not bad, but nowhere near the 60 percent threshold that would put it among the best of the best concepts we've tested. And for a general-audience action movie that we're trying to put in theaters, it ideally needs to be testing at, or close to, that "best of the best" level—otherwise the financial risk will exponentially increase.

After the respondents read and rate the concept of *Critical Conditions*, we use that baseline to start testing different details about the film that might boost (or depress) interest. We call this measuring the *sequential lift*. First, we tell respondents the film will be directed by Michael Bay. Suddenly, "definite" interest shoots up to 61 percent. What we just learned is that the concept for the movie on its own is very good, not great—but when it's a Michael Bay picture, it's a much surer bet.

Next, we want to learn to what degree casting might have an impact on interest in the movie. We're considering three actors for the role of Joe Fernandez: a big-name action star who is a pretty obvious choice and would require a hefty paycheck; a TV actor coming off a hit show who could be hired for substantially less; and Pedro Pascal, a popular actor who straddles the film and TV worlds. We ask our respondents to rate their interest in seeing the movie if it starred each actor. The TV actor depresses "definite" interest below our initial concept-only rating—we shouldn't cast him, even if he would cost considerably less than the other two. The big-name action star keeps "definite" interest steady—not detracting from the concept, but also not bringing anything new to the table. Pedro Pascal, on the other hand, moves the needle in a positive direction—up to 65 percent. We also test two potential actresses who could play Joe's wife. One doesn't change "definite" interest levels. She would be fine to cast—no harm, no foul. But the other option is a clear winner—pairing Pedro Pascal and Zoë Saldaña gets "definite" interest all the way up to 70 percent.

Finally, we ask our respondents to consider the entire *Critical Conditions* package, from written concept, to director, to actors. We're looking for their overall impression of the project, any concerns they have about the story, and if it's worthy of being seen in theaters versus at home.

Here's what we learn after parsing all the data: the movie appeals slightly more to men, though it still registers above 60 percent "definite" interest with women. It appeals to all ethnicities, though it demonstrates strongest interest among Hispanic-Latino audiences, likely due to the potential casting of the lead characters. It should carry a PG-13 rating, since parents who were surveyed said it would be a great family film for their older kids. As we hoped, it's a movie for everybody.

Beyond capturing interest, the survey also provides insights into audience expectations for the film. High production values are a must, with respondents interested in seeing nonstop and heroic action from start to finish. Clearly, Michael Bay will knock that out of the park. We also need to pay attention to how the wife is portrayed in the script—female respondents said they want her to be a true partner in the action, not a passive victim. We can use these findings to improve the storyboards and script before we even go into production.

Over the next few weeks, we run additional Capability Tests in key international markets. Country by country, respondents return the same enthusiastic levels of "definite" interest in *Critical Conditions*. We have all the makings of a global blockbuster. But we must remember: our test is the result of a very specific set of inputs. For our movie to reach its fullest potential, Michael Bay needs to direct, and Pedro Pascal and Zoë Saldaña need to star. If we lose Bay, or Pascal or Saldaña are unavailable, we need to reevaluate the level of "definite" interest in our concept. But if all stays the same, we just exponentially increased our chances of success.

CHAPTER 4

Feathered Fish Can Neither Swim Nor Fly

I AM CONFIDENT THAT THE GENRE of a movie is an important consideration in your choice to see it. You want to feel comfortable that what you're going to see will fulfill your expectations. After all, if you're going to see a horror movie, you're going there expecting to be scared. If you're choosing an action movie, you hope it's going to be an adrenaline rush. And if it's a comedy, you expect you will be laughing your ass off. Whether or not those expectations are realized has a great deal to do with your giving the movie a thumbs-up or a thumbs-down.

When I conduct a research screening, I typically let audience members know the genre of the movie beforehand so they can judge whether it is the "kind" they would like to see. Showing a horror movie to people who would never pay to go see a horror movie is not helpful. After respondents have seen the film, the third question on the survey each one of them answers is "Considering what you knew about the film before tonight, how did it compare to your expectations?" If they came in expecting a comedy and they did not find what they saw to be very funny, they would most likely answer, "Not as good as I expected," and be hesitant to recommend it to others.

But there are times when I screen a film where the audience is unprepared for the clash of genres they will be watching. For example, when a movie is trying to be both a horror and a comedy, it can often become confusing for the audience. They are unprepared for what they are seeing and don't quite know how to place it. They haven't seen a trailer or been exposed to any word of mouth. A movie that is identified as a single genre or easily understood subgenre has the greatest opportunity to succeed.

The popularity of genres is not fixed. Like the length of women's skirts, the thickness of men's ties, and the color of kitchen appliances, they go in and out of fashion. In the 1920s the advent of sound led to the popularity of musicals, comedies, dramas, and gangster movies. The 1930s brought on the popularity of horror and adventure films. The 1940s saw film noir and dramas taking in the most box office dollars. The forties through the end of the fifties were also known as the golden age of the Western. War movies also grew in popularity during, and for a time after, World War II. In the 1950s, adventure films took over the box office and had a good run until the 1960s, when comedies gained popularity, especially when targeted to the baby boomer generation. As the years continued into the 1970s and beyond, the appeal of disaster and science fiction movies ebbed and flowed as did action, animated, adventure, fantasy, superhero, and horror films.

According to industry data website the-numbers.com, since 1995, in the US and Canada, the most popular genre in terms of box office dollars has been adventure, accumulating a little over $67 billion in box office, with action movies in second place with a little over $60 billion. The combined total for the next four most popular genres—comedy, drama, thriller/suspense, and horror—is actually less than the combined box office performance of adventure and action genre films.

There are genres that have generally understood and accepted subgenres. Consider comedies, which can be grouped into action comedies, romantic comedies, buddy comedies, road comedies, slapstick comedies, dark comedies, and other subgenres. These movies work for audiences when they blend, rather than clash, genres.

FEATHERED FISH CAN NEITHER SWIM NOR FLY

I'm not saying a movie can't be successful when it ventures into mixed-genre territory, but in so doing it becomes more dependent on a creative marketing campaign, and upon the movie itself delivering in its execution. But I can name so many films that were mixed genre that never worked, because they're often "feathered fish" that neither swim nor fly. In other words, they don't really fall into one category or another. They're not funny *enough*. Or not scary *enough*. Most often, but not always, the audience wants a movie to lean into one genre more than the other. If they are shelling out full price for a theater ticket, they want to be sure.

Disney's 2023 *Haunted Mansion* was not a box office success, earning $117 million worldwide against a reported budget of at least $200 million. The film had a poor opening weekend, earning $33.3 million globally, which was Disney's worst opening of that year. A Reddit poster summed it up: "It's like they were going for *Pirates of the Caribbean* but instead made a movie that's borderline inappropriate for kids under twelve. To make it worse, it doesn't have any scares or thrills to keep everyone else happy."

The 2017 animated faith-based movie *The Star* is another example of one that struggled to find an audience. It was a Nativity story but with a different spin, told from the animals' perspective. An all-star cast came together to voice the characters, including Tyler Perry, Oprah Winfrey, Kelly Clarkson, Steven Yeun, Keegan-Michael Key, Christopher Plummer, Ving Rhames, and Zachary Levi, among others. Mariah Carey performed the lead song. Seemed like it had potential—a fresh take on a familiar story, big-name pedigree, and targeted for Christian families as a holiday movie outing. Yet when it was tested the audience perceived that it was closer to a Sunday school lesson than an entertaining theatrical experience. Well intended, beautifully executed, with a lot of talent, but a feathered fish. It was educational but not fun or funny enough, two of the most important criteria for a successful movie in the animated family film genre. There was little humor in it, and certainly not the level of comedy required to satisfy parents and kids alike. Most limiting in its potential was that it played very young as opposed to the blockbuster films in its genre that satisfy a broad age range of kids, teens, parents, and even general-audience moviegoers without children. Although it was meant to be enjoyed by the whole family, and released during the Christmas season, it had limited success, grossing just over $63 million globally.

A further challenge with a feathered fish movie is deciding the audience to whom the movie will be marketed. A comedy audience could be very different from a horror audience. Think about the trailer for a horror comedy playing in front of an audience that has come to the theater to see a horror feature and the same trailer playing in front of a comedy feature. Through the preshow trailer audits we conduct at theaters, we collect the responses that audiences have to trailers. We can see that such a trailer could be seen by one part of the moviegoing audience as not funny enough and by another part as not scary enough. We've all been at movie theaters watching trailers, and at the end of each preview you can sense whether the audience is going to see a movie or not based on their reactions. Most feathered fish movies receive a kind of mixed response—from sighs to grunts to titters to WTFs—but few garner the consensus that movies with a clear genre, or movies for everybody, receive. Moviegoers can tell from the trailer that something is off about the film. Hopefully what's "off" is interesting enough to persuade them to see it. And that's why feathered fish movies are harder to market.

Everything Everywhere All at Once is clearly an example of a feathered fish genre movie, but it worked. It worked because of its extraordinary execution of a complex idea and a mixed genre. It's a bold, brash, in-your-face movie. The potential to achieve the box office success that movie did achieve was simply not visible in its idea or in its script. The movie did $143 million in global box office, with $77 million in North America alone. It was written and directed by Daniel Kwan and Daniel Scheinert, who produced along with Anthony and Joe Russo and Jonathan Wang. I truly believe that if you gave five other filmmakers the same exact script to execute, you easily could have had five failures, while in the hands of Kwan and Scheinert, et al., it worked.

I think the project, with its difficult-to-define genre, would have died early in development at many studios. I recognize that if research had been conducted at this early stage, it would have likely received very low Capability Scores. I think part of the success of the movie was the very fact that it couldn't be easily placed in one genre or another. I contend that it wasn't the way it opened that made it successful but rather the way it held on, because of how people talked about it. To be fair, *Everything Everywhere* was a polarizing movie. People loved it, and there were also a significant number of people who hated it. But the people who loved it *really* loved it and fervently talked about it.

The numbers support the notion that *Everything Everywhere All at Once*'s success was driven by how people talked about it. It premiered in March 2022 to a raucous positive reception at the South by Southwest Film Festival. Directly after that, it opened in only ten movie theaters and did a strong average of fifty thousand dollars per theater over that opening weekend. By its third weekend in release, it had expanded to over a thousand theaters and grossed over six million dollars, and for thirteen consecutive weeks grossed more than one million dollars each weekend. People both loving and hating it generated discussions that led to many moviegoers deciding they had to see it themselves to form an opinion. At the 95th Academy Awards *Everything Everywhere All at Once* was honored seven times and won Best Picture of the year.

Following *Everything Everywhere*'s Best Picture win, another brilliantly executed feathered fish, *Poor Things* (fantasy, horror, sci-fi, romance, comedy) was nominated for eleven Oscars. Going back a few years, 2014's *Birdman* was a brilliantly executed feathered fish. It won four

Oscars, for Best Picture, Best Director, Best Screenplay, and Best Cinematography. It earned $103.2 million globally. And this was a movie that Box Office Mojo describes as "A washed-up superhero actor attempts to revive his fading career by writing, directing, and starring in a Broadway production." The audience's enthusiasm for these films is evidence that a feathered fish movie, when well executed, can have strong playability.

MOVIE MARKETERS WORK AT FINDING the most effective messaging strategy to meet that objective. A major studio marketing head regularly told his executives that they weren't in the "truth in advertising" business, they were in the "getting asses into seats" business. For example, everything you have seen about a movie—the trailer, the publicity, and the digital campaign—gets you to buy a ticket for what you believe to be a creature horror film. You go to the theater and watch, in fact, a comedy horror feature with few creatures. The marketing team did its job in that they got you into the theater. The movie? It might be a disappointment to some given their expectations. But to others, if it is executed well, it might not be what was expected but is entertaining enough. Movie marketing traditionally works with known genres, often using consumer research to test messaging alternatives. Take a well-accepted genre, action comedy. The marketing team may start out with a trailer that mirrors the movie itself in how it blends the action and comedy elements in the movie, and yet that trailer gets "meh" feedback. That may lead them to alternatives, messaging the movie as more of a comedy with some action, or as an action movie with some comedy. They find that they're going to generate the most interest among ticket-buying moviegoers with the "action movie with some comedy" sell. They did what they were supposed to do and got customers to buy tickets. Some of those moviegoers are going to be happy, and some disappointed, based on their expectations.

The marketing of a feathered fish movie presents its own unique challenges. The marketing team may initially try to make the campaign work, messaging that the movie is a blended genre. That approach seldom to never works when the goal is to maximize opening weekend box office revenue. As the cost of marketing a movie is a significant contributor to the financial risks a studio is taking when it considers green-lighting a picture, a feathered fish project faces challenges in getting a green light.

According to coauthor Bob Levin (former head of Worldwide Marketing for Disney, Columbia/Tri-Star, and MGM), "In 1994, I was heading marketing at Disney, and we were working on *I Love Trouble*, starring the biggest movie actress at that time, Julia Roberts, and the popular Nick Nolte. Genre? It was a romantic-action-comedy-thriller, a bona fide feathered fish. Its execution failed, achieving only 22 percent on Rotten Tomatoes' Tomatometer. We chose to open it over the four-day July Fourth weekend in hopes of maximizing its box office. It came in fifth place, and over the four days grossed just $12 million. During the rest of its run, it grossed only an additional $18 million and was never released internationally."

Levin continues: "The trailer for the movie failed, as it tried to blend all the elements: chemistry and comedy repartee between Roberts and Nolte, mixed with action set pieces and threatening thriller elements—a mishmash that just didn't work. TV spots were created to target different audiences with different looks at the film: an action spot, a rom-com spot, a thriller spot, even a critics' endorsement spot. The problem was that even in a short thirty seconds, those single genre spots couldn't hide the failure of the movie itself."

The renowned film critic Roger Ebert wrote, "Roberts and Nolte's relationship is so featherweight, so delicate, that it keeps getting ground up in the wheels of a conventional thriller plot. This lightweight stuff all works, in its own way, but I'm not sure it fits easily into a story that also involves the two of them almost being crushed to death by an elevator, among other close calls."

In 2017, once again two big movie stars, this time Tom Hanks and Emma Watson, were paired in *The Circle*, a drama-mystery-sci-fi-thriller. It grossed a total of $40 million, evenly split between domestic and international. Movie journalist Anne Thompson wrote, "*The Circle* is a feathered fish. The movie is neither the sort of smart and edgy indie that A24 could market, nor a glossily entertaining commercial studio vehicle. It doesn't appeal directly to younger Watson fans or older Hanks fans. *The Circle* therefore satisfies neither critics nor mainstream audiences. It's what industry insiders like to call a 'tweener.'"

While the movie *The Blind Side* has been revealed to be less than the true story that it was presented as when it was released in 2010, it was hugely successful, grossing more than $300 million globally. The film's star, Sandra Bullock, won the Oscar, the Golden Globe, and the SAG award for the year's best actress. The *Los Angeles Times* ran a story about the movie at the time of its release, with the film's writer/director John Lee Hancock describing the low point of his development of the project, initially with Twentieth Century Fox. Though the studio denies his account, he says he understood the studio's unease with "a feathered fish" that didn't fit their marketing pigeonholes: "It's not really a sports movie, although it's got sports in it," Hancock says. "It's also not a chick flick," he says, though it was written for a female star. "My take on it was . . . there was something for everybody. That's a suspicious thing for people to hear. They don't trust that."

I find it interesting that when we do polling among moviegoers exiting a theater, we often find the exit scores for a comedy or horror movie are somewhat lower than the scores received when we did the research screening of that movie. I believe the reason is that since there are a good number of subgenres or subcategories within comedy and horror movies, the studio pushed most folks into believing it's one thing when it's really another. As mentioned earlier, in comedy you have farce. You have slapstick. You have erudite and witty comedy. You have black comedy. You have romantic comedies, teen comedies, R-rated sex comedies. In horror, you have creature/alien horror; slasher horror; and exorcism, vampire, and zombie horror. There's also psychological horror and "torture porn." Each one of those brings out a different kind of audience.

The reason those movies often don't get rated as highly, when compared with their screening scores, is that in marketing a film, the studio often needs to pick a lane, trying to appeal to the widest audience within the genre. For me, when you say comedy, I know what I like. I don't like farce. I don't like black comedy. I like slapstick and comedy that's smart and witty. But let's say a marketing executive must market a farce and hides that it's a farce because he knows most people don't like farces. I think it looks pretty funny, I go see it, and I'm disappointed. It looked like a comedy, but the subgenre, farce, that it really is was "hidden" to get as many butts into seats as possible.

The result of the marketing team doing its job might actually hurt the movie's staying power in theaters. Think of it this way: they market the movie for what it truly is, and fifty people come to see it. All love it and it has great playability, but to a small audience. They find a marketing message with greater appeal to a broader audience and a hundred people come to see it. The longevity, or "legs," would not likely be as strong, but the overall opening weekend box office results would likely be stronger.

The marketing team must pick a lane, because if they don't, or if they pick a wrong lane, the movie can all too easily fail financially. Most filmmakers are artists, and yet the financial risk of failure should be a strong consideration for them if they want to be in show business. If they get their movie made and it doesn't have a specific lane that the marketing team can communicate, then that team will pick the path with the greatest potential to succeed. But that will also affect what people think about the film.

Tony Sella, former head of marketing at Twentieth Century Fox for decades, recalls the years he worked in Disney's marketing department before joining Fox. "Three out of the five years I was there, we were number one in domestic box office with the least number of releases," he says. "We were going up against Warner Bros., who had as many as twenty-five releases, and we had maybe half that number. And why did our movies outgross theirs? My whole theory is that we knew what we were selling: high-concept, single-genre movies. It's like when you go to a grocery store and there's this hybrid fruit made up of ten different fruits that you can get for free. Or you can buy an orange for a dollar. And you'll take the orange. Because people want to buy the fruit they know."

Sella has been guided as well by the likes of Jeffrey Katzenberg and Steven Spielberg. He told me that he'd never forget Katzenberg saying, "Sell them the *perception* of the movie they want to see," and Spielberg saying, "Always lead with science fact, not science fiction." Because calling it science fiction slips it into a genre that people will close the book on right away.

In picking a genre lane, a marketing team can discover that a movie has unexpectedly changed genres in its transition from script to final execution, and in so doing has altered its appeal. *Pretty Woman* was written as a black comedy for adults. Its box office success came from being directed by Garry Marshall. He started his career in the 1960s writing for *The Lucy Show* and *The Dick Van Dyke Show*. He gained fame for developing *The Odd Couple* into a successful TV show, and then went on to create *Happy Days*, *Laverne & Shirley*, and *Mork & Mindy*. He's also known for directing a string of successful comedy hits throughout his career. Marshall changed the tone of *Pretty Woman*, leaned into the chemistry between Richard Gere and Julia Roberts, and changed the ending from bleak to romantic and hopeful. In so doing, a movie that in different hands might have appealed only to a limited adult audience became a four-quadrant movie, going on to become a $463 million worldwide success.

When the Disney marketing team came into the first *Pretty Woman* research screening, they were planning for a campaign targeted to adults, and, given the movie's genre, a modest marketing campaign. The film at that time was titled *3000*, the dollar amount the hooker (Roberts) was being paid for her week of services. And then they sat and watched an entirely different movie from the one they expected, and experienced an audience that was explosive in their positive reactions throughout its hour-and-fifty-nine-minute running time. After the movie was over, the marketing team huddled and realized the movie they had to market was not the movie they had expected to market. It was, for marketing, a feathered fish in that the film that began as a movie about an off-the-street call girl who's paid to spend a week with a guy was turned into a clearly defined romantic comedy with broad appeal. In fact, one of the surprises was that parents allowed their underage daughters to see the movie despite its R rating, which contributed to its box office success.

They confronted the dissonance between what the movie was about and how the movie was executed. This led to a lot of discussion about the need to change the title. Jeffrey Katzenberg, then Disney's president, saw the movie that Marshall directed as a Cinderella story, offering as an alternative title *Princess of the Boulevard*. The marketing team was not enthusiastic about that choice and went to work looking for something different. Levin eventually landed on the title *Pretty Woman*, and that, coupled with featuring the Roy Orbison pop hit "Oh, Pretty Woman" in the film, was key to broadening the appeal to a wide audience. The story goes that when the movie's writer, J. F. Lawton, saw the film, he looked at Katzenberg and unhappily said, "But that's not my movie!" Katzenberg advised him that in the future if he wanted to control what he wrote, he would need to direct it as well.

HOW TO SCORE IN HOLLYWOOD

MANY FILMMAKERS ARE STILL very much attracted to the unexpected nature of a feathered fish movie despite the challenges it poses. Young filmmakers, who want to be the "next big thing" and want to be seen as hip and cool auteurs, are especially attracted to the unconventional and the atypical. Many newer filmmakers view a single-genre movie as sort of being overly conventional, a "programmer." But in terms of the general moviegoing audience, it's simply a safer and less risky bet to make a single-genre movie.

The potential global box office performance of movies is a key factor in deciding how much to spend on making and marketing a film. Single-genre movies—the ones that give marketing a clear lane—have become even more important, as they easily set up for global messaging. Taking the year 2023 as an example, the five most successful films were not feathered fish. Each clearly had a lane in which it was marketed: *Barbie* (comedy), *The Super Mario Bros. Movie* (adventure), *Oppenheimer* (drama), *Guardians of the Galaxy Vol. 3* (superhero), and *Fast X* (action).

In 2012, while Sella was at Fox, the studio released *Abraham Lincoln: Vampire Hunter*, based on a popular graphic novel, although catering to a niche audience. Box Office Mojo carries the logline for the movie as "Abraham Lincoln, the sixteenth president of the United States, discovers vampires are planning to take over the country. He makes it his mission to eliminate them." Its genre identified it as action, fantasy, and horror. I think we all can agree, *feathered fish*!

Sella thought that the title was totally impossible to overcome. "I mean, who didn't laugh when you heard it? And this wasn't a comedy! A decision was made that a stylistic production approach—some fast cutting and weird music—would somehow help illustrate the title and then they'll get it. Of course, that didn't happen. The idea of Abraham Lincoln, of all people, in this fantasy-action-horror movie was an impossible marketing challenge. I recently went back and looked at the trailer for the movie and I'm like, 'How could I possibly have put that out into a theater?' I remembered the production cost being somewhere around $70 million. My job? Do whatever I had to do to get people to want to see this movie. There was a lot of excitement at the studio driving me to want to succeed. It had a hot director adapting a book written by a bestselling author. But in the end, the feathered fish of it all was impossible to overcome."

Vampires were at the core of another feathered fish movie, *Twilight*. Rob Friedman is an industry veteran who co-led Lionsgate and Summit studios. Earlier in his career, he had been at Paramount Studios as vice chair and COO, as well as serving as president of worldwide marketing at Warner Bros. Pictures. Friedman told me that when he was at Summit and first heard that a *Twilight* movie was in development, he immediately thought of it like "*Romeo and Juliet* in the vampire world."

A bit of background: Karen Rosenfelt was copresident of production at Paramount. In 2005, Paramount restructured, and as part of her exit deal Paramount gave her the opportunity to take a few of the properties she'd been developing. One that she chose was *Twilight*. It had been a long time in development with a couple of failed scripts, and had never reached a senior executive pre-greenlight discussion at the studio.

"Remember that during the development process the books hadn't taken off the way they did once production was underway," Friedman says. "Erik Feig, Summit's head of production at the time, was pitched the movie. He met with me and said he thought it'd be a cool movie to make for around $30 million to $40 million. Erik and I talked and agreed that if the movie wound up doing $60 million at the box office, we'd make a nice chunk of change."

Friedman gives a great deal of credit to Feig in acquiring the movie rights for Summit. "A lot of work went into getting it," he says. "Author Stephenie Meyer felt burned by the Paramount development process. She felt she'd lost all control. To his credit, Erik worked with her to set up the 'Stephenie Meyer bible' to make sure the movie would be true to the original book, her vision. And everything in that bible seemed doable."

Friedman told me about the moment he realized that *Twilight* would become a pop culture sensation. "On vacation in Costa Rica, I noticed that women of all ages were reading *Twilight* books around the hotel pool. The marketer in me got excited when I realized that mothers read the book before their daughters could read it, and then they gave it to *their* mothers because they loved it so much. You could see the buzz, this whole phenomenon occurring as the books were passed from generation to generation. If the light hadn't gone on at that point, I was in the wrong business."

The subsequent four *Twilight* movies earned a total global box office of more than $2.5 billion.

This brings me to a more recent vampire-inspired example, the critically acclaimed *Sinners*, released in the spring of 2025. Written and directed by Ryan Coogler of *Black Panther*, *Creed*, and *Fruitvale Station* fame, the film follows twin brothers who, after serving in World War I, return to the Jim Crow South to open a juke joint. There, they face more than racism when a horde of vampires shows up.

On the surface, *Sinners* was a feathered fish, because the first half was structured as more of a drama that sets up the characters and time period and the latter half was most certainly a horror/vampire movie. But this film had a lot going for it. The story was layered with allegory and embellished with terrific music and steamy romance, and featured stellar performances from an ensemble cast led by Michael B. Jordan in dual roles as the two brothers.

Furthermore, it benefited from a very smart, well-executed marketing strategy from the team at Warner Bros., who most certainly picked the right lane. They made a conscious decision to play down the human drama and musical elements and leaned heavily into a horror/vampire positioning to pull in genre fans. Ryan Coogler and Michael B. Jordan were leveraged in digital media with punchy public relations messaging. Importantly, there were dedicated efforts to communicate to African American moviegoers, who responded to the cultural aspects of the story and turned out in big numbers over opening weekend. Critical buzz, with an exceptional 97 percent Rotten Tomatoes score, and positive word of mouth provided huge momentum in the second and third weeks of release and beyond. *Sinners* collected upward of $365 million on a reported $90 million production budget. Betting on the filmmaker and the star turned out to be the right gamble—and a very good payday—for the studio.

THERE IS CLEARLY A PLACE for the unconventional and the feathered fish, as *Sinners* proved, but films such as these especially need to be made with fiscal discipline. In assessing the potential of such films and how much money to put at risk, I respond with my strong belief that they should make money if they are made for, and marketed for, the right price. I am not standing in the way of cross-genre films, but I am saying know the potential audience for such a movie, know the marketing challenges facing getting people into those movie seats, and make and market it at a price that reflects a reasonable potential return. In the epilogue, you will read a great deal more about this idea of assessing the risks in deciding a movie's budget.

RELEASED IN 2019, *Hustlers* is a good example of a film that embraced its mixed genre and was developed smartly to expand its potential audience and make money. It grossed over $157 million globally, with a production budget of just over $20 million.

"If you look at *Hustlers* as just a stripper movie and you run 'stripper movie' through any data analytics, it will tell you you're probably going to fail," says Adam Fogelson, chair of Lionsgate Motion Picture Group and former chair of both Universal and STX. "But we didn't see it as a stripper film, which is a dangerous statement to make because the lead characters are strippers, and if it doesn't work you can look silly. But we honestly didn't believe it was a stripper movie. We believed it was a female empowerment movie. We believed it was a female *Wolf of Wall Street*, with a huge *Robin Hood* component. It was a film celebrating female empowerment and body positivity and sex positivity. And it was a spectacular embrace of Jennifer Lopez's larger brand. While her feature film career had been, with a couple of notable exceptions, sort of largely in the romantic comedy space over the last bunch of years, her brand as a businesswoman, and her brand as a 'celebrity,' was all about strength and bravery and balls. And this movie was going to give her an opportunity to demonstrate that."

In 2000, Columbia Pictures released the movie *What Planet Are You From?* With a total global box office cume of $14 million, it's the poster child for a feathered fish movie made and marketed for the wrong price. With an estimated production budget reported between a low of $55 million and a high of $75 million, the movie is rumored to be one of the biggest—if not *the* biggest—money losers in the studio's history. Directed by EGOT (Emmy, Grammy, Oscar, Tony) winner Mike Nichols, it starred Garry Shandling, Annette Bening, Greg Kinnear, and Ben Kingsley. Nichols and studio head John Calley were best friends, having collaborated on *The Remains of the Day*, as well as on *Catch-22*, *Postcards from the Edge*, and *The Birdcage*. There was gossip at the time that this was a big payday for Nichols, which influenced his decision to take it on. Upon its release, the *New York Times* critic Elvis Mitchell wrote: "*What Planet Are You From?* wants to be sweet and dark at the same time, but it is as distant as a planet's satellite."

Roger Ebert also didn't know what to make of it: "Here is the most uncomfortable movie of the new year, an exercise in feel-good smut. *What Planet Are You From?* starts out as a dirty comedy but then abandons the comedy, followed by the dirt, and by the end is actually trying to be poignant."

It was also virtually unmarketable. Shandling plays an alien outfitted with human reproductive equipment who's sent to Earth to impregnate a human woman so his race can conquer the planet. But when he becomes aroused, a loud whirring noise emanates from his pants. The movie was rated R, and the trailers and TV spots couldn't really get into the darker side of the movie. And the lighter comedy that could be used wasn't very funny.

All advertising for all movies must adhere to standards set by the MPAA (Motion Picture Association of America), the same organization that gives movies their ratings, and there are strict rules that must be followed. Anything that hints of lewd or graphic content will be flagged and rejected, particularly during family viewing hours before 9 p.m. The MPAA reviews all advertising for movies, regardless of the medium, and must approve it before it can be used.

Given that the movie was, in Ebert's words, "feel-good smut," a movie where the joke was a noisy penis, the advertising for the movie could only get MPAA approval if it didn't get close to revealing the basic joke of the plot. The resulting advertising was dull and just not funny.

Nichols complained about the marketing of the movie to the president of the studio's marketing division, and to Calley as well. Due to the MPAA restrictions, none of the TV spots were able to create much moviegoer interest in buying tickets to see the film. Everyone knew the movie was headed toward disaster, but as it came closer to its opening, Calley decided to put more money into the television advertising budget to try and get the movie to open. It opened to $3 million.

HOW TO SCORE IN HOLLYWOOD

ADAM SANDLER STARRED IN TWO MOVIES, one year apart, that were both feathered fish. The comparison of box office performance between these two underscores the importance of committing to a genre lane.

Released in 1999, *Big Daddy* was a comedy drama in which Sandler's character adopts a kid for all the wrong reasons. The movie did a global box office just shy of $235 million. The marketing for the movie chose its lane—comedy—and audiences weren't disappointed. The second movie, released in 2000, was *Little Nicky*, a comedy fantasy. It did a global box office of $58 million. Sandler played the son of the devil sent to earth to bring his two brothers back to hell. The trailer couldn't hide the feathered fish nature of the movie. The execution couldn't save that marketing miscue. Its opening weekend grossed $16 million; compare that to *Big Daddy*, which opened to over $41 million.

In 2013, *Jack the Giant Slayer*, a reworking of the Jack and the Beanstalk tale, was released. It fared poorly, dropping 65 percent after its opening weekend, resulting in a worldwide box office of $197 million. Of course, that figure doesn't sound so low, but its production budget was nearly the same—$195 million. Adding in marketing costs, it was a big financial disappointment. An executive close to the movie explained to me that taking the well-known tale in a different direction produced a movie that was neither fish nor fowl. It wasn't executed for the younger audience that found the classic tale appealing, and the older audience, having outgrown fairy tales, saw the movie as having little to no appeal.

So for the general audience, the movie wasn't a cool "want to see," and for parents it seemed not to have been made to entertain children. For the family audience, there was a disconnect between the storybook that parents read to their children at night and this movie that brought it to life.

Except for Disney, live-action fairy-tale adaptations may be a genre-bending feathered fish burial ground. The 2020 film *Gretel & Hansel* grossed less than $25 million in worldwide box office. Roberto Benigni's 2019 *Pinocchio* grossed less than $25 million globally. Even though *Red Riding Hood* made $90 million on a $42 million budget, once you factor in P and A (prints and advertising), that's hardly a windfall.

Compare those box office achievements to what Disney does when it adapts a fairy tale into a live-action movie. *Alice in Wonderland* (2010) grossed more than $1 billion globally. *Maleficent* (2014), a revisioning of *Sleeping Beauty*, grossed just shy of $800 million worldwide. And 2017's *Beauty and the Beast* grossed close to $1.3 billion globally. Obviously, the power of the Disney brand helps it dodge the feathered fish syndrome that most often leads to problems at the box office.

However, Disney is not completely immune when it comes to feathered fish releases. In 1984, when new leadership came to the studio, the animation team was finishing the misguided film *The Black Cauldron*. Made for $44 million and released in the summer of 1985, the movie grossed $21 million and was never opened outside the US.

In the opening of his review, Roger Ebert called attention to the feathered fish problem this movie faced with the audience: "The best of the Disney animated features were not innocent children's entertainments but bloodcurdling stories of doom and obsession (with a few smiles along the way, of course). They only looked innocent because they were cartoons. Reflect for a moment on the Island of Lost Boys in *Pinocchio*, or what happened to Bambi's mother. The great Disney cartoons contained all of the fearsome possibilities of the Grimm fairy tales—or, for that matter, of life itself. Only in recent years have the Disney feature cartoons grown pale and innocuous, as part of the general delusion that harmless means colorless."

And there was the problem Disney's marketing department faced. "The movie was made for an audience that hadn't come to a Disney animated movie since their childhood," Bob Levin says. "And the audience that identified themselves as fans of Disney animated movies saw *The Black Cauldron* as too scary and violent for their children to see. To me, it didn't fit into what was considered to be an animated movie, and thus to the audience, it was a feathered fish. The trailer didn't attempt to sugar-coat the nature of the movie, and the poster carried the headline 'Hidden by darkness. Guarded by witches. Discovered by a boy. Stolen by a king. Whoever owns it will rule the world. Or destroy it.'"

The failure of *The Black Cauldron* led to serious discussions at Disney about closing down the feature animation department. That didn't happen, and just under four years later the success of *The Little Mermaid* gave birth to what some call the renaissance of Disney animation.

Three movies that fit into the dilemma of feathered fish films stand out for coauthor Levin from his tenure as head of marketing at Disney, Sony Pictures Entertainment, and MGM: *Dead Poets Society*, *Jerry Maguire*, and *Windtalkers*.

"As a movie marketer," Levin says, "I at times faced the challenge of successfully marketing movies that were not by their very nature feathered fish, but if we were not careful in how we marketed them could have been perceived as such by consumers, and in so doing would have undermined the opportunity they had to achieve the box office success they did."

Dead Poets Society was a 1989 Disney release under the Touchstone Pictures banner. The logline on Box Office Mojo reads: "Maverick teacher John Keating returns in 1959 to the prestigious New England boys' boarding school where he was once a star student, using poetry to embolden his pupils to new heights of self-expression." Not exactly the movie you would expect to be the fifth highest-grossing movie of the year, achieving a worldwide box office of close to $236 million. The writer, Tom Shulman, won the year's Best Screenplay Oscar, while Robin Williams was nominated for Best Actor. Peter Weir was nominated for Best Director, and the movie itself was nominated for Best Picture. A key positive in this very well-made movie directed by Weir was the casting of Robin Williams as John Keating. And there also began the challenge to not compromise the marketing approach, and in so doing make the film appear to be a feathered fish.

"From the first research screening, we realized that we had a movie that would play strongly across a wide audience," Levin says. "And yet on the surface, if not presented properly, it could be perceived as a small movie appealing only to an upscale educated audience. The title alone was a possible obstacle to widening the film's appeal. Three uninviting words—Dead. Poets. Society. To the studio, the movie was akin to other prep school movies, such as 1939's *Goodbye, Mr. Chips*. The studio preferred retitling the movie *The Unforgettable Mr. Keating*. Given its strong Playability, the studio also wanted to move it from a fall release, the time in which 'important' movies are thought to be released, to the summer, when 'popcorn' movies are filling the screens.

"I went to the film set in Delaware to let Peter and Robin know of our decisions. The three of us went to dinner after they wrapped shooting, joined by Robin's then wife, Marsha. Early discussion was how excited we all were about how the production was going, and how special the movie was going to be. When I told them of the studio's plan to change both the title and the release date, they were stunned. They viewed those decisions to be indications that the studio was dumping the movie. Dinner not yet served, they got up and in protest exited the restaurant, leaving me alone at the table.

"Eventually, we kept the title but moved to a June release. While the movie gets into some very dramatic moments, including a suicide, we saw that the real opportunity to draw in the audience was playing to Robin's popularity as a comedian. A good three-quarters of the trailer is Robin being Robin as we locked the movie into the comedy lane. The marketing messaging hinted at more, though, showing Robin as an inspiration to his students. It was a struggle with the filmmakers to have them see the sense in why we picked the comedy lane, but we never compromised. If we had, that compromise could have made the movie seem like a feathered fish—comedy, coming-of-age, drama—and would have likely greatly reduced its chances for the success it ultimately achieved."

Jerry Maguire (1996) was a huge success, earning close to $275 million at the global box office. Tom Cruise won the Golden Globe award for Best Actor, and he earned an Oscar nomination for Best Actor as well. *Jerry Maguire* was also nominated for Best Picture, Best Screenplay, and Best Editing, and Cuba Gooding Jr. won the Oscar for Best Supporting Actor.

"When I joined Sony Pictures Entertainment as worldwide head of marketing, the positioning of *Jerry Maguire* as a sports movie had been agreed upon," Levin says. "The trailer that was being constructed focused on Tom's character being an adrenaline-driven, type A sports agent who burns himself out. In testing the trailer, it did gain interest with moviegoers, but with most of the interest and excitement coming primarily from older sports-loving men. The movie had a lot of dimensions to it—sports, romance, comedy, drama. While it had all those *elements*, it wasn't a feathered fish. It worked beautifully and we had the opportunity to attract a much larger audience than the sports-world positioning was doing. We created a new trailer, repositioning the film as a romance set in the high-stakes, high-stress world of athlete management, centered on a movie star, Tom Cruise, whose character, Jerry Maguire, goes through a major change in his approach to life. This reframing expanded the audience as it moved the movie into a lane with strong appeal to a wide audience and avoided a feathered fish marketing approach, which could have resulted if the messaging had lacked focus and presented a little bit of this and a little bit of that—as in a little romance, a little sports, a little comedy, and a little drama."

FEATHERED FISH CAN NEITHER SWIM NOR FLY

Windtalkers, the 2002 World War II action drama starring Nicolas Cage, was a feathered fish. Originally scheduled to be released shortly after 9/11, the studio decided its violence was misplaced in the aftermath of the terrorist attack on the US.

Excerpts from Roger Ebert's review lay out the feathered fish nature of this movie:

> *Windtalkers* **comes advertised as the saga of how Navajo Indians used their language to create an unbreakable code that helped win World War II in the Pacific. That's a fascinating, little-known story and might have made a good movie. Alas, the filmmakers have buried it beneath battlefield clichés, while centering the story on a white character played by Nicolas Cage. The moment you decide to make** *Windtalkers* **a big-budget action movie with a major star and lots of explosions, flying bodies, and stuntmen, you give up any possibility that it can succeed on a human scale. The Navajo code talkers have waited a long time to have their story told. Too bad it appears here merely as a gimmick in an action picture.**

Levin joined MGM to lead marketing and distribution in June 2001. In preparation for a December release that year, most of the marketing work had already been done on *Windtalkers* before his joining the studio. He recently told me how it felt to be in a situation where all the pressure was on marketing to save the day.

"Following the 9/11 terrorist attack, I believe the decision not to release the movie on its original December 2001 release date proved to be fatal," Levin says. "MGM's senior management argued that there was no place for an action-packed war movie so close to 9/11. Changes in release dates are always called into question, and in the case of *Windtalkers*, I think it was a misguided decision. In the aftermath of 9/11, I think its portrayal of American heroism would have been welcomed. Importantly, by staying on the original release date the movie would have benefited from the media coverage that surrounded the group of surviving Navajo code talkers being brought to Washington in July 2001 to receive Congressional Gold Medals—presented to them in the rotunda of the Capitol by then president George W. Bush.

"A year later, in the run-up to the movie's new release date in June 2002, the Navajo code talkers were an old story that received little to no coverage. They are what made the story interesting, but with a $115 million production budget, MGM needed a big hit. The direction was set for me: sell an action-packed war movie focused on Nic Cage as virtually a one-man army against the Japanese. In fact, neither the trailer nor any of the creative advertising ever even tried to explain the meaning of the movie's title, and all the publicity plans featuring the Navajo code talkers were stale."

Levin continues: "The movie did a worldwide gross of $77 million against a reported $115 million production budget. I think moviegoers were simply not interested in a violent war movie that seemed to lack any compelling storyline or a specific enough villain/antagonist.

"In addition, this was all happening when the studio needed *Windtalkers* to succeed as it contended with a less-than-stellar box office track record since it had begun to distribute and market its own movies in 2000. Since doing so, it had little success to speak of other than *Legally Blonde*, the Reese Witherspoon hit. The pressure everywhere at the studio was intense. Senior management needed *Windtalkers* to be nothing less than a grand slam. I think in comparison with *Saving Private Ryan*, which was a huge international hit, *Windtalkers* looked weak. No story. Just a lot of violent action. *Ryan* was a war movie standard that *Windtalkers* just could not come close to living up to. I believe that if *Windtalkers* had been made for half of what it cost and centered on the fascinating stories of the Navajo code talkers, it would have made money. Its box office failure was laid at the feet of marketing, of course, and I was fired."

BY ITS VERY NATURE, every musical is a feathered fish, as each one, while a genre of its own, a musical, is combined with a story that is identified as a separate genre. Consider, for example, the Steven Spielberg–directed *West Side Story*, released in 2021. Its genre is listed in Box Office Mojo as crime, musical, romance. The movie received critical acclaim and scored 92 percent on Rotten Tomatoes' Tomatometer—a testament to Spielberg's brilliance. Yet the movie never caught on, generating just $76 million in global box office. Was the Romeo and Juliet story of two people who fall into forbidden love out of touch with current audiences? Was the portrayal of the Latino community out of touch with how Latinos culturally identify? Whatever the reason, it simply did not connect with the audiences that were ready, postpandemic, to come out of their homes and sit with others to watch it in a theater.

Another theory as to why the remake did not excite audiences in the first place is that the 1961 movie was near perfect. Why remake perfect? And I think most people, particularly older moviegoers who remembered the Jerome Robbins–Robert Wise original fondly, felt the same way.

What achieved greater financial success was the 2012 release of the musical *Les Misérables*. As the story of its development was relayed to me, the producers did what was needed to give the movie a chance to succeed, knowing they were at risk with its feathered fish nature. "We were in the pre-greenlight process on 2012's *Les Misérables*," says Adam Fogelson. "I thought everyone—our Universal team, Working Title, Cameron Macintosh, our director, Tom Hooper—had put together an exceptional theatrical proposition for that movie. It met every criterion I have for when a stage musical is worth being reimagined for the screen. Everything about the script they had written, the cast they had put together, the idea of having the actors perform the songs live and really capturing authentic performance in that—all of it was absolutely stunning. But we were at a crossroads when the ingoing budget of the movie would have required the film to become the third highest-grossing musical in history to make an appropriate return on investment. And as much as I loved the film, on the Universal side—and by the way, this was not a fight; it ended up being a real partnership—the conversation was, 'What moments in this film would we love to have but are not actually essential for an audience who won't be comparing what they see on screen to the script we're currently reading?' We worked with the team to be thoughtful about which moments should stay, and which moments should go, and got it to a place where it was an amazing business proposition that was then thoroughly reinforced by how spectacularly it performed."

Les Misérables grossed $442 million worldwide on a budget reported to be just over $60 million. Fogelson and the filmmakers understood the risks of a musical movie, the feathered fish of it all, and found a responsible way to make it work for them.

It may be that audiences have redefined what they consider to be a movie musical. Of the fifty top-grossing movie musicals of all time, worldwide, thirty-three are animated films, twenty-one of which were released in the last twenty-five years. I can look back to 1989 and Disney's release of *The Little Mermaid* as a time when audiences once again embraced musical theater delivered through the movie medium. Primarily the medium of animation.

Since it opened in 2003, the stage musical *Wicked* has grossed more than $5 billion globally, and is currently the fourth-longest-running show in Broadway history. The audiences that fall under its spell are of all ages, as the show caters to young people, adults, and families. And now the first of two movies, *Wicked*, was released at Thanksgiving 2024. Its source material is the 1995 book *Wicked: The Life and Times of the Wicked Witch of the West*. That book is based on L. Frank Baum's 1900 novel *The Wonderful Wizard of Oz*, which was brought to the screen as *The Wizard of Oz*, starring Judy Garland. To Universal's credit, *Wicked* brought enough appeal into its marketing material to easily be a movie for everyone.

This is a movie founded in fantasy, not drama, and not the real-life of 1950s New York as in *West Side Story*, or the early 1800s as in *Les Misérables*. While not animated, *Wicked* is firmly in the genre of the hit fantasy musicals produced by Disney, though all or most of the others were animated. Its trailer, with a strong musical score, has no songs sung directly to camera. It's a fantasy that reminds viewers of its connection to *The Wizard of Oz*, and at the same time has a feel of magic reminiscent of the *Harry Potter* series. It's what now should be considered the redefined, in fact elevated, musical genre for our time.

From the 1930s through the 1950s, musicals as a genre were at their highest level of popularity throughout the Western world. Musicals from that era such as *Meet Me in St. Louis* or *Singin' in the Rain* were entertaining and fun. *Wicked* is a return to a musical being entertaining and fun, rather than dramatic and at times even dark.

A feathered fish movie can work if it is brilliantly executed and/or marketed. In most cases, the feathered fish is metaphorically marketed with either its wings clipped so it can swim, or its fins taped back so it can fly.

CHAPTER 5

Fix It Before You Shoot It

THE TITLE OF THIS CHAPTER MAY SEEM LIKE A NO-BRAINER, but script issues are often overlooked or minimized in the tidal wave of energy required to get a film off the ground and into production. Big studios are under the gun to come up with a slate of movies each year, and the best of the ideas, some still not fully baked, are green-lit with the assumption that any shortcomings will be resolved before the cameras roll. Sequels to hit films seem like a sure bet, even when flaws in the screenplay haven't been completely ironed out. Amy Pascal, the astute producer and former chairperson of the Motion Picture Group at Sony, spoke honestly when she said, "Lots of times you make movies because you were pressured into it, or because you had another movie with that filmmaker, and it made so much money there was no way to say no. But it's like anything else in life. You want to believe that you're doing it for all the right reasons, even if you're not."

Perhaps more than theatrical studios, most of the streaming services are challenged to keep up with demand, pumping out fresh content monthly to retain their current subscribers and lure new ones. Despite first-rate talent, both in front of and behind the camera, movies produced for in-home viewing have fallen under a dark cloud of "quantity over quality." I hear it time and again in my focus groups and see it on surveys that test audiences fill out: "Good for a night at home, but I wouldn't pay to see it in a theater." The streamers have upped their game and now try to produce fewer, better pictures. But those initial perceptions are difficult to overcome once they are seated in the minds of viewers.

My advice to any filmmaker, and certainly to any studio executive involved in the green-lighting process, is to make sure you are absolutely, unquestionably, entirely in love with the script *before* starting principal photography. Yes, there can be fixes on the fly, but they are not necessarily easy to make. Given the number of voices involved in seeing a movie through to completion, there can be debates about how to address a script problem. And once the camera is rolling, the clock is ticking, and the meter is running. Cha-ching! At that point it's costly to make changes. Then there's that old saying that has been bandied about Hollywood forever, "If it's not on the page, it's not on the screen." It applies to this day. Directors are bound to the script, and while they certainly have the latitude to shoot alternative footage, they are working within a finite number of days to accomplish what is outlined in the screenplay. Adding anything else can add days to the shooting schedule, and time overruns are budget killers (not to mention black marks on their reputations).

Years ago, I conducted screening research for Savoy Pictures, an independent studio that made films costing roughly half the average production budget that the major studios were spending. From what I understood, the company's business model was predicated on limited financial exposure on the front end (theatrically) and greater financial reward on the back end (cable, syndication, and home video). Savoy did not get first dibs on the best movie scripts. One that came its way was for a movie called *Exit to Eden*, which was riddled with problems. It was based on an Anne Rice novel, and Garry Marshall, who was just coming off his blockbuster hit *Pretty Woman*, was interested in making it. The decision-makers at Savoy convinced themselves to move forward, figuring the problems with the script would be fixed and the jokes would get funnier in the hands of good comedic actors and under the watchful eye of such a talented director. Well, unlike a fine wine, the script did not improve over time. The finished film just didn't work. It did not test well, it did not open well, and it made back only a fraction of its production budget during its theatrical run.

Just a year later, I witnessed the same thing happen again. Same studio, different director. Fresh off *The Fugitive*—a very successful big-screen adaptation of the television series starring Harrison Ford, Tommy Lee Jones, Sela Ward, and Julianne Moore—director Andy Davis came calling with a new script that he had written himself and wanted to direct. It was called *Steal Big, Steal Little*, and it was in trouble. The department heads at the studio (many of whom were friends of mine) were scratching their heads trying to make sense of it. But Davis persuaded those at the very top of the studio that he would deliver a movie that was much better than what they saw on the page. Based on his recent success and their desire to forge a relationship with a filmmaker whose career was on the rise, *Steal Big, Steal Little* was green-lit and produced. History repeated itself—it didn't test well and failed at the box office, earning a meager one-tenth of its production budget. You can probably guess what happened to that independent studio. Savoy Pictures filed Chapter 11, and that was the end of that.

In no way am I saying that execution doesn't matter. Talented filmmakers often elevate the screenplay as they bring it to life. Garry Marshall was a wonderful director, one whom I adored personally and whose films are classics—*Pretty Woman*, *Beaches*, *Runaway Bride*, *The Princess Diaries* (both one and two), *Valentine's Day*, and *New Year's Eve*. I mean, come on! But if the script is just plain flawed, it's going to be an uphill battle at best, and more likely a disaster.

HERE'S A MUCH HAPPIER STORY TO SHARE. In the early fall of 2021, I received a phone call from two of my all-time favorite clients and friends,

Broderick Johnson and Andrew Kosove, the cofounders and co-CEOs of a very successful independent production company, Alcon Entertainment. It's the company behind *Blade Runner 2049, Arrival, P.S. I Love You, Prisoners, Dolphin Tale, The Blind Side,* and several other films that have grossed in the $100 million to $200 million range and turned hefty profits.

On the day of this call, Johnson and Kosove were excited because they had acquired the rights to Garfield, the Monday-hating, lasagna-loving star of the world-renowned comic strip, several TV series, video games, and feature films. It had been an arduous negotiation that was years in the making, involving the original creator of the *Garfield* comics, Jim Davis; the comic strip syndicators who had "discovered" him, Viacom, which owned the parent company (Paws, Inc.); and the producer who was orchestrating the sale. It was a big deal for Alcon because it is rare that an independent company gets the opportunity to purchase globally established IP.

Kosove said, "When you buy a piece of IP, you're buying a piece of property that you think has certain fundamental elements that give you a chance. In the case of Garfield, it's an almost universally known brand, and those are hard to find. You can walk down Santa Monica Boulevard, and nine out of ten people will say, 'Of course I know Garfield!'"

Johnson added, "The fact that it's known gives you the turbo power to do something special and reach a really broad audience."

A new Garfield movie was in the works, and Johnson and Kosove were calling me because they were already starting to think about a timeline for research, even though it was still early in the development process. I assured them that it wasn't too early. While I was happy for them, in the back of my mind I knew they would have to reinvigorate a dusty legacy brand for a contemporary family audience, and research could guide them. I told them about an early testing capability offered by my company that would allow them to preview a very rough version of the film to parents and kids using EngineWorks, the media lab facility at our Valley Village, California, headquarters that's equipped with two small forty-eight-seat theaters. It would require only an animatic, which is a rough preview consisting of mostly black-and-white renderings with temporary voice talent, plus the imaginations of the recruited audience. These early tests had worked very well for other clients, and I knew this research could be helpful for *The Garfield Movie*.

The vision that Alcon had for the new film was to make it fully animated, unlike the two Garfield movies that Twentieth Century Fox had released in 2004 and 2006. They had been hybrids that included live-action and animation, and I'd worked on both. A fully animated movie, they explained, would feel new and fresh to audiences and have more connectivity to the original comics and TV shows, which fans loved. They had a concept that had been blessed by Jim Davis, which reunited Garfield with his biological father, an entirely new character. Based on an early script, Johnson and Kosove brought on director and visual effects expert Mark Dindal, who was experienced in animation with credits on movies including *Chicken Little* and the original *Aladdin* and *The Little Mermaid* films. The story evolved further when Dindal asked writer David Reynolds, with whom he had worked on *The Emperor's New Groove*, to develop a "director's pass" of the screenplay, and they worked together to flesh out the story a bit more. A heist aspect was added to the script, a rough animatic was produced, and in October 2021, we conducted the first test.

Johnson was out of town and unable to attend, but Kosove and a couple of other Alcon executives were there, along with Dindal, Reynolds, and the film's producers. This group, and members of the Screen Engine staff, were seated behind two-way mirrors, looking in on forty-eight children and forty-eight parents who were seated in their respective theaters. Tension and excitement were palpable as the movie—just rough drawings but with dialogue and temporary music, as mentioned above—began to play.

The theaters are equipped with ViewTrac technology, Screen Engine's proprietary system for capturing audience engagement in real time, as participants watch content. There were dials at each seat and attendees were instructed to turn them up when they liked what they saw and down when they disliked or felt bored with what they saw. Their collective responses were calibrated and graphed. On huge screens in the back room, we could see where audience investment kicked in, which jokes landed, and which did not. The parents were also outfitted with VX (viewing experience) biometric wristbands, wirelessly connected to cameras and microphones in the theater, additional equipment we often use in our EngineWorks facility. These devices monitor subliminal engagement based on three measures: heartbeat, facial expressions, and audio responses. The output from the bracelets was also graphed, and provided one more measure of how the content was resonating. After the movie was over, all ninety-six participants filled out surveys, and we conducted focus groups to hear their firsthand thoughts about what they had just viewed. The results were not great. Kosove remembered calling Johnson afterward and telling him, "We have a movie that doesn't work."

Yet from my years of experience, I had a sense that Alcon and the filmmakers were headed in the right direction, because although they were clearly rattled by the results of that first round of research, certain aspects of the film were well received. The qualitative feedback that we got from those ninety-six participants was enlightening, and I saw that the filmmakers were listening. The storyline features a Garfield character much younger than the lazy, sarcastic cat that is so familiar to and beloved by audiences. That issue needed to be addressed, and as their research partners, one of our key recommendations was to lean into the origin story and position this new film as a prequel to everything that came before it.

What was really gutsy, though, was Alcon's commitment to do what was right for the movie. After that test, they went right back to work on the script, taking eight months to reconceive the storyline and spending a whopping $800,000 on a new animatic that we would test in June 2022. Kosove said, "Well, we had no choice at that point. We had already procured distribution from Sony and were committed to making the movie. The only question was how to efficiently get to a better version of it. Clearly, that was to continue to rewrite and board it and not begin to animate." Giving the research credit, he said, "What we were able to do with your assistance was identify aspects that were very positive, so that we could understand, in context, what wasn't working and begin to ideate the changes needed."

Johnson recalled a conversation with Sony chairman Tom Rothman, who struck *The Garfield Movie* distribution deal with Alcon. Rothman told them to "measure twice and cut once." Johnson said, "We were already ahead of that. If you're a major studio, you can keep spending money until the movie is perfect. As an independent, we needed to control our costs and be very disciplined."

"We are businesspeople," said Kosove. "It's a lot cheaper to draw than it is to animate. We needed to get this right in an animatic form before going to animation, or risk going over budget by tens of millions of dollars."

The second test proved much better than the first. Garfield's origin story was distinctive and gave the audience something to grab on to. Sequences that had not worked were removed—Jon's girlfriend in the first version, Garfield's jealousy of her, scary (and not funny) alley cats that were the villain's sidekicks, and food fantasies that interrupted the flow of the story. There was additional work to be done, though. The villain, a vindictive white cat by the name of Jinx, required some finessing, and the movie still wasn't funny enough.

"That's when we made a decision that was extremely fateful and important," said Kosove. "We brought on Lee Eisenberg and Gene Stupnitsky, who are tremendous comedic writers, having run *The Office* TV series for a number of years. They were comedy punch-ups. What they cleverly did was to increase the comedy by building on the foundation and taking every joke a little further, as opposed to unwinding the whole thing."

With certain fixes, the animatic was updated and tested once more before the animation process began. Then the actual voice talent was brought in to record their parts: Chris Pratt as Garfield, Samuel L. Jackson as his biological dad, and Hannah Waddingham as Jinx, along with Nicholas Hoult, Ving Rhames, Cecily Strong, and other well-known actors in the supporting roles. In the role of Jinx, Waddingham did a magnificent job recording a sassy song called "I'm Back," which was used as an introduction to the villain. However, it was the only musical number in the entire picture, and the test audience felt it slowed the story and seemed out of place as the only performed song. The tough call was made to take it out of the film, although it can be heard in all its glory on *The Garfield Movie* original soundtrack.

At various stages of completed animation, the movie was tested several more times with larger audiences in regular theaters. Alcon and the filmmakers continued to listen, learn, and refine. Johnson and Kosove give a lot of credit to the director, Mark Dindal, who has a great sense of story, stayed calm throughout the entire process, and was open to hearing new ideas.

On May 19, 2024, Alcon hosted the world premiere of *The Garfield Movie* at the historic TCL Chinese Theatre on Hollywood Boulevard. The stars of the film turned out to support the opening. Many of the invited guests were decked out in Garfield orange, and yes, lasagna was served at the party afterward. The film opened to the public the following Friday, outperforming the competition over Memorial Day weekend in terms of number of tickets sold. It enjoyed successful runs in nearly every corner of the world, took in hundreds of millions of dollars, and proved that Alcon's vision of the Garfield brand satisfied moviegoers across cultures and languages.

FIX IT BEFORE YOU SHOOT IT

"You cannot fear the input of your customer," said Kosove. "This is an extremely challenging business. The reason we had this outcome and we're all sitting here in a good mood is that we made the film for a reasonable price point and worked so carefully in animatic form to get the story correct before we went to animation."

ALCON ENTERTAINMENT DID ITS HOMEWORK EARLY, and it paid off in dividends. For live-action movies, we often conduct "table script reads," a method that emulates the live table reads that every movie and TV episode undertakes with the assembled cast to sharpen a script before the cameras start rolling. With table script reads, we bring in actors to read the script, including a narrator who voices the setup and scene descriptions between dialogue. All are professional actors—usually well-trained voice-over artists who know how to bring text to life, as in a podcast—although none are the cast members who will eventually portray the characters in the film. This process is typically done in the same small theaters that Alcon used for *The Garfield Movie*, equipped with our ViewTrac dials and keypads. An audience of forty-eight movie viewers is seated, listens to the reading, and uses the dials to register their engagement. However, the reading is always recorded, and if our clients want a bigger audience or a more geographically diverse group of participants, we can easily recruit online participants to view the recording at home on their computers, using the arrow buttons in place of the ViewTrac technology.

After the reading is finished, the audience completes surveys, and we conduct a focus group to glean additional commentary from the participants. Table script reads provide early insight into the appeal of the storyline and characters, identify confusion and pacing issues while they can still easily be addressed, and gauge overall satisfaction, particularly with the ending. It is surprising how well the participants visualize what is on the page when the script is performed by these well-trained professionals. Some close their eyes periodically and can be seen smiling or nodding at what they hear. Table script reads are just one more tool in the toolbox for mitigating risk before the big money is spent.

ANOTHER EXAMPLE OF A FILM that would have benefited from preanimation testing is 2020's *Sonic the Hedgehog*. Hindsight is twenty-twenty, as they say. Like Garfield, Sonic is a renowned IP, and bringing the character to the big screen was an excellent idea. Sonic was introduced to the world in 1991 as a Sega video game. Based on the popularity of what would become a hugely successful franchise that includes gaming and several television series, Paramount Pictures developed a feature film. In early 2019, the studio conducted a couple of small test previews on a still-unfinished version of the movie with very rough animation. The recruited audiences were delighted to see the character Sonic in a full-length feature, alongside his new best friend on Earth, Tom (James Marsden), and the evil Dr. Robotnik (Jim Carrey). But the screenings revealed issues that needed to be addressed. The stakes weren't high enough and Sonic's personality and attitude weren't quite right. The tonality of the film also needed to be finessed.

At the end of April, the first *Sonic the Hedgehog* movie trailer launched with finished animation and there was an explosion of online criticism about the character design. Interestingly, at those early previews, there was little to no pushback on the look of the Sonic character, perhaps because I prepared the test audiences in a preannouncement that the rendering was extremely rough, encouraging them to use their imagination.

Producer Neal Moritz said, "When we put our first trailer out, it was one of those days where you had to say, 'Here's the good news. We've had more views than almost any trailer ever. The bad news? Everybody who saw that trailer agreed that the design sucked.'" The issue was with the more-realistic-than-expected rendering of Sonic's character, which had humanlike teeth and different eyes from its video game counterpart.

"During the initial *Sonic* test screenings, we didn't have any of that reaction," Moritz said. But the message from the general public was loud and clear: changes had to be made. "I had to go into a meeting with Paramount the next day and beg them for a bunch more money and to delay the release of the movie so we could completely redo the character." To the studio's credit, they jumped into action, and within ten days of the online trailer launch, we were conducting focus groups at our Screen Engine facility to understand exactly what fans and superfans of the franchise expected Sonic to look like. We got the answer—without question, in his big-screen debut, the titular character needed to be consistent with the way he looked in the video games.

Paramount agreed, and Moritz confirmed that many additional months and a significant amount of money would be invested to set things right. Had early testing of the Sonic character rendering, personality attributes, and script been done beforehand, it would have informed the first version of the film and everything that followed. At the end of the day, the studio stepped up and funded the necessary changes. The character imagery was brought in line with fans' expectations, and much of the film was restructured to address other issues that the early screenings divulged. It probably wound up being some of the best money Paramount ever spent. *Sonic the Hedgehog* opened to a whopping $58 million in the US and went on to gross $319 million worldwide. It spawned a sequel, *Sonic the Hedgehog 2*, that did even better—topping more than $400 million at the global box office. And there was more to come. *Sonic the Hedgehog 3* continued the saga, opening domestically a few days before Christmas 2024, expanding into worldwide territories five days later, and adding nearly half a billion dollars to the franchise's global box office during its theatrical run. A very good investment, indeed.

Another example of fix it before you shoot it.

HOW TO SCORE IN HOLLYWOOD

DRILLING DOWN INTO THE ELEMENTS OF A GREAT SCRIPT, I cannot emphasize enough the importance of character setup and development. Some of the toughest problems to overcome once the film is shot and assembled center on character issues. In the editing process, it's fairly easy to fix something that doesn't work if it requires trimming a scene, substituting a different take, or recording a new line of dialogue. It's far more difficult to make a character more likable or a villain more threatening, particularly if the footage needed does not already exist. There are a couple of basic rules about characters.

The audience must invest in at least one of the main characters. This means feeling an emotional connection to them, investing in their journey, and rooting for them to overcome an obstacle or achieve a goal. Amy Pascal believes that even more than story, characters are the foundation of success. "Movies are about characters," she said. "People go to the movies for emotional reasons, and what drives the emotion is who the story is about. The characters are the whole deal." Who can argue, given her track record not only as the producer of the *Spider-Man* and *Venom* movies but also as the former head of Sony, where she green-lit *American Hustle*, *Captain Phillips*, *Zero Dark Thirty*, *Moneyball*, *The Social Network*, *The Da Vinci Code*, and *Cloudy with a Chance of Meatballs*.

Todd Black, also a heavyweight producer, agrees with Pascal. He has many character-driven successes under his belt, including *The Equalizer* franchise, *The Pursuit of Happyness*, *The Taking of Pelham 123*, and the 2016 remake of *The Magnificent Seven*. For his company, Escape Artists, specializing in independently financed film and television, it's all about character. "We work really hard at characters, and I think when a movie is successful, it's because audiences like one or more of the characters," he said. "It can be a bad guy, a good guy, one that you're either rooting for or rooting against, or connecting with in some way. You can relate to them, or you want to be like them, or you admire them, or they're sexy, or they're whatever. And one of the things Jason [Blumenthal, his partner at Escape Artists] and I always talk about with writers and directors is we must make sure that whatever story we're telling, no matter the genre, we have got to like and, importantly, delineate the characters. I have a secret when I read scripts. I cover the characters' names when I'm reading, and if I don't know which character is saying what, then I know there's a problem."

Leading characters should have qualities that invite emotional attachment. Thinking about some of the greatest ones of the last five decades, it's easy to identify why audiences championed them. They are brave (Indiana Jones), resourceful (Ellen Ripley in *Alien*), cool (James Bond), endearing (Forrest Gump), funny (Ron Burgundy in *Anchorman*), smart (Hermione Granger in *Harry Potter*), or an underdog (Rocky Balboa). But they don't necessarily have to be admirable or even likable. Many successful and well-respected films feature unlikable protagonists, some earning major critical acclaim for the actors in those very roles. Joaquin Phoenix as Arthur Fleck in *Joker*, Margot Robbie's Tonya Harding in *I, Tonya*, Charlize Theron's portrayal of killer Aileen Wuornos in *Monster*, Forest Whitaker as Idi Amin in *The Last King of Scotland*, and Cate Blanchett as Jasmine in *Blue Jasmine* are a few that come to mind. I think part of the reason these performances were so highly praised is that despite being a deranged psychopath, a cheater, a serial killer, a ruthless dictator, and a self-absorbed socialite, these characters engaged us and made us want to follow their stories. Emotional attachment spans a broad spectrum, even encompassing characters we love to hate.

Imperfect characters are reflective of real life and often bring a certain authenticity to the story.

In *Hope Floats*, a film I tested long before I started my own company, Sandra Bullock played a former prom queen and cheerleader, Birdee, who returns to her hometown in Texas after discovering her husband, the former high school quarterback, is having an affair with her best friend. Everyone in the small town knows about the affair, and Bullock's character arrives back at her mother's house humiliated and depressed. Adding to Birdee's misery, many of her former schoolmates remember how snobbish she was in high school and relish the queen bee's downfall. Her eccentric mother, played by the great Gena Rowlands, tries to be supportive, but midway through the story she suffers a heart attack and dies. As expected in a romantic drama, Bullock's character eventually finds love and a new lease on life, providing all the beats to please the core female target audience and genre fans. But at the first test screening, it did not. The audience did not feel enough empathy for Bullock's character, and some, like those catty women in the small town, turned against her. During the test screening process, moviegoers told us that Birdee did not express enough grief, especially over the loss of her mother.

As a brilliant solution to the character issue, director Forest Whitaker shot a new scene that fixed the problem. By that time, Bullock was already on to her next project and had changed her hairstyle, but she was willing to do whatever was needed for her character. So the new sequence featured her on the morning of her mother's funeral, fresh from a shower with her wet hair braided. She needs something to wear to the funeral and goes into her mother's closet to look through the dresses. Most are colorful, but she finds a beautiful black dress and pulls it out for a closer look, then holds it up to her face to take in her mother's scent. In a solitary, heart-wrenching moment, she crumples against the wall and breaks down in tears, sobbing in grief. That one addition to the story made her entire character more human and vulnerable for the audience. The next time the film was tested, it played significantly stronger. Moviegoers warmed to Bullock's character, had far more empathy for her, and her happy outcome—a new love interest and a new start in life—felt earned.

FIX IT BEFORE YOU SHOOT IT

Reshoots are not always possible, and in fact, they are difficult to get approved. Stars are often unavailable, sometimes already working on their next film in a remote location or with a new look. Studios may be unwilling to spend the money a reshoot requires, which can run into the millions of dollars. And release schedules are locked well in advance, so there may not be enough time to go back and reshoot or shoot new footage. Getting the characters right at the script stage is clearly the best path, and that means giving the audience someone to care about and invest in.

More recently, my company tested *tick, tick... BOOM!* The 2021 film was directed by the incomparable Lin-Manuel Miranda and produced by Imagine Entertainment, Ron Howard and Brian Grazer's company. The story centers on a young man struggling to make his mark in the competitive world of musical theater. He is hardworking and talented but filled with self-imposed pressure to achieve his goal by the age of thirty. As his anxiety mounts, he rejects well-meant suggestions from friends and alienates many of them. He becomes harsh, and at times, inconsiderate. Ultimately, he achieves his dream, but he doesn't live long enough to enjoy the accomplishment. In an early cut of the movie, it wasn't disclosed until the end of the story that he was a real-life person, and while his name, Jonathan Larson, is not well known, his achievements have been widely celebrated. He was the young composer, lyricist, and playwright behind *Rent*, who tragically died of an aortic dissection at the age of thirty-five on the day before the show was first previewed off Broadway. When it moved to Broadway, *Rent* went on to win three Tonys and the Pulitzer Prize for Drama, all awarded after Larson's death.

When the movie was first previewed, there was resounding praise for Andrew Garfield's performance in the leading role. But the test audience found his character rather unlikable, and they had trouble rooting for him or feeling good about the posthumous acclaim that Jon Larson's work achieved. Overall, the response to the entire movie was mediocre. The filmmakers went back to work. Lin-Manuel Miranda protected the integrity of the real-life story but was open to making the changes required to get the audience behind the character. In this situation, the issue was addressed without requiring reshoots.

In the next round of testing, a new opening with narration and B-roll (supplemental footage) established right from the start that the film is based on the life of Jonathan Larson, noting his accomplishments and early death. While most in the audience did not know Larson's name or his life story, the earlier reveal of the true story basis and orientation to the real-life character made him more captivating from the outset. It provided a strong reason to continue watching, which is particularly critical to Netflix, the platform upon which the movie would play. Additionally, it helped that some of Jon's unpleasant behavior was pared back, softening him a bit, although the new introduction made the audience more willing to forgive him. In the revised cut, Jon came across as far more relatable and sympathetic, a character worth rooting for, largely by providing that context up front. At that subsequent test screening, positive impressions of him skyrocketed, and the film played remarkably better.

On a personal level, *tick, tick . . . BOOM!* was my favorite film of 2021, and I was thrilled when it received three Oscar nominations, including one for Andrew Garfield's portrayal of Jonathan Larson.

THIS BRINGS ME TO ANOTHER POINT. **If you have a third-act problem, it's often a first-act problem as well.** This is a very common issue. The setup to the story and to its characters is critical to audience satisfaction and almost always ties into the payoff at the end. Moviegoers must be on solid ground in terms of understanding the characters' backstories and motivations, the rules of the world in which they live, and what is at stake for them. Those "breadcrumbs" must be dropped early in the story (the first act) and must continue to build throughout. Otherwise, the characters' outcomes ring hollow, no matter how victorious they are at the conclusion of the story. You can't expect the audience to feel good about the ending if it doesn't feel earned. That feeling of satisfaction requires a deep understanding of a character's original situation, what they're up against, and what they learn or accomplish as the storyline develops. Moreover, as they watch, the audience is taking mental notes and anticipates that anything of importance that is set up in the first act will be paid off at the end, a convention that moviegoers have come to expect.

Couper Samuelson, who is the head of features at Blumhouse as mentioned earlier, has a very good grasp of third-act issues being tied to the first act. This is especially true in horror films: because the experience of watching them is, by design, so distressing, the audience has an even greater need for character growth and catharsis. But if the audience doesn't fully understand who the characters are at the outset, they have nothing to measure their growth against in the finale. Samuelson explains: "One way of underscoring this growth can be to take a 'value-negative' element from earlier in the story and transform it, through decisive action by a character, into a 'value-positive' aspect at the end." Let me unpack that idea.

I previously referenced *Halloween*, the 2018 film that reinvigorated the franchise, and the concept we tested, which led me to encourage the studio to pay Jamie Lee Curtis what she wanted in order to resurrect her Laurie Strode role. The ending of that film, as originally written and produced, did not work. It featured a showdown between Laurie and Michael Myers in which she shoots at him and misses, and he is last seen slinking off into the woods. When the film was first previewed, the test audience was expecting a more spectacular fight and wondered why Laurie's daughter, Karen (Judy Greer), and her granddaughter, Allyson (Andi Matichak), were such bystanders after the audience had spent so much time investing in those characters. Those of us involved in the test screening could feel the disappointment in the theater, after what had been a terrific response until that point. The filmmakers quickly realized that reshoots would be needed to make the ending more satisfying.

Samuelson reflected on the insights gleaned from that first test screening. "The ending is never just the ending. There's something in the body of the movie, often in the first act, that needs help."

In this installment, we learn that Laurie's obsession with Michael had ruined her daughter's childhood. She forced Karen to train and prepare for the day that Michael would return, to the point where the state stepped in, declared Laurie an unfit mother, and removed her child from her home. Now an adult with a daughter of her own, Karen has rejected her mother's odd behavior. Karen's teen daughter, Allyson, hardly knows her grandmother at all.

Says Samuelson, "It was only in retrospect, watching the movie with an audience, that we fully realized *Halloween* was about the way trauma will flow from generation to generation. Laurie was totally screwed up by the events of 1978. She locked herself away like a hermit and didn't have love, didn't have family, because she thought she needed to be vigilant for Michael's return. We had to figure out a way to heal all three generations of Strode women."

While the crux of the story centered on confronting the slasher who has escaped from a psychiatric hospital and is on his way back to Haddonfield, the filmmakers realized that the strained family dynamic also needed to be addressed and overcome as part of delivering an emotionally satisfying conclusion. The audience never simply wants the hero to defeat the villain. They want the hero to do it in a way that *means* something, emotionally speaking.

Samuelson continued. "Laurie needed to beat Michael, but in a way that healed the pain she had caused her daughter and her granddaughter. As a result, we had to reshoot not just the ending but also pieces earlier in the movie because we hadn't really defined Allyson and Laurie's relationship. We knew Allyson was interested in having a relationship [with her grandmother], so there's a scene where they meet outside a football practice. It's reminiscent of a scene in the original film where Laurie sees someone out there and it's Michael. This time, Allyson sees someone out there and it's Laurie." At that point in the story, Laurie is a value-negative presence in Allyson's life, so it makes sense that Laurie would appear to Allyson in a way that was unsettling to her—just as Laurie was unsettled by Michael in the middle of the 1978 film. In the scene that follows, Laurie gives money to Allyson and encourages her granddaughter to leave town and avoid being a part of what will surely occur when Michael resurfaces. Laurie is counseling Allyson that she never confront the trauma of her grandmother and her mother.

Having better defined Laurie's dynamic with her granddaughter, the filmmakers gave the same treatment to the relationship with her daughter, Karen. "We also shot a flashback of what Karen's life was like as a child. She talks about what she went through and then we show flashbacks of a young Karen. One of the things that often helps is taking an object that has a value-negative connotation in the story and inverting it in the ending. In this situation, it was the gun that Karen was forced to train with by her militant, fucked-up mother that became a source of trauma for her. At the end, when she's stuck in the basement, and Michael is upstairs and she wonders whether she's going to have the strength to take him on, Karen looks over and sees that original gun and it even has her initials on it." The filmmakers referred to that prop as the "Roy Hobbs gun," a reference to the 1984 Robert Redford baseball film where the hero uses a seemingly special baseball bat that had also been associated with trauma: the bat had been cut from the tree near where Roy's father died.

"Just to fully magnetize it as a value-negative thing," Samuelson says, "when Karen sees it, the audience knows that's going to be the hardest thing for her to do, to fire the gun that was the source of so much trauma. In fact, in the scene, the door to the upstairs is open. She's waiting for Michael, and she screams out, 'Mom, help us! I can't do it! I'm sorry, I can't do it.' The audience is subconsciously thinking about the flashback when they hear that. They think of a desperate little girl, which is what she was. And Judy Greer happens to be a first-ballot, hall-of-fame, incredible actress. The audience understands completely how hard it is for Karen to fire that gun. They think, 'Oh shit, she's not going to be able to do it!' And then, even worse, Michael hears Karen and now *he*, too, knows she won't be able to do it. So he steps in to come get her and then her face drops, and she says, 'Gotcha,' and shoots him. She was able to use this thing that was genuinely a horrible memory—and it's not just the gun, it's her whole childhood—and metabolize it in the moment and turn it into a value-positive thing, luring Michael into her line of fire, with the flip of a switch. The audience loses their minds. It was like a religious experience."

The film ends with a spectacular finale, and that helps as well. Michael is gravely wounded and has fallen into the basement. The house is rigged with security bars and gas valves, which Laurie controls, and as three generations of Strode women escape, it goes up in flames. What was initially perceived as Laurie's prison, a fortress that she built to protect herself, is actually the trap she set for Michael—value negative to value positive. When I presided over the next test screening in suburban New York, the scores went up by a nearly unprecedented eighteen percentage points.

Samuelson references *Get Out* as another example of his thesis. I rewatched the film after we chatted, and if you haven't seen it in a while, I implore you to watch it with his "value negative to value positive" explanation in mind. Samuelson's insight adds deeper dimension to the satisfaction you will feel at the end of the movie, when the main character,

Chris (Daniel Kaluuya), escapes. Samuelson explained more about Chris's backstory than you might get from watching the film just once. He was a latchkey child whose mother worked at night and his routine, when he was at home alone, was to watch television for hours on end.

"Chris was left alone one night when he was nine years old. His mother didn't come home, and he was watching TV. He worried that something was wrong, but if he made the phone call to the police, he might find out that it was true, that something bad *had* happened. And he was paralyzed with fear. He couldn't bear to do it, he couldn't face it, and so he didn't call. And it turns out that his mom had been in an accident. But even worse, *because* he didn't call, no one came to rescue her, and she died cold and alone." Young Chris's anxiety is given extra detail when we see the nervous child scratching at the armchair as he watches TV: value negative.

In the film, Catherine Keener's character hypnotizes the adult Chris, now her daughter's boyfriend, under the pretense of helping him quit smoking, although she is really preparing him as the family's next target for brain transplantation. She uses his guilt about his mother's death to control him. In the scene, as she stirs a cup of tea as the trigger for hypnosis, he falls into a trance and tumbles into a void where he sees Keener's character in a television set. The audience gets a glimpse of what he might experience as his identity and his consciousness are subsumed into "The Sunken Place." Later in the story, he discovers the Armitage family's diabolical plan to transplant the brains of their aging relatives into the bodies of their young Black victims, and realizes he is next. The terror that he briefly experienced under hypnosis will now become permanent.

Samuelson continues: "Watching the film, the audience is thinking there is no way for Chris to overcome this. Consciously, they know Chris has the issue of these psychos who are going to take over his body. Unconsciously, the audience also understands that Chris's own particular vulnerability about his guilt at what happened to his mom will make it doubly hard for him to win. He will be helpless, and no one will rescue him." And so, in his anxiety, Chris again scratches at the armchair he's strapped to.

Unlike when he was a child, this time the scratching yields a small but crucial discovery: the armchair has cotton stuffing. When the evil son (Caleb Landry Jones) reenters to bring Chris into surgery, Chris is able to overpower him. Why? Because he has taken this value-negative thing from his childhood (the guilt-induced anxiety that resulted in his nervous habit of scratching the armchair) into a value-positive thing: he has filled his ears with the cotton so he won't hear the trigger of hypnosis. As Samuelson says, "He is not just overcoming his own internal demons, he's literally being saved by the most value-negative symbol for Chris's entire race: the crop of slavery! The entire value negative is inverted."

Samuelson's value-negative/value-positive proposition does not apply exclusively to the films he produces with Blumhouse. He brought up another excellent example, *Aliens*, the sequel to the 1979 horror sci-fi film *Alien*. In the original Ridley Scott–directed film, Sigourney Weaver's character, Ripley, is the only survivor of an expedition to explore a faraway celestial body called LV-426, where a hostile alien entity attached itself to a colleague and invaded their spaceship, the *Nostromo*. At the end of the first movie, Ripley escapes in the ship's shuttle, destroys the *Nostromo*, and blasts the alien monster into space. She then puts herself into stasis for the return to Earth—lights out. *Aliens*, the James Cameron sequel released seven years later, opens with Ripley finally being rescued and awakened, fifty-seven years after her ordeal on LV-426 but looking none the worse for the passage of time, thanks to hypersleep. Her superiors do not believe Ripley's story about a hostile alien life-form and hold her responsible for destroying the expensive *Nostromo* star freighter and its payload. She is stripped of her position as a flight officer, and the only job she can get is working the cargo docks, running loaders and forklifts. First act, value negative.

Ripley is miserable and agrees to accept a dangerous mission that will return her to LV-426, but only after she is offered the chance to have her credentials reinstated. Samuelson says, "In the finale, it's her ability to operate the mechanical loader that allows her to survive against the matriarch xenomorph." Third act, value positive! Though very few audience members will be consciously aware of this negative-to-positive inversion, they tend to feel it. Next time you rewatch a movie you love, from *Aliens* to *The Natural*, I challenge you to keep Couper Samuelson's thesis in mind and see if you can figure out how the filmmakers have designed the story so characters transform objects from value negative to value positive.

Michael Arndt, the Oscar-winning screenwriter of *Little Miss Sunshine*, put together a wonderfully informative lecture called "Endings: The Good, the Bad, and the Insanely Great." He and Couper Samuelson must be cut from the same cloth, because their philosophies are in sync. In his lecture, Arndt talks about the alchemy of creating an "insanely great ending." He posits, "It should be both surprising and positive. But the most important thing is, you want your ending to be meaningful. A lot of stories are not as clear or articulate as they could be in terms of what the underlying set of values are, or in creating a drama out of two competing value systems that are embedded in those stories."

THE CHARACTERS THAT AUDIENCES GET BEHIND are typically protagonists. Yet protagonists need something to fight against, a foe or an obstacle to overcome. This leads me to another key component of a well-developed script. **Great stories almost always include a formidable villain.** The threat—whether human, monster, disaster, or some other force working against the achievement of a goal—needs to be powerful and believable. When villains are characters (human or creatures), their motivations should be revealed. I cannot begin to count the number of movies I've tested that have ill-defined villains. Audiences are always pulled out of a story and feel unsatisfied when they do not understand what the villains are after. The stakes—what is at risk if the villain succeeds—need to be both high and specific. Conquering the world, for example, is high stakes but not specific. Movie viewers crave well-rounded villains with distinct motivations and clearly defined lengths to which they will go to achieve them. In a horror movie, the haunting is never scary *enough* if we don't know what the ghost wants. But if the entity's objective is fleshed out, perhaps by including a revenge element, or a score to settle with the living before crossing over, or a new host body that is needed, the stakes become more terrifying.

TONY SELLA, WHOM I MENTIONED in the previous chapter, is the GOAT: the greatest-of-all-time creative marketing executive, or certainly one of them. He's known for the visually arresting campaigns and brilliant taglines that he spearheaded at Twentieth Century Fox. During Sella's tenure with the studio, he led the marketing efforts for *Avatar*, *Planet of the Apes*, *Mr. and Mrs. Smith*, *X-Men*, *Night at the Museum*, *Wolverine*, *Taken*, *Ice Age*, and scores of other films. I've always said he can sell the shit out of any movie, including some that were, well . . . shit. Still, as those who work in that end of the business know, even movies that turn out to be enormously successful can be difficult to position. Imagine figuring out a way to market a $200 million–plus movie about blue people. The stakes couldn't have been higher, yet Sella nailed it, and *Avatar* went on to become the highest-grossing film of all time.

Abraham Lincoln: Vampire Hunter, one of the "feathered fish" highlighted in chapter 4, was an entirely different story, a hard-sell genre mashup with a title that sparks a double take. Most people would instantly know that the slavery-abolishing sixteenth president of the United States would be the good guy in this movie. But who is the bad guy? Vampires? Really?

As mentioned earlier, Sella lamented when he rewatched the trailer years later: "It was all Abe the protagonist, and no evil antagonist. So the concept and the struggle were lacking. In classic horror/action films, the antagonist and their mission set the stakes." The film certainly had more issues than just the trailer. But Sella's point is a good one—even before seeing the film, prospective viewers should know what's at stake. What is the protagonist up against? Who is the nemesis and what is it after?

Couper Samuelson hedges a bit more than Tony Sella when discussing villains and their motivations. He thinks the audience needs to understand what animates a villain, but not to the point of demystifying him or her. Samuelson points to *The Black Phone*, a Blumhouse horror/thriller about a man who abducts children and keeps them in the basement of a house for a few days before killing them. There is a disconnected wall phone in the basement, which strangely rings from time to time, with calls from the boys who have been murdered by the sadistic villain. Directed by Scott Derrickson—who has a stellar track record with *Doctor Strange, Sinister, The Day the Earth Stood Still,* and *The Exorcism of Emily Rose* to his credit—it stars Ethan Hawke as The Grabber (villain) and newcomer Mason Thames as Finney, a young boy who is his latest victim. The filmmaking and acting are top-notch, and Thames is magnetic as the boy who is trying to escape.

At the first research screening, the test audience was befuddled. "The audience was wondering what The Grabber is doing," says Samuelson. "Why didn't he just kill these kids? Why wait three days?" But Scott Derrickson thought it was best to keep his motive ambiguous. "I kind of agree," says Samuelson. On a previous Blumhouse hit, *The Invisible Man*, the audience had had a similar curiosity about the villain: Why was he so obsessed with the heroine (played by Elisabeth Moss) that he would go to such lengths to stalk and scare her? Though the studio wanted to shoot an additional scene answering that question, the writer-director, Leigh

Whannell, came up with a more elegant (and economical) solution: he recorded an ADR (automated dialogue replacement) line of the heroine asking that very question to the villain's brother and henchman (played by Michael Dorman): "Why me?" The brother's answer: "Because you left." In other words, the villain couldn't countenance the loss of his girlfriend. In a subsequent test screening, the audience no longer wondered about the villain's motive.

Derrickson found a similarly elegant way to address the same question in his film. There's a scene in the movie where The Grabber leaves the door ajar and Finney sees his opportunity. He is about to escape, but then the phone rings and it's a call from one of The Grabber's dead victims, a boy who warns Finney not to escape because that is what The Grabber wants. He wants Finney to leave so he can punish him. But Finney leaves anyway and runs down the street screaming for help. The Grabber pursues him, catches up to him, stands over him, and says, "Night-night, soldier boy." Then he strikes the boy and there is a blackout.

"In Scott's view, The Grabber was probably a Vietnam vet," said Samuelson as a way of explaining why he calls Finney "soldier boy." But that backstory is not part of the film. So to help the audience understand the villain's motive without being too specific, the director came up with the idea of relooping (adding off-camera lines to) the phone call. In the next cut of the film, the boy who calls Finney warns him not to escape, this time adding, "He wants you to be naughty." Then, in the revised cut of the escape scene, when The Grabber catches up to Finney, he says "Night-night, naughty boy."

"All of a sudden, the audience understood that he wants kids to break the rules so he can punish them," said Samuelson. "It's sort of crazy, but it provided a unifying worldview of the villain. To me, that's what's important. In *The Black Phone*, he was filling his emotional hole."

FIX IT BEFORE YOU SHOOT IT

AND THEN THERE ARE THOSE SCRIPTS that are flawed beyond repair. Producer David Permut reminds me of a film that, even after extensive reshoots, simply could not be saved. It was many years ago and we were both coming up in Hollywood. I conducted so many screenings for *The Marrying Man* (I believe sixteen was the final number) that Permut joked he was going to make me an associate producer on it.

It all started at the restaurant La Scala in Beverly Hills, where the thirty-six-year-old Permut met famed playwright, author, and screenwriter Neil Simon for what Permut anticipated would be a social lunch. Therefore, it came as a big surprise when Simon produced a thick envelope and told Permut that he had written a script for his next movie and wanted Permut to produce it. After lunch, Permut called his assistant and told her to clear his entire afternoon. Racing back to his office, he hunkered down on his sofa and read Simon's script. "I liked it very much," he said. "I knew I had to move quickly with Neil, so I called him that same afternoon and said, 'Let's make this picture.'"

At that point in his career, Permut had a first-look deal with United Artists, meaning he was contractually obligated to offer them first dibs on any script he was planning to develop. UA had provided him with a Beverly Hills office and was paying his overhead. But as he recalled, the studio was in a state of flux with a revolving door of executives at the top. No one was taking responsibility for green-lighting, and as such, UA was passing on every script that came through its doors. "So Disney chief Jeffrey Katzenberg smartly made a second-look deal with me," said Permut. "Once UA formally passed on *The Marrying Man*, I drove out to Disney like Willy Loman with the script in the trunk of my car. I called [Disney production executive] Ricardo Mestres and Katzenberg from the parking lot and told them I had a gift to deliver. When they heard it was a Neil Simon script, they said, 'Come right up!' This was on a Friday and the deal was closed that weekend."

On the heels of getting the go-ahead, Permut's assistant felt he had earned a long-overdue vacation. She encouraged him to go to Hawaii. On the plane, using the old-fashioned 1990s-era phone that required a credit card, Permut had a shocking conversation with Neil Simon, who told him, "I want out." Apparently, an announcement of the deal to make *The Marrying Man* had hit the trades, and veteran comedian Alan King was threatening to file a suit against Disney, Neil Simon, and David Permut. Permut pulled the trade publications from his briefcase to try to make sense of what was happening. "I'm reading this on the fucking airplane on a leisurely trip to Hawaii that my assistant talked me into. I landed in Hawaii, called her, and told her to get me back on the next flight out."

When he returned from his twenty-six-minute visit to Hawaii, Permut put the pieces together. He discovered that at a celebrity tennis tournament in Palm Springs, Alan King had shared a story about a man named Harry Karl who was the heir to a shoe store fortune. Karl had been married to Debbie Reynolds, and after they divorced, he went on to marry another four times, including twice to an actress named Marie McDonald, who was known around town as "The Body." While King was holding court, several people were within earshot, including a few other popular comedians and Neil Simon. Simon thought the idea would make an interesting movie and assumed Alan King was joking when King suggested they partner on it. Well apparently, it was no joke. To get *The Marrying Man* underway, a financial settlement and "thank you" credit at the end of the movie finally squared things with King, but it was only a precursor to the trouble that would plague the picture.

To be clear, Neil Simon's script was not the Harry Karl story. It borrowed very loosely from the real-life events. In the movie, a rich playboy (Charley, played by Alec Baldwin) is engaged to the daughter of a movie studio owner. At his bachelor party in Las Vegas, he meets a gorgeous nightclub singer (Vicki, played by Kim Basinger) who is Bugsy Siegel's moll. After Bugsy Siegel catches them in bed together, he makes Charley marry Vicki, even though the two hardly know each other. When Charley's fiancée finds out, she gives him time to disentangle himself from the shotgun marriage and agrees to marry him as planned. Charley divorces Vicki, but in a subsequent chance encounter, sparks fly between them, and he marries her again. It doesn't work out, they split up again, and then they meet yet again. Oy!

"It was flawed from the beginning because of the repetitiveness and redundancy of the premise," Permut said. "He married her and divorced her, married her and divorced her. Where do you wind up in the third act? How do you top this infatuation? The core idea is flawed."

I asked Permut what he saw in the script in the first place. I thought it was a one-joke movie when we first previewed it. Looking back all these years later, Permut acknowledged that he was a young producer at the time, "and it was Neil Simon, one of the foremost writers in the world." Permut wasn't the only one who bought into the script, and both he and the studio executives did everything in their power to fix it, albeit after it was already shot. As mentioned, I tested it over and over again, each time with adjustments that attempted to address the problems. At one point, the studio approved a ten-day reshoot based on the test audience feedback.

What Permut will not talk about but was reported in the press—including in an April 5, 1991, article written by Steve Weinstein in the *Los Angeles Times* titled "The Worrying Man of 'Marrying Man'"—were the big problems unfolding on the set. The two stars, Kim Basinger and Alec Baldwin, first met when they were introduced to each other at the initial table read. Like the characters they portrayed in the film, sparks flew. Reportedly, the lovers argued with the crew, tempers flared, furniture was thrown, and people were banned from the set. The budget ballooned and despite the costly reshoot, nothing could save *The Marrying Man*.

"I felt like I was in a war zone every day on that movie," Permut says. When it wrapped, he had T-shirts made that said, "I survived the reshoot of *The Marrying Man*," which he gifted to every member of the crew still standing at the end of production.

CHAPTER 6

Danger Signs along the Road to Completion

TEST SCREENINGS HAVE ALWAYS BEEN AT THE CENTER of my career and still account for a big part of Screen Engine's business. My previous book, *Audience-ology: How Moviegoers Shape the Films We Love*, delves deeply into research conducted on films before they are released and the multitude of insights that test screenings reveal. The filmmakers and all the stakeholders on the studio side who are responsible for greenlighting, financing, producing, distributing, and marketing the movie can walk away from those early previews with a treasure trove of information about how well their film plays and the enthusiasm that movie consumers are likely to express when encouraging friends and family to see it. Importantly, as discussed in previous chapters, changes can still be made to address any issues that surface from the research before the film is locked. Some films require reshoots, but more often fixes can be made with edits, and by using ADR (automated dialogue replacement), different music, or footage that exists but was left on the proverbial cutting room floor.

It is through the test screening process that I have identified several danger signs that can have an impact on the reception a movie receives from the ticket-buying or streaming-subscribing public. These are the typical complaints we hear from test audiences, and while you may wonder why these problems weren't identified and fixed before the film was assembled, sometimes it is impossible to anticipate an issue beforehand.

A joke that seems hilarious on paper or during the initial table read may fall flat in the finished film. An explanation of a plot point that seems abundantly clear to those who have lived with the script for years can raise questions from moviegoers who are hearing it for the very first time. This is why virtually all big studio movies and most independently produced ones are put through the test screening process before they are released. Fresh eyes provide the very best litmus test.

Perhaps the most common danger sign is pacing, usually **slow pacing** in places that causes the viewer to feel fidgety or even completely disengage. Often when we test films we can sense boredom in the auditorium as audience members shift in their seats and people get up to use the restrooms or refill their drinks. This often happens during sequences that go on for too long or rely too heavily on exposition that does not move the narrative forward. For movies that are previewed in standard theaters (which is where a majority are tested), we have personnel stationed outside the auditorium doors who log the precise time that participants leave for bathroom breaks or to buy concessions. Afterward, we review the log to see if there was a flurry of "audience traffic" at a certain time. That observational information is passed along to the filmmakers so they can examine the scene(s) where the audience disengaged. For movies previewed in our facility, we have the ViewTrac dials that capture in real time exactly where the participants lost interest.

We also use the VX bracelets, developed in partnership with Sony, that I referenced earlier. I've worked with many biometric devices over the years. Most capture only one of several measurements—facial expression recognition, eye tracking, heartbeat/pulse monitoring, galvanic skin response, or audio intensity (the level of laughs, gasps, or sighs). Our proprietary wristbands monitor three in a single device—facial expressions, heartbeat, audio reactions—and they are easy to pop on, do not require any special wiring, and provide a reliable algorithm to graph engagement and emotional response to the content. Any movie that is tested includes questions about pacing on the survey that audience members complete afterward, providing quantitative data on the percentage who felt the film moved just right, too fast, or too slowly, along with feedback on specific scenes or areas of the story that dragged.

It's very common to have complaints of slow pacing during the beginning of movies where time is devoted to character introductions and story setup. The audience is always waiting for that first big moment to hit, which is often the "inciting incident"—the conflict that is ignited, the murder that sets off the investigation, the journey that gets underway, the obstacle that is thwarting the goal—and if it takes too long to get there, viewers get antsy. For theatrical films, moviegoers are captive. They have paid for their tickets and will remain in their seats even if their engagement is delayed longer than they would like. But for streamed movies, there is always the risk of tune-out. Platforms like Netflix, Amazon, Disney+, and Apple TV+ know exactly how long they have to "hook" their audiences, typically within the first ten minutes, before viewers reach for the remote to find something better to watch. These viewers are eager to connect with the story and need something powerful to grab on to at the outset.

Aside from the beginning, pacing issues will crop up anywhere in a film where it takes too long to get to the point, where information feels redundant, an emotional beat is repeated, or where a joke or situation overstays its welcome. It is important to know that criticisms of pacing are not always the same as criticisms of length. Pace and length are two distinct measures, and we ask about both on our test screening surveys. An audience may feel that certain parts of a story lost some steam but that overall, the length of the picture felt just right. Still, when there are pervasive criticisms of slow pacing in multiple parts of the movie, perceptions that it seemed too long will often follow. Lengthiness is mostly an *overall* assessment or feeling, that when all is said and done, the movie seems indulgent or overwrought.

SOME VERY FINE MOVIES have benefited from judicious trims, and others have undergone more extensive surgery during the months between first cut and release date. *The Woman King* is an example of a terrific, crowd-pleasing movie right out of the gate that became even better once length issues were addressed. It is the critically acclaimed, historically inspired story of an all-female regiment of warriors in 1823 defending the West African kingdom of Dahomey against the neighboring Oyo Empire that had raided its villages and enslaved its people. The characters in the film are mostly fictional, but the story has its roots in true events. The idea to bring it to life on the big screen originally came from actress Maria Bello after a visit to West Africa, and she persuaded heavy-hitter producer Cathy Schulman and force of nature, producer, and actress Viola Davis to develop it. Schulman's company, Welle Entertainment, and Davis's JuVee Productions produce movies and television content that appeal to diverse audiences, so *The Woman King* was right in their wheelhouse. TriStar Pictures was on board as the production and distribution partner and its president, Nicole Brown, championed it all the way through. The film is beautifully crafted by director Gina Prince-Bythewood (*Love & Basketball, The Secret Life of Bees, The Old Guard*).

Viola Davis is a tour de force in the movie, portraying General Nanisca, the leader of the women warriors. Schulman says, "Viola was a major advocate from the very beginning. She wanted to do an action-type film and a physical part. Most important, the idea that there could be a power center in a film that was entirely made up of Black women, and particularly dark-skinned Black women, was an enormous passion for her and for me and for all of us. It was a bold thing to go into the marketplace with that kind of picture because there was a lot of skepticism that it would be accepted by a general audience, and it could work with its mostly Black cast. The truth was the movie is in a genre that is familiar, like *Braveheart* or *Gladiator*. It's not completely foreign; it just looked different. *Black Panther*, which I think was an extraordinary film in its own way, opened the door for an exploration of something more grounded and historically based, which was our movie."

When the film was first tested in Chicago to a blindly recruited audience, it received an enthusiastic response. Moviegoers felt the story was intriguing, the performances were top-notch, and the action/fight scenes were spectacular. But because it lasted well over two and a half hours, there was pushback on the length and criticism that certain scenes went on for too long. The spans between battle sequences seemed to give permission to some attendees to take a bathroom break, and the audience traffic was about double what we typically see during a screening, even for a movie that is two-plus hours long.

The filmmakers took the test audience feedback to heart, trimmed about ten minutes, and tested again. The response remained strong, but there were still many complaints about slow pacing. To their credit, another seventeen minutes were cut, and the movie came together beautifully. At the final test screening, audience traffic was down to one-third of what it was at the original preview, meaning the vast majority of moviegoers stayed glued to their seats throughout the duration of the film, even though it was still over the two-hour mark.

I totally understand how difficult it is to trim nearly a half hour from an epic story, and I'm not cavalier about the tough decisions that director Prince-Bythewood and the talented editor, Terilyn Shropshire, had to make throughout that process. Each frame is precious to those who have dedicated months, if not years, of their lives to birthing a movie. But here is why it is so important to keep pace and length in check: when the audience stays engaged, they remain in the world and alongside the characters depicted. This is an underlying reason why we love movies. They transport us into worlds we never thought we would visit. *The Woman King* takes us back two hundred years into a little-known kingdom in West Africa where heroic women banded together, trained, fought against the brutality of the slave trade, and defied the odds.

What was great about the testing process on *The Woman King*, and what Prince-Bythewood did so masterfully, was to listen to the audience without sacrificing the integrity of the film. *The Woman King* was released in September 2022 and opened to a respectable $19 million, taking in nearly $100 million worldwide and generating accolades from critics and audiences alike. It earned a whopping 94 percent critics' score on Rotten Tomatoes, and a virtually perfect 99 percent audience score. If you haven't seen it, the spectacular fight choreography is reason enough to watch, but the characters, performances, and incredible story will also leave a lasting impression.

"This was a process that in many ways had to do with pace and length," Schulman says. "The most common reality we experience through testing is that audiences refuse to be bored. They *should* refuse to be bored! I am a huge proponent of that. That is why we are working in this art form. If you want to make a painting or a sculpture, be my guest, and let people decide how long they want to stand around and look at it."

The Woman King was recognized with award nominations and went on to win AFI's Movie of the Year. While it was not nominated for an Oscar—and some argued that it should have been—there's a funny story about producer Cathy Schulman and those esteemed awards that has nothing to do with this chapter but reveals a little more about her career and her personality. Cathy was also a producer of the 2005 film *Crash*, a poignant dive into class distinctions and racial tensions in Los Angeles, cleverly told through intertwining character storylines. It is the type of film that sparked discussion when it was in theaters, and it received a Best Picture Oscar nomination the following year. Yet it was up against some stiff competition, and Schulman didn't think her picture would actually win, so she was reluctant to write an acceptance speech. On the day before the awards, Schulman's publicist, Howard Bragman, called her to say the Vegas odds had gone her way. She asked, "What the heck are Vegas odds?" Bragman said, "They're the ones that matter. You really could win this thing." So Schulman prepared a speech.

The following day, in a hurry to dress and get to the awards show, Schulman called out to her husband, "Hey, that speech is on my computer. Will you print it out and put it in your jacket pocket? It's open." Her husband went to the computer, pressed the print button, and put the paper in his pocket. At the awards, Schulman didn't look at the speech for fear it might jinx the odds. In fact, she was so sure that *Brokeback Mountain* would win that she didn't hear Jack Nicholson's announcement of the Best Picture winner. It wasn't until the director of *Crash*, Paul Haggis, elbowed her and whispered, "You better move fast; we don't have a lot of time," that it even registered in Schulman's brain that their movie had won.

Schulman said, "So many things happened in those few moments. It's hard to rest in a moment of glory. The minute you're up there, you're thinking, 'Is this real? Do I have imposter syndrome? Will I ever be able to do this again?'" Onstage, Schulman looked down at the paper her husband had handed to her, and with horror saw that it was not her acceptance speech but rather a page of statistics on the genocide in Darfur! She had been doing research for her next film, a documentary she was producing, and had left her notes open on her computer. "I guess I had forgotten that I had been working on *Darfur Now*, which I'm very proud of, and not on my speech."

Interestingly, Schulman had been traveling on the awards circuit during 2005 and often ran into the same group of people who had movies that were nominated that year. George Clooney's film *Good Night, and Good Luck* was also a Best Picture contender, and he gave Schulman some advice. He told her that if ever she ends up onstage and feels nervous, she should just look at the person in the center of the first row and try not to think about the crowd that is really out there. Now, on the Academy Awards stage without her speech and with nearly forty million viewers watching, Schulman looked out into the audience and there, sitting smack in the middle of the first row, was none other than George Clooney. "That gave me the courage to give my speech," she says.

Cathy Schulman and I have known each other for decades, and I've conducted the test screenings on most, if not all, of her films. In addition to her producing credits, she served as president of Women in Film for eleven years, and from time to time teaches graduate-level film classes at Chapman University and UCLA. The day after the 78th Academy Awards ceremony, I was scheduled as a guest speaker for Schulman's evening class at UCLA. All day, I waited for a phone call telling me that the class was canceled. Straight off her Best Picture win for *Crash*, I knew Cathy must have been out all night doing press coverage and celebrating with her partners on the film. Well, the call never came, so at the end of the day I drove to the UCLA campus in Westwood half expecting that Cathy would be a no-show. When I arrived, there she was in the classroom, along with a gleaming gold Oscar statue, surrounded by her students. We had a wonderful time taking photos with the statue and the very deserving producer who brought it home.

RETURNING TO ISSUES that will impact a film's playability, not all pacing issues pertain to scenes that drag or feel repetitive. Test audiences will also complain about **fast pacing**, parts that move too quickly, especially if they feel they've missed crucial information or did not have enough time to enjoy a twist or reveal or a moment of victory. Impressions of fast pacing are often a proxy for confusion.

George Tillman Jr., who has directed important films like *Men of Honor* and *The Hate U Give*, recalled that he could feel when a particular film of his, *Notorious*, was moving too quickly. "It was a film where things were just too tight, where the cut was moving very fast and trying to get through the material, trying to keep people on the edge of their seats," he said. "I like to sit in the middle of the audience, and I just remember there was a feeling. I didn't even need to see the surveys. I felt like, ah, I've got to slow things down."

The 2009 film depicted the life story of the Notorious B.I.G. (rapper Christopher Wallace), and going into the first test screening, Tillman knew he needed additional footage to flesh things out. But he was trying to stay within the budget approved by the studio, Fox Searchlight. The first test preview was conducted without the extra scenes that Tillman wanted to shoot. "It was a small friends-and-family screening," Tillman said. "But some of those people were not my family or my friends." He laughs hard as he recalls walking into the theater and seeing people who worked in the cafeteria or the bookstore on the studio lot. But that is exactly the kind of audience that is recruited for a friends-and-family screening, and seeing those faces wasn't the only reason for his nervousness. He knew the movie needed the additional photography.

"It's a tough situation for a filmmaker," Tillman said. "The story of the Notorious B.I.G. is so interesting, and people didn't know a lot about his life at that time. The audience was invested, and they wanted to be there in the theater, but you could tell they wanted more. I could sense we were moving too fast, and the audience wasn't sitting with the characters and didn't have time to live with them. They wanted to feel like they were listening in on conversations. We needed a few more scenes to make the cut sing." Based on those early results, Tillman got what he needed.

Speaking of George Tillman Jr., he wrote and directed one of my all-time favorite films, *Soul Food*, which did not have pacing issues at all but is worth mentioning just for the fun of it. I remember testing it in Marina del Rey, California, to an extraordinary response. *Soul Food* was the best food-themed movie I had ever seen, and after the screening, I was starving. So I raced to a nearby restaurant afterward for a late dinner before it closed. With my mouth still watering from what I had just seen at the theater, I arrived at Aunt Kizzy's Back Porch, specializing in "down-home cooking," to feast on chicken and dumplings, corn bread, and mac and cheese. That movie captured the notion of family . . . and made me so hungry!

"I remember that screening vividly," says Tillman. "That was a film I made for Fox 2000 with Laura Ziskin, who was amazing. The film was a very personal experience for me. That was my family. That's where I grew up, with those Sunday dinners and soul food. I had seen *Eat Drink Man Woman*, but there wasn't anything like that to represent African Americans. You must keep the audience in mind when you're making a movie, but sometimes, as a filmmaker, I make one for myself. I have a story I want to tell. I need to get it out there. And that was my experience with *Soul Food*. The audience can feel the authenticity of the material, and when you're being honest with your storytelling, it becomes an audience movie."

ON TEST AUDIENCE SURVEYS, it is not uncommon to see complaints of slow pacing at the beginning, and even persisting into the middle of the story, followed by criticism of the very same film as pacing too quickly at the end. Audiences need time to follow the pieces that come together as things wrap up, or just to sit with the denouement for a moment or two.

When the story reaches its climax and resolves too quickly, even if everything makes sense, there will be comments that the ending feels "abrupt." I recently worked on a family movie that had a very exciting scene at the end where the good guys won, and the bad guys were defeated. There was a heartwarming moment with a good message, but even so, moviegoers weren't feeling it. The ending had all the right ingredients, but the timing was so quick they felt they were missing something. Those story beats—the battle, the victory, the protagonists expressing their feelings for one another, and the moral payoff—just needed a little more "air" so the audience could appreciate each one.

Parts of a story that move too quickly can cause **confusion**, which is another common danger sign. Unanswered questions and story threads that are introduced but not completed to satisfaction can cause the audience to feel frustrated and cheated. There is a difference between "good confusions"—aspects of a story intentionally left ambiguous to spark discussion or to create intrigue and/or heighten suspense—and "bad confusions," which detract from movie viewers' enjoyment and can pull them out of the picture. I remember when we tested *Where the Crawdads Sing*, which includes a murder mystery, some audience members were a bit confused when the dead man's necklace is found decades later inside a book that belonged to Kya, the main character. That reveal strongly suggests she killed him and got away with it, a crime that many would find forgivable given that he tried to rape her and continued to threaten her even after she fought off the attack. Still, the revelation was a bit opaque, and I'm certain that it was a creative decision by the filmmakers to divulge her hand in the villain's death without spoon-feeding it to the audience. I would categorize that as a good confusion.

On the flip side, there are many examples of confusions that diminish audience enjoyment. I conducted research on a tasty arthouse film that was extremely well acted and featured outstanding production values.

But it never tested well. At each preview, one-third or more of the audience walked away feeling confused because the dialogue was accented and difficult to understand, the secondary characters popped in and out of the story without being well established, and the jumps in time were disorienting. The filmmakers made many attempts to address the issues, reassembling scenes in a more linear fashion and adding cards (bits of text that appear between scenes in a film) to delineate the years. But confusion remained widespread, and while it found its evangelists, I'm not convinced that the film ever achieved its full potential.

Flashbacks can also generate confusion, especially if many are used throughout a film. I remember years ago talking to Gary Lucchesi, the esteemed Hollywood producer (*Million Dollar Baby*, *Primal Fear*, *The Age of Adaline*, and the *Underworld* franchise) and former president of the Producers Guild of America. Before forming his own production company, when he was still head of production at Paramount, Lucchesi oversaw the 1991 movie *Dead Again*. It was directed by and stars Kenneth Branagh as a nineties-era private detective who is trying to establish the identity of a mute woman, played by Emma Thompson, who is suffering from amnesia. Thompson's character has nightmares about the bloody 1949 stabbing of a woman whose husband was sent to the electric chair for her murder. Within this twisty crime/mystery, the 1949 storyline is told in flashback, and the husband and wife are also portrayed by Kenneth Branagh and Emma Thompson.

When the movie was previewed to a test audience, two major issues surfaced. First, moviegoers were totally confused by the transitions back and forth in time, and second, they felt the murder scenes were far too violent. Lucchesi says, "I went home after the screening and I'm eating Häagen-Dazs wondering why we made this movie. The next day I was talking to Sydney Pollack, who was the executive producer, and we were trying to figure out what to do. We came up with the idea of changing the flashbacks to black and white." That single change not only distinguished the 1949 scenes from the 1990 scenes but also helped tamp down rejection of all the blood in the murder scenes. When the revised cut was tested, the scores doubled versus the first screening, and the film was locked.

My company recently tested a film that is a modern-day noir, wherein the same actor plays two different roles, and the premise relies on flashbacks to dole out clues to a mystery. Confusion persisted at every screening, and some of the audiences' questions pertained to the flashbacks. Lucchesi's story about *Dead Again* reverberated in my mind. Unfortunately, the solution was not as simple as changing the flashback scenes to black and white.

Films about hauntings will often generate high levels of confusion if the rules around the ghost appearances, powers, and behaviors are inconsistent. The same thing applies to aliens or any other type of monsters that require world-building. The audience will go along for the ride as long as boundaries are drawn. But if the rules are not well established, or if they change midstream, viewers will feel confused and may be pulled out of the story.

THIS BRINGS UP ANOTHER DANGER SIGN: betraying the movie rules. Regardless of the genre, once the parameters of behavior and setting are established, any glaring deviation will be a red flag. Not only will it spark confusion but the audience will also feel as though the rug has been pulled out from under them. They are buying into a premise, often one that requires a suspension of disbelief, so to veer beyond the guardrails of what has already been planted in their minds is disruptive. For example, if an antihero's special power is strength, and that power is clearly delineated in the first and second acts, the character cannot suddenly teleport through a wall in the third act after using only his brawn up to that point. That would be a betrayal of the rules, and the audience can turn against the film.

ANOTHER CRITICISM THAT CAN ARISE from test screening research centers on perceptions that a film contains **cheesy or corny moments**. Sometimes these pop up as dialogue that does not seem organic, humor that is silly rather than clever, or interactions between characters that come across as forced. These miscalculations spark impressions of inauthenticity, which at best take moviegoers out of the story for a beat, and at worst can make the audience feel downright uncomfortable. Moviegoers can smell the cheese from a mile away. The character in a horror movie that walks toward the strange sound when the lights go out? A trope! The action hero who survives a fall from four stories with little more than a scratch? Ridiculous! The pickup line that is slicker than an oil spill? Cringey!

I worked on a film where the two leads had little chemistry and the actors themselves looked uncomfortable during their intimate scenes, generating comments from test preview attendees that those sequences seemed cheesy. How was the audience supposed to buy their romance if the characters looked like they were faking it? Unfortunately, short of recasting and starting over, there wasn't much that could be done to remedy that particular problem. Still, in most cases where there are complaints of cheesy content, those issues can be addressed by truncating a scene, deleting it altogether, or switching out a line or two via ADR.

Another situation that borders on cheesy is what is known as a "hat on a hat." This is when a point is made and the audience gets it, but something else is added unnecessarily to drive the point home again. The expression has its origins in comedy. Stand-up comedians are wary of adding another joke to a bit that is already working because it detracts from the original material that was funny on its own. The same thing can happen in movies. If the joke is funny enough, let it breathe. Putting another "hat" on it will often trample on the laughter. Similarly, adding a second twist to one that already works can diminish the impact of the first surprise.

I am a big fan of Emerald Fennell, who wrote and directed *Promising Young Woman* and several episodes of the series *Killing Eve*. She also portrays Camilla Parker Bowles in *The Crown* and has a number of other acting roles to her credit. Fennell makes the kind of entertainment that people want to discuss, and her films stay with me for days after I see them. My company tested her 2023 film *Saltburn*, which had that effect on me. It is the story of a young man, Oliver (Barry Keoghan), who attends Oxford University and becomes infatuated with a handsome, charismatic, wealthy classmate named Felix (Jacob Elordi), who invites him to his family's country estate for the summer. The film is a layered commentary on the idle rich and those who desire that lifestyle, and it pushes boundaries in more ways than one. In the film, Oliver is awkward, especially when he first arrives at the estate and does not know the protocols of aristocratic society. Felix's parents seem forgiving if not oblivious, but the butler (Paul Rhys) is onto him, knows that he does not belong in the family's social circle, and seems to delight in making Oliver uncomfortable. At breakfast on the first morning he's there, Oliver requests eggs, and the butler deliberately serves them runny, which Oliver finds repulsive.

I don't want to say too much more about the film because if you haven't seen it, you should. It is full of delicious twists and turns, some of them shocking. At the end of the story, there is a particularly memorable scene where Oliver dances naked through the mansion to the song "Murder on the Dancefloor"—and kudos to Barry Keoghan for his brilliant performance—signaling his newfound comfort in the social stratosphere. In the original cut that was tested, there was a final scene after the naked dance where Oliver sits down to breakfast and the butler again sets eggs in front of him. Runny eggs. I thought it was in the film to make a point, that even though Oliver had settled into the lifestyle that he aspired to, the butler still called him out, in a passive-aggressive manner, as undeserving. But when I watched the final cut again months later, I saw that the egg scene at the end had been deleted. I've always wondered if the talented Ms. Fennell thought bringing back the runny eggs was a hat on a hat. When we test another one of her movies, I must ask!

ANOTHER KEY DANGER SIGN IS **dissatisfaction with the ending**, which can be the kiss of death in terms of positive word of mouth. When it comes to conclusions, there are two types of satisfaction, and each is equally important. *Intellectual* satisfaction pertains to questions being answered, characters' outcomes explained, loose ends tied up, and the storyline generally made whole. Was the mission accomplished? Journey completed? Crime solved? Villain caught? Intellectual satisfaction is critical, and yet it is rarely enough. Ideally, endings must also be *emotionally* satisfying. Did the characters have a moment of triumph? Was justice served? Was a lesson learned? Was the reward earned? I find that it is very rare to get a high score from a test screening audience if the ending does not satisfy on both intellectual and emotional levels.

Endings do not necessarily need to be wrapped and tied with a bow. Certain aspects can be ambiguous, especially if the intent is to spark discussion, leave the audience guessing (in a good way), or tee up a sequel. To this day, people continue to debate the conclusion of Christopher Nolan's 2010 mind-bending *Inception*. Was it reality or a dream? And that's a wonderful aspect of the movie. Across the globe, there was excitement to see the film just to be part of that conversation. But if the conclusion is not satisfying *enough*, on both the intellectual and emotional levels, moviegoers will often leave the theater feeling disappointed, and negative word of mouth will likely follow.

Producer Cathy Schulman agrees. "I'm obsessed with endings because I really believe what people feel as they leave the theater is most crucial. Endings are the hardest part to get right in every film. That's been my experience producing thirty-plus movies."

My company tested *A Quiet Place: Day One* before its release in summer 2024. The third installment in a hugely popular franchise, the movie leverages the terrifying alien invasion established in the first and second films, where even the most minuscule sound attracts ferocious monsters that are killing off the human species. Except for Djimon Hounsou's character, the third picture features an entirely new cast. None of the Abbott family members from the 2018 and 2020 films (portrayed by John Krasinski, Emily Blunt, Millicent Simmonds, and Noah Jupe) return in this third one. From the very title, *A Quiet Place: Day One*, prospective moviegoers understood that this was a prequel.

Not surprisingly, test audiences loved the suspense and scares depicted in the third film, and the urban New York City setting felt fresh and different from the isolated, rural locales of the first two installments. Seeing huge crowds of people reacting to the invaders in the early days of the attack, skyscrapers and bridges being blown to pieces, and panic in the streets, was an absolute thrill for the attendees at the early previews. The new characters, Samira (Lupita Nyong'o), her scene-stealing emotional support cat, Frodo, and the traumatized young man she befriends, Eric (Joseph Quinn), played extremely well. In the film, Samira is a terminal cancer patient who knows she has limited time left. Her dying wish is to revisit the neighborhood where she grew up, and Eric accompanies her through the city, narrowly escaping the monsters as they quietly make their way to her old apartment building, then to Samira's favorite pizza place (now destroyed by the alien invaders), and to the jazz club where her father once played piano.

In the first version of the movie that was tested, Samira says goodbye to Eric in the third act and hands her beloved Frodo to him. He heads toward the river, from where he knows he can make his way out of the city because the monsters cannot swim. Producer Andrew Form described what followed in that early cut. "The next scene is Eric by himself walking toward the beach. He looks out over the water and sees land on the other side. He finds a white box and puts the cat into it, and just starts to swim, pushing the box across the water by himself. Cut to Samira. She's walking down the street with her headphones on. She pulls the headphones off, music plays at full volume, and the screen goes black."

That ending was intellectually satisfying. The audience understood that Samira's journey was over. She was going out on her own terms, knowing that her cat and her friend would get to safety, and choosing the time and place to end her life rather than allowing the cancer to decide. It was meant to be an empowering end for a strong character. But the audience didn't feel emotionally satisfied. It was a sad outcome for Samira, and some felt she should have at least tried to escape with Eric and Frodo. A few even rejected the implication of her death by suicide.

Form continued: "We knew the audience was on the journey with these two characters, and their relationship was working on every level. So we asked ourselves, 'What are moviegoers really craving?' We knew we needed to ratchet up the ending, give them some excitement, some jeopardy, and something to overcome at the end. We also wanted to include a nice genre element to wrap up the movie." The executives at Paramount agreed, and it was decided that new footage would be required to provide an ending that would deliver on all fronts. With careful editing and additional photography, the revised ending featured more heightened suspense, a huge action sequence, and a heartwarming moment of emotionality to pair with the intellectual payoff.

Earlier in the movie, there was a boat of survivors out on the river, and that aspect of the story was brought back in the third act. Form said, "We put the two characters, Samira and Eric, in jeopardy on the FDR Drive. That scene was new. There are creatures close, bearing down on them, and we have no idea what Samira is going to do. The threat is there, and the audience is on the edge of their seats." In additional footage reminiscent of John Krasinski's character in the first movie saving the lives of his children, Samira finds a crowbar and smashes the windows of abandoned cars along the FDR Drive, diverting the attention of the monsters so Eric and Frodo can get to the boat. "Eric sees his moment," said Form, "and takes off. Unfortunately, he makes a noise and now the chase is on in his direction. He has to run for his life. It's him with the cat, running down that pier as the creatures are coming toward him at full speed. At the last second, he dives into the water. We all know the creatures can't swim, so once he hits the water, he is safe. He swims to the boat, and we see that he is rescued. To us, that was satisfying and exciting."

Once the audience knows Eric and Frodo have made it to safety, the story goes back to Samira, who revisits the jazz club where her father had once performed and spends a moment looking at an old photograph of herself as a child with him. She smiles and cries. Meanwhile, on the boat, Eric finds a note from Samira in his pocket, thanking him for bringing her home (obviously to the places she had loved most) and telling him to take care of her cat. These heartwarming beats raised the level of emotionality at the conclusion. The very last scene is similar to the original ending. Samira walks into the street and plays the blaring music, except in the final version, there is a quick cut of a monster looming in the background.

While the revised ending of the film was still sad, Samira's death was counterbalanced with those poignant moments of happy memories and gratitude. The audience knows that she is at peace. Clearly, there is hope for the survivors, including Eric, Frodo the cat, and Djimon Hounsou's character, who is on the boat. Not only did the test audience evaluations of the ending skyrocket with the new footage but ratings of the story and the characters also increased sharply. The work, time, and expense that were required to make the ending more emotionally satisfying undoubtedly fueled positive word of mouth. The film opened strongly to $52 million in the US and has taken in more than five times that amount on a worldwide basis.

WORLD WAR Z IS ANOTHER MOVIE that benefited from a revised ending. At the time, Marc Evans was the president of production at Paramount, where he oversaw the creative development of that picture, as well as other blockbuster films in the *Mission: Impossible*, *Transformers*, and *Star Trek* franchises. He knows big-action tentpoles, and it's interesting to hear him reflect on *World War Z* and what led to major reshoots before it was released.

"At the end of the day, we all collectively made a big mistake with the third act of that movie," Evans said, "and we all saw it. The producers, the director, we knew it. We were under pressure from all around the business to make movies big in order to compete."

The storyline in *World War Z* centers on a mysterious plague that is turning the world's population into zombies. Brad Pitt portrays a former United Nations investigator who is pulled into service to help find the origins of the disease so a vaccine can be developed. His involvement in the investigation takes him around the world and within inches of his life as he encounters zombie attacks that are wiping out entire cities. Through his various encounters, he observes that the zombies do not go after the seriously injured or terminally ill, apparently because those compromised humans would not be strong enough to host the virus and further its spread.

The original ending featured Pitt's character engaged in a huge battle with the zombies in Russia, surrounded by a group of elderly people who are immune to infection because they are weak and sick. Before the picture was even tested in front of an audience, the filmmakers knew they had a problem. It was a hard-learned lesson, and Evans readily admits, "It was a crazy, massive fight at the end which delivered no emotional payoff. We didn't see it on paper because it's the third act of an action-heavy movie. We were looking at what Marvel was doing and what Michael Bay was doing with *Transformers*. Of course, being big was wrong. It needed to be small. It needed to be personal. And that is really what very smart, creative people, plus the limitations of going back to shoot, taught us. You don't always have to be big." Writers Damon Lindelof (of the *Lost* TV series fame) and Chris McQuarrie (*The Usual Suspects*, and later the *Mission: Impossible* movies) were brought in to help with rewrites. They dialed down the action and ramped up the tension and emotionality of the third act. Paramount agreed to fund the reshoots.

In the revised ending of the film, Brad Pitt's character wants to test his hypothesis about illness providing immunity to a certain vulnerable population. Inside a World Health Organization facility in Wales that has become infested with zombies, he and his colleagues stealthily try to get to a storage area that holds pathogens. Their intent is to infect themselves with a disease for which there is a cure to see if it camouflages them from the zombies. However, they become separated, and Pitt's character alone comes face-to-face with a zombie. In a riveting sequence, he injects himself with an unknown pathogen that is at hand and then approaches the zombie. The zombie sniffs him but does not attack, does not bite. Then

Pitt's character walks down the hallway to a soft drink machine, creates a racket as he opens it and allows the cans of soda to spill out onto the floor, and walks triumphantly toward an onslaught of zombies who are attracted to the noise. The zombies lumber right past him, ignoring him as the music swells. His theory is proven.

The final scenes show him being vaccinated, perhaps the antidote to whatever he injected himself with to make it appear that he was sick, then reuniting with his family in Nova Scotia. Those heartwarming moments are intercut with shots of survivors around the world finally receiving a vaccine, and Pitt's narration about buying some time so that humanity has a fighting chance of survival.

When the film was retested, it performed extremely well, aided in no small part by its intellectually and emotionally satisfying ending. It opened to a huge response in summer 2013, taking in $66 million over its first weekend, and more than half a billion dollars worldwide during its theatrical run.

ANOTHER DANGER ZONE pertains specifically to comedies and other genres that rely on humor like action comedies and romantic comedies—**jokes that don't land**. Great comedy filmmakers like Judd Apatow and Sacha Baron Cohen are prepared for this, and they are meticulous when it comes to testing their films. They often include more jokes than they actually need in their first cut, gauge the test audience's response, then trim back to get rid of what doesn't work as well, and tighten to get the comedic timing just right. They will shoot backup takes and alternate punch lines so if one version of a comedy bit doesn't work, they have others at the ready to substitute. When we test their films, I find they usually care more about listening to the audience than about the actual scores on the surveys. In the theater, they set up night vision/infrared cameras so they can capture the audience's reactions and review the video afterward to help guide their edits.

When all the jokes work from the get-go, it's always a special night in the test screening business. Monica Levinson has produced several of Sacha Baron Cohen's pictures, and she and I have often reminisced about the first test preview of *Borat*, which we were both lucky enough to experience. It was conducted in Marina del Rey, and I'm not sure that anyone could have predicted the response. It was absolutely raucous. During the naked fight scene, perhaps better described as the "teabag" scene, people jumped out of their seats in waves, like at a ball game. Levinson says, "There was one guy who got up and just ran up and down the aisle screaming with his arms up. I've never seen an audience react in such a way. It was insanity. In my life, I've never seen a movie play so well! We all had to go out after that screening and just sit and reflect. And it was our first preview!"

Personally, I thought the way Twentieth Century Fox distributed the movie was genius. They were criticized by many for not initially opening on enough screens, giving the impression they did not have enough faith in what they had. But nobody knew the Borat character then. So they opened the film on only a semi-wide or limited number of screens, let the word of mouth build, and sure enough, it exploded the next weekend. Levinson said, "I got that Saturday-night call from Sacha saying, 'You're not going to believe this, but we're number one.' And I said, 'With eight hundred screens we're number one?'"

To this day, *Borat* is one of the funniest movies I've ever seen. Monica Levinson went on to produce *Brüno* and *Borat Subsequent Moviefilm*, and had producing roles on *Old Dads*, *30 Minutes or Less*, and *Zoolander*. While she also produces films in many other genres, she knows her way around comedy and has seen her share of jokes that landed and others that have missed. I asked her what it is like working with Sacha.

"It's amazing. He's brilliant. And I never want to say no to him. I want the creative process to flow. The writers' room needs to create; they need to keep coming up with ideas. He needs to be able to have that umbrella and figure out how to either make it work, or not. And sometimes we shoot things that are not going to work, but we need to be able to have options and the ability to try."

NANCY KIRHOFFER IS ONE OF the most respected postproduction professionals in Hollywood. She has worked on *Booksmart, Molly's Game, The Prestige, Blockers, Being the Ricardos, The Trial of the Chicago 7, I Feel Pretty,* and *My Sister's Keeper,* along with more than 150 other titles. She oversees the convergence of three principal elements of a movie—the picture, the sound, and the music—working across departments to assemble the final product that we eventually see on the screen. It takes on average about six months after wrap to bring a studio movie to finish, although most are tested much sooner than that—about ten to twelve weeks after filming is completed, when there is a director's cut. Kirhoffer attends all the test screenings on the films that she handles, often guiding the filmmakers through the process, which can be quite anxiety producing for a director. She knows the importance of regular moviegoers' eyes on a picture, and the need to listen to warning signs that might emanate from early test audiences.

"It's a very scary thing," Kirhoffer says as she describes the headspace of a filmmaker. "You've spent all this time in prep. You've spent all this time in production, which is super exciting. You have all these people doing amazing things and it's like a big love fest. You're creating and you're exhausted in the best possible way coming out of production. And then you go into post and all of a sudden, it goes from being very big to being very intimate in the cutting room. At that point, directors have usually only seen dailies and they haven't seen it cut together, and oftentimes they're like, 'Oh my gosh, it's not what I thought it was.' I believe the director's cut is hallowed ground, a time for the director to just marinate in their movie, to relax, to see it all from a different perspective. There may be something you love as a filmmaker because you were on the set the day you created it and it was beautiful and funny and wonderful, so you put it in your cut, yet you're not really sure if it's working. But an audience is going to tell you the truth!"

In the gentlest way possible, Kirhoffer tries to prepare the filmmaker, and especially if it's a first-time director, for the loss of control they will feel when their movie is turned over to an audience. She begins early on, emphasizing the importance of the testing process and telling the director that this is a gift, a time to learn. I love that! I tell filmmakers the same thing—the test screening is *their* laboratory. Certain filmmakers will conduct their own test screening first, either with "friends and family" or with a recruited audience of regular moviegoers, but without the executives from the studio in attendance. This gives them an opportunity to gauge how their initial cut is playing and allows them the privacy to make any adjustments before the large team of studio brass weighs in with their opinions.

Kirhoffer remembers working on *Neighbors 2: Sorority Rising*. Based on the great success of *Neighbors*, as previously discussed in the first chapter, a second film was in the works very soon after. Nick Stoller was once again the director. Stoller, Evan Goldberg, and Seth Rogen wrote the screenplay for the sequel, and most of the characters initially conceived by Andrew Cohen and Brendan O'Brien appeared in it, including Rogen and Rose Byrne at the center of the story. *Neighbors 2* leverages the same basic premise as the first film, but instead of hell-raising fraternity boys, it is wild sorority girls who move in next door.

Kirhoffer says one of the biggest surprises of her career was when

Neighbors 2 was tested, and the jokes didn't land. "I'd seen it a couple of times and we all thought it was hilarious, just like the first one. But what we learned in the preview process was that the stuff boys got away with, girls really didn't." Stoller, Goldberg, and Rogen took it all in and rebounded like the professionals they are. "These guys are brilliant," Kirhoffer says of the writing team. "And so they wrote some new scenes, and they tweaked the characters." The film was tested several more times to guide the new content. "It was hilarious in the end."

Neighbors 2: Sorority Rising was never the huge hit its predecessor was, and I contend the difference was the big idea that tapped into those life-changing transitions between college and parenthood that made the first movie so special but perhaps didn't seem as fresh the second time around. Still, the sequel was made for $35 million and took in a respectable $108 million worldwide.

CHAPTER 7

Balancing the Art and the Audience

AFTER READING THE LAST FEW CHAPTERS, you may have reached certain conclusions about research and movies. I hope you don't think of me only as a data junkie, or as someone who believes that movies are paint-by-numbers projects or that blockbusters can be created in a lab by combining a bunch of specific inputs to create a specific output. If you do, I can assure you that nothing could be further from the truth.

I've always been an artist at heart. As a teenager, I traveled back and forth from New Jersey to New York City for acting gigs. I was what they called a triple threat: I acted, I sang, and I danced. Even when I stepped away from being a performer and began to get more involved in the research side of the entertainment business, I still felt the pull to create. I've produced twelve television movies of my own so far, as well as a documentary. I know what it's like to fall in love with a project. I know what it's like to spend years turning an idea into a reality. And I know what it's like to make pretty much no money doing it.

That was the story of *Wild Iris*, a 2001 television movie I produced. It was a passion project, one that had been sparked more than eleven years earlier when I read the script for an unproduced play called *Bluebird Bridals*. The story was about a woman whose life fell apart after her husband's suicide, forcing her and her teenage son to move in with her overbearing mother, who runs a bridal shop out of her home. It was a compelling slice-of-life narrative that felt similar to movies like *Fried Green Tomatoes* and

Steel Magnolias, which were hits at the time. I was deeply committed to turning *Bluebird Bridals* into a film.

But the road to making the movie that would become *Wild Iris* was long and winding. By the time the stars finally aligned almost a dozen years later, moviegoer tastes had changed significantly. I knew that my tender domestic drama didn't stand a chance of making money in theaters. But I still thought it could find an audience, and my partners and I eventually got Showtime and Paramount to agree to finance and distribute it. We lined up a killer cast, headlined by Gena Rowlands and Laura Linney—two absolute treasures who would eventually both be nominated for Outstanding Lead Actress in a Miniseries or Movie at the 54th Primetime Emmy Awards (with Linney eventually winning). It also featured a young Emile Hirsch, appearing in only his second film, as the teenage son.

It ended up being a happy story: my passion project got made, it got well-deserved award recognition, and after splitting the producer's fee with my partners, I made a whopping $25,000 when all was said and done. I was fortunate enough to form a lifelong bond with my dear friend Gena Rowlands, who passed away the night before I finished this very chapter. I wouldn't trade the experience of knowing her for anything. I would make that movie all over again.

But I wouldn't make another movie *like* it again. This is an important distinction. My experience making *Wild Iris* was creatively fulfilling, and it remains the project I'm most proud of. But it wasn't financially sustainable, especially when you consider how much time went into bringing it to fruition. Financially speaking, you're not going to have much of a career churning out dozens of movies like *Wild Iris.*

This experience points toward an inescapable truth about making it in Hollywood: you need to find the right balance between the spirit of your art and the needs of your audience.

BALANCING THE ART AND THE AUDIENCE

LET'S GET ONE THING OUT OF THE WAY AT THE TOP: you'll be hard-pressed to find anyone in Hollywood making movies solely because they want to make money. Sure, there's money to be made—but there are far easier ways to do it, ways that don't involve spending years of your life toiling away on a single script, or being sequestered away from your family for months on set. However cynical you may be about the film industry as a capitalist venture, I can assure you that people are in this business because they love the art of moviemaking.

"I have to love a movie to sell it," producer Brian Grazer told me. "When I go into a meeting with a studio, I know I have to make the case for the *why* of this project. Why now? Why with this group of talent? Why with this investment of money? I have to answer those questions for myself first."

The projects that spark Grazer's interest are the ones that move him. "The soul of something, the emotions that connect to the human heart—that's what interests me. I concentrate on universal themes, like love." Grazer's films have covered everything from brotherly love (1991's *Backdraft*) to romantic love (1993's *For Love or Money*) to the love of family (1989's *Parenthood*) to the love for an underdog (2005's *Cinderella Man*), and even the love for an unlikely hero (2001's *A Beautiful Mind*). His passions have even helped him sell movies based on the strength of universal themes alone. "I was once told by the president of a studio that the script I wanted green-lit wasn't good enough. I pushed back and asked her to pretend the script was good enough. Did she believe in the story's theme of love?" The studio ended up making the movie.

When it comes to picking projects, producer Amy Pascal is chasing a similar feeling. "It's like falling in love, a chemical attraction to something," she told me. "I only work on movies now that I want on my tombstone."

She couldn't help but rave about some of her upcoming projects. "I'm excited about making *Cleopatra* with Denis Villeneuve. It's one of the greatest stories ever told, and I've been working on it for twenty years. It seems like it could be as big as anything." She also has high hopes for the movie adaptation of Andy Weir's acclaimed novel *Project Hail Mary*, which has Ryan Gosling attached to star. "It's about an astronaut and his relationship with an alien. They both try to save the world! That book excites me, and I know it will be made into a great movie."

But passion alone doesn't guarantee that a project will pan out the way you hope it will. "I think everyone has things they fall in love with, and I'll give you one of mine: 2003's *Big Fish*," said veteran studio executive Peter Schlessel. The film, directed by Tim Burton, was about a son trying to make sense of his dying father's life. "If it was good, we would know how to get it out there. If it was great, it could be *Forrest Gump*—it had the potential to be something ridiculously, unbelievably special. It was not the kind of movie I would've usually supported. But I believed in it so fully that I pushed, pushed, pushed." Schlessel eventually moved forward with the project at Columbia Pictures, with a reported $70 million budget. "We probably green-lit it for a little bit too much money, and we probably were too lax on certain things because of what I saw as the potential." The movie only grossed $66 million in the US and a total of $123 million globally.

Schlessel's experience with *Big Fish* points toward the reality of moviemaking: it's not just about the artistry. It's also about creating projects that can find an audience.

Nicole Brown agrees. "Some filmmakers seem to be more dedicated to speaking solely to their vision and discounting feedback from moviegoers. Then, if their movie doesn't realize its full box office potential, it's often hard to accept that perhaps some of their missed opportunity lies in their inability to listen to the audience."

BALANCING THE ART AND THE AUDIENCE

I ONCE SAT ON A PANEL, hosted by the Writers Guild of America, that was geared toward writers from the LGBTQ+ community. An audience member asked a question about what kind of movies they should write to be successful. One of the panelists kicked things off by saying, "Follow your heart! You can only write from your heart." This was a popular answer—it got big applause from the crowd. But I knew it only hit on half of the equation.

"Writing from the heart is your ticket to entry, but it's a little naive to think that's all you need to succeed. If you want to pay your rent, you have to listen to the marketplace," I told the audience. "Believe me, if 'gay' movies made money every time out, Hollywood would make nothing but gay movies. But that's not the world we live in."

I got some applause, though not nearly as much as the other guy. But my statement has been proven true time and again—most recently with the rollout of *Bros*, a 2022 comedy starring Billy Eichner and Luke Macfarlane as two commitment-phobic gay men who fall in love.

Nick Stoller, the director of the project, talked with me about how the movie came together. "I had been interested in the idea of a romantic comedy about two men for a while." Stoller, who is straight, wanted to partner with an LGBTQ+ voice on the project to ensure authentic representation. He soon found that creative partner in actor and comedian Billy Eichner. "We both wanted it to be really funny and very real, heartfelt, and honest, which is what I've tried to achieve with all the movies I've done," Stoller said. They also agreed that Eichner should star in the project. "Billy is just so funny, such a comic genius. I thought about it, honestly, as a comedy vehicle for Billy Eichner—not as a gay romantic comedy. I thought of it the way I think of *Forgetting Sarah Marshall* as a comedy vehicle for Jason Segel, or *Neighbors* as a comedy vehicle for Seth Rogen and Zac Efron."

HOW TO SCORE IN HOLLYWOOD

My company conducted the test screenings for *Bros*, and I loved it from the beginning. It was terrifically funny, with real insight and heart. It was produced by Judd Apatow, who has a strong reputation for producing well-received, commercially successful comedies like *Trainwreck*, *Bridesmaids*, and *Knocked Up*. Critics showered the movie with praise, resulting in an 89 percent Fresh score on Rotten Tomatoes. Audiences who watched it agreed, delivering it an A rating on CinemaScore and an eighty-six (out of one hundred) Index Score on PostTrak. But the number of moviegoers who actually turned out to theaters was disastrously small: *Bros* opened to just $4.8 million in the US, on its way to an anemic $14.7 million worldwide gross.

What went so wrong? Much of the promotion for *Bros* centered around it being a groundbreaking, unapologetically gay film that didn't shy away from sex. It was the first gay romantic comedy from a major studio—featuring an all-LGBTQ+ cast—brought to life by Billy Eichner, the first openly gay man ever to write and star in his own major studio feature.[1] But focusing so heavily on these firsts left little room for promoting the strong comedic elements of the film that could have appealed to a wider audience.

The commercial failure of the movie stung for all involved. According to Eichner, "Straight people, especially in certain parts of the country, just didn't show up for *Bros*. And that's disappointing, but it is what it is."[2]

"Gay men were the primary group who saw it in a theater. It's not like he said something that was a lie or incorrect," Stoller said in an interview.[3] "People saw it and thought, 'That story's not my story. Why would I go see that?' But we thought it would have bigger reach than that, based purely on the testing. All three tests sparked fascinating conversations and people clapped. It's why the studio spent a lot of money. They didn't spend it because they thought the movie would be good for the world. They spent it because it's a really entertaining movie."

BALANCING THE ART AND THE AUDIENCE

I RECENTLY CAME ACROSS an interview with Rick Rubin, famed record producer and cofounder of Def Jam Recordings, that struck a chord with me. When approaching a project, Rubin said, "The audience comes last. I'm not making it for them, I'm making it for me. When you make something truly for yourself, you're doing the best thing you possibly can for the audience." My ears really perked up when he pivoted to my world: "If you go to the movies, so many big movies are just not good. It's because they're not being made by a person who cares about it. They're being made by people who are trying to make something that they think someone else is gonna like. And that's not how art works. That's something else. That's not art. That's commerce."

I have complicated feelings about Rubin's assessment. On the one hand, I completely agree with the idea that every project needs a beating heart in it. It needs a champion. It needs someone who believes in it, who loves it, who lives and breathes it. But in all my years of experience making my own projects and working with Hollywood's greatest luminaries, I've never met a project that *didn't* have someone who treated it like their own precious baby.

I'm not just talking about auteur-driven passion projects, either. I've made movies as a producer for the Lifetime network that were birthed out of research that told us women-in-jeopardy thrillers would sell. My producing partners and I would sit around a conference table, brainstorming all sorts of outlandish plots, trying to find the right combination of elements that would draw the most eyeballs. But you better believe that when it came time to make those movies, I was fully invested in making them the best damn woman-in-jeopardy thrillers the world had ever seen. I loved those movies. I *still* love those movies. Every one of them has a piece of me in it.

With that being said, I have no issue with Rubin's assertion that the audience should come last when you create art. Lest you think this invalidates the entire book you've read up to now, let me be clear: while I wholeheartedly believe that the audience should be involved in every movie, they don't necessarily have to be taken into account during the *conception* of a project.

George Lois, the famed advertising impresario of the twentieth century, was a fountain of creative ideas. He was credited with naming Stouffer's Lean Cuisine and the "I Want My MTV" campaign, designed dozens of covers for *Esquire* magazine, and worked on ad campaigns for Xerox, Jiffy Lube, Pepsi, ESPN, and other iconic American brands. He coined the phrase "The Big Idea," which became synonymous with groundbreaking advertising, and used it to title one of the books he wrote. He offered some great advice in that book, which I proudly own and refer to from time to time. A few of his principles resonate strongly with me, and I'd like to share them here for those of you who've been challenged to come up with your own big ideas:

- Teamwork might work in building an Amish barn, but it can't create a big idea. Be confident of your own edgy, solo talent.

- Reject analysis paralysis. Get the big idea and think it through—it all fits, you know it's right, you know it's ambitious and aggressive, it thrills every cell in your body. Trust your gut.

- Reject group grope. Decisive, breakthrough creative decision-making is almost always made by one, two, or possibly three minds working in unison. Collective thinking usually leads to a stalemate or worse.

- Drive your big idea to the very edge of a cliff. Creativity is the ultimate adrenaline rush. If you have what you consider a fantastic concept, you must drive it to the precipice. But if you go too far, you plunge to a fiery (and embarrassing) death. The real challenge is knowing when to stop ... but you must take the risk.

- Never listen to music when you're trying to come up with a big idea, especially if you're a music lover. Music you consider great is involving and transformative, carrying you away to someplace you don't want to be when you need to solve a specific problem with a communicative idea.

Pretty heady stuff from a brilliant mind, so I felt compelled to include it in this chapter.

When Kent Broadhurst wrote the play that inspired *Wild Iris*, I can assure you that there was no consideration given toward what a future audience might think about it. That was a passion project, sparked out of Kent's lived experiences and his own wholly unique creative vision. That's the genesis of all great art.

But when it came time to turn that play into a film, that's when we had to start thinking about who and how big the audience for his passion project would be. Otherwise, we risked making it for way too much money. That's why I've never been precious about *art*-art or *commercial* art. It's not an either-or proposition. Every movie, no matter what its genesis, should be able to have a soul *and* produce a profit.

In an article for *The Ankler* entitled "Flops for Dummies," Richard Rushfield chastised Hollywood for condemning those who take creative risks and fail, citing the backlash to Francis Ford Coppola's *Megalopolis* and Todd Phillips's *Joker: Folie à Deux*. Rushfield's point was that industry insiders take pleasure in the box office failures of others. Instead of praising Coppola for underwriting his own passion project and Phillips for taking a "wild swing" on the heels of delivering the 2019 megahit *Joker* to the silver screen, those box office failures were ridiculed by the very people who work in the same company town. Rushfield also blamed the investor class and "big data" for its myopic view of what it takes to create great entertainment. I, too, disavow the mean-spirited vilification of any movie, and especially the work of illustrious filmmakers like Coppola and Phillips. But I'm also realistic and know that every big creative risk is followed by a financial day of reckoning. Accountability should not stifle creative vision, but if you're on the losing end, there will be consequences.

There's an uncomfortable truth about working in Hollywood: if you want to keep making movies, you need to keep making money.

We're all working in the movie *business*. We're not in the movie *art*. It's the nature of the beast. Unlike a painting, which can be created from a single artist's vision and displayed in a single buyer's home, movies are the culmination of hundreds of artists' work and designed for mass consumption. A film isn't really a film until it's out in the world—until it can be viewed, dissected, discussed. The audience, and how it receives a film, becomes part of the art itself. There's no divorcing the two.

Illumination CEO Chris Meledandri echoes these thoughts: "Filmmaking on this scale is the *commercial* arts. It's the ability to find the balance between the artistic and the audience." Illumination's raison d'être is creating crowd-pleasing animated films for audiences of all ages, and Meledandri is pragmatic about what that means. "We are spending well north of $100 million, between filmmaking and marketing, on every movie we make. We have a responsibility to return on that investment—to make things that are going to engage and delight audiences. If we do that, we earn the right to keep making more films."

This reality is why Amy Pascal was careful to distinguish between the choices she makes today as a producer and the choices she made when she ran Sony's Motion Picture Group. "When I ran the studio, there were all sorts of movies that I wouldn't want to spend years of my life getting made. But as a businessperson, I knew they were commercial and smart to make."

But the desire for commercial success can sometimes lead studio chiefs to green-light movies that don't strictly have an artistic reason to exist. After finding success with *Venom* and *Venom: Let There Be Carnage*, Sony used its motion picture rights for Marvel's *Spider-Man* characters to move ahead with solo movies about ever more tertiary characters—with ever more diminishing returns. *Morbius*, the 2022 film starring Jared Leto as a biochemist who inadvertently infects himself with a form of vampirism, made only $167 million at the worldwide box office—a disappointing result for what was meant to be a tentpole in Sony's superhero universe. Things got worse with 2024's *Madame Web*. Star Dakota Johnson's press tour for the film quickly became consumed by rumors she disliked the project.[4] By the time the movie, about a paramedic who develops clairvoyant powers, was released, it was dead on arrival—opening to just $15 million in the US and barely eking out $100 million worldwide.

Countless sequels that were approved solely to recapture the magic of a prior success have also been rejected by audiences: 1997's *Speed 2: Cruise Control* ($164 million worldwide) versus 1994's *Speed* ($350 million worldwide); 2003's *Dumb and Dumberer: When Harry Met Lloyd* ($39 million worldwide) versus 1994's *Dumb and Dumber* ($247 million worldwide); 2005's *Son of the Mask* ($60 million worldwide) versus 1994's *The Mask* ($351 million worldwide); and the list goes on. Furthermore, the sequels featured only half (Sandra Bullock but not Keanu Reeves in *Speed 2*) or none of the original cast.

After years of working in audience research, I can tell you with complete certainty: people know a cash grab when they see it. My company once ran a Capability Test on a potential film reboot of a popular 1980s television show. The twist for this project was that it would be gender swapped, with two female leads instead of the two male leads that were in the original project. There was just one problem—the test audiences hated the idea. They completely rejected it, saying it felt like a soulless gimmick.

Once the results came in, the producer, who was unaware the studio had commissioned the Capability Test, found out about it and called me, livid. *How could you help kill this project? People don't even know who is going to be in it! We are going to get two A-list actresses to star!* I gently had to tell him: We're not trying to kill the project—we're just letting you know the risks of making it. People don't know who is going to star, but they're not buying into the premise and are wholesale rejecting the idea of a reboot. Once you get the actresses lined up for the project, we can test it again and see if it makes a difference.

He never wound up making the movie. Probably the right call.

The makers of the *Divergent* franchise weren't so lucky. Hot on the heels of smash hit young-adult book adaptations like *Harry Potter* and *The Hunger Games*, Lionsgate Films thought they had a similar slam dunk on their hands with *Divergent*. The three-book series, about a young woman who lives in a dystopian society divided between five factions, spawned two successful films: *Divergent* ($288 million worldwide gross) and *Insurgent* ($297 million worldwide gross). This led the studio to believe that there was enough demand to justify splitting the final book in the series, *Allegiant*, into two separate films: *Allegiant* and *Ascendent*.

This move wasn't without precedent: the final films in both the *Harry Potter* franchise (*Harry Potter and the Deathly Hallows*) and the *Hunger Games* franchise (*The Hunger Games: Mockingjay*) were split into two parts. But consumers were tiring of what they saw as a studio cash grab. Additionally, the *Divergent* series never reached the same level of popularity as these other properties, and the *Allegiant* novel—which ended with the death of heroine Tris Prior—had not been well received by the series' fans.

It wound up being a perfect storm that doomed the franchise. *Allegiant* opened to just $29 million in the US, far below the $50 million–plus openings of the first two films, before grossing just $179 million worldwide. It was such a precipitous decline that the studio considered ending the series with a TV movie instead of a theatrical release.[5] But after the movie's original cast declined to participate in the project's move to the small screen, *Ascendent* was shelved entirely—and the *Divergent* film series never received a proper conclusion.

How do decisions like this get made? Amy Pascal reveals the slightly cynical truth she's learned after so many years in the business: "I've gone through many green-lighting processes. So often, internal politics are involved, shaping decisions." Often, data gets wielded as a weapon to drive whatever the most desired outcome is. "No head of a studio who desperately wants to make a movie ever says the numbers don't pencil out. Not ever," she says. "If you want to make a movie, you find a way. And if you don't want to make a movie, then you use the data as justification to pass on it. Anyone on that green-light committee can interpret the numbers to arrive at the decision they want."

No wonder film testing sometimes gets a bad rap.

IN JANUARY 1991, Jeffrey Katzenberg, then chairman of Walt Disney Studios, sent a ten-thousand-word memo to his bosses, Michael Eisner and Frank Wells, along with the studio's most senior executives.[6] It was Katzenberg's take on what he saw as the biggest challenges facing the movie industry, and his best ideas about how to solve them. It was an instant conversation starter, especially after it was leaked to the rest of the industry via *Variety*. Even though the document is more than thirty years old, it's still surprisingly resonant today—especially when it comes to our discussion about the relationship between art and audience.

For Katzenberg, crafting a successful movie came down to the passion of the people involved. "Most other jobs exist to create products that are purely functional. While any profession can have its rewards, the range of impact in producing shoes or cars or toothpaste is limited. Our product has no function other than to entertain," he wrote. "The best of our output has come to be something that consumers will treasure for years and years. Since we want the final result of our efforts to inspire a sense of passion on the part of our consumers, it is imperative that we feel an equal measure of passion in its production. It's magical for the audience, and it should be magical for us."

This mentality led Katzenberg to be skeptical about the benefits of audience testing. He wrote that testing "can be dangerous, because it can lead us to trust the test rather than trusting our instincts. How often has a film tested 'off the charts' and failed to do well at the box office? Inoffensively pleasant films can test misleadingly high. We get excited . . . and then they fail to perform to our inflated expectations. Testing has the aura of science about it. And there is nothing scientific about the movie business."

I'll be honest—this take from Katzenberg surprised me. So much so that I had to consult my coauthor, Bob Levin, who happened to have served as the president of worldwide marketing at Disney during the Katzenberg era. He revealed a more complicated picture than the memo suggests.

"Here's what reading this memo again all these years later reminds me of," Levin said. "Despite what he says about testing, Jeffrey was dedicated to research in both the production and marketing of Disney, Touchstone, and Hollywood Pictures movies.

"When I agreed to take the job at Disney, I had no expectation that research was so heavily used in these processes," Levin said. "After accepting the position, I was sent a stack of research screening reports for a yet-to-be-released movie, *The Journey of Natty Gann*. There had been more than a half dozen screenings done on this movie alone, and I soon found out that this was more usual than not. I had never seen such importance placed on research results, even in all my previous years as a senior ad executive."

This reliance on research extended far beyond just testing a movie's playability. "There was a lot of importance placed on weekly tracking research of moviegoer awareness, interest, and choice in seeing movies coming to a theater," Levin said. "In many cases, I was instructed to add money and buy more television spots if tracking research was weaker than expected." Research also helped develop trailers, TV spots, and even posters. "Jeffrey would ask for changes, sometimes very small changes, based on research results—and then test once again.

"By 1991, he may have concluded that 'there is nothing scientific about the movie business.' But in the practical day-to-day terms of producing and marketing films, it didn't stop him from buying a lot of research and paying a good deal of attention to the results," Levin said.

I'm grateful for Bob's firsthand account of the role research played during the Katzenberg years at Disney. But how do we square this with what Katzenberg himself wrote in his famous memo?

I think a lot of the vitriol against research comes down to optics. Movie testing often has a bad reputation among the more art-minded side of the industry because of its reliance on numbers. This makes it all too easy to lump research testing in with the bean counters from the accounting department.

But it's important to remember that behind these numbers are the real opinions of real people—people who represent the millions of other people who are (hopefully) going to plunk down their hard-earned cash to watch your movie. So when it comes to knowing what is going to engage and delight, there is no more powerful tool than audience research.

GRAHAM KING—who has produced films like *The Town*, *The Aviator*, *There Will Be Blood*, and, of course, *Bohemian Rhapsody*—learned about the value of audience testing early in his career, from none other than legendary director Martin Scorsese. "He loves to preview movies; he loves to hear what an audience has to say about his films," King shared. "He said to me, 'Kid, everyone you showed this movie to that's in our world will either placate you or they're out for you. It becomes personal, or they have some kind of ulterior motive for your movie. So if you really want the truth, you've got to show it to the guys on the street. You've got to show it to the people who are not in this town and not in this industry.'"

What can I say: Scorsese nailed it. Of everyone involved in the moviemaking process, only the audience comes into a test screening without an agenda. They don't care whose idea a movie was, or what went into making the thing. They aren't concerned with whether it will make money or receive critical acclaim. They just want to be entertained. That makes their feedback some of the most honest and valuable you can find.

Oscar-winning director Ron Howard has a keen understanding of finding balance between the art form and what the audience wants, shedding light on just one of the reasons for his success as the director of more than three dozen films, many of which reached blockbuster status at the box office. "This is a mass medium," he said. "This is about the way a story communicates to a large number of people, millions and millions. It is a dance, and it must be undertaken with real thought and consciousness."

BALANCING THE ART AND THE AUDIENCE

As a final-cut director, Howard does not compromise. He considers himself the keeper and protector of the story. But he also listens to the audience and likes that I encourage him to use test screening feedback to make informed decisions. "One thing I have control over is the storytelling," he said. "I use the materials that I've been able to gather through the filming to try to 'land the plane,' to make sure that it reaches the audience. It's a communication [that's] meant to achieve a connection with them. And once I've done that to the best of my ability, I feel that for an audience that chooses to watch, there's a really high chance that they're going to enjoy it, that they're going to appreciate it, and they're not going to feel like they wasted their time."

We chatted about Howard's impressive body of work, including *Night Shift* (his very first collaboration with longtime partner and producer Brian Grazer); *Parenthood*; *Apollo 13*; *Ransom*; *A Beautiful Mind*; *Rush*; *Thirteen Lives*; and his latest picture, *Eden*. "It begins with art and that desire to communicate," he mused. "Every story has a set of principles and narrative values. Whatever the tone you've chosen, whatever the genre, it's still art. When you start sharing it with an audience, the challenge is to understand how the ideas are being delivered and what it's adding up to. When you get the answers back, it's sometimes pretty heartbreaking to you as a creative person, but if you understand the information and the feedback that you're getting, you then get to make a value judgment. You get to make those informed decisions."

I asked Howard to explain his superpower, but he insisted he really doesn't have one. When pressed, the best I could get from this amazingly talented filmmaker centered on what he brings to others. "Innately, I think I have a story sense that aligns with audiences," Howard said. "I'm interested in what stories have to say, what they can offer to an audience, what kind of performance opportunities they might give actors, and where there are places to let the special effects or the music or the cinematography really shine. I try to create an environment where the creative opportunity is maximized."

Howard's approach has met with huge success. He is one of the highest-grossing film directors in Hollywood, with more than fifty titles released in nearly as many years, some recognized with Academy Award nominations and wins. He shared a funny story with me about the night he won the Oscar for *A Beautiful Mind*. Six years prior, in 1996, another film he directed, *Apollo 13*, was nominated for Best Picture. It didn't win. Mel Gibson's movie *Braveheart* took home the award that year (and Gibson won for directing). At the time of the ceremony, Howard was directing Gibson in *Ransom*, so the two were working together every day. "He felt bad," said Howard. "He was thrilled to win, but he knew it was a disappointment for me."

Fast-forward to 2002: Howard's 2001 picture, *A Beautiful Mind*, was nominated for seven awards, including Best Picture and Best Director. Just before the ceremony, Howard ran into Gibson, who told him he would be presenting the award for directing. "I'm handing you the Oscar, buddy," Howard remembers Gibson saying. Howard asked him, "How do you know?" and Gibson replied, with a twinkle in his eye, "Oh, I know!" Of course, Mel Gibson did not know who the winner would be. Those decisions are kept under very tight wraps until the announcement is made on the night of the broadcast. But Howard was well aware that Mel can be pretty outrageous and might pull a fast one. He wondered if his name would be called, even if it wasn't the name inside the envelope that Gibson would be opening. "It's just not beyond the realm of possibility," Howard said, laughing.

On the night of the Academy Awards, sure enough, Howard was announced as the winner of the directing award for *A Beautiful Mind*. As he made his way toward the podium, he was trying not to trip and wondering if he would remember everything he wanted to say. He managed to get through his speech and then, as he was leaving the stage, a thought sent a chill down his spine. He turned to Gibson and said, "Show me that card!" Thankfully, when he looked down at it, the name he saw was Ron Howard. In addition to his award for directing, he won the Best Picture Oscar for *A Beautiful Mind*, and there were also wins for Russell Crowe, Jennifer Connelly, and writer Akiva Goldsman.

"I'VE LEARNED A LOT FROM EVERY TEST SCREENING I'VE EVER DONE," producer Neal Moritz said. "You work in this kind of shell for years, putting so much time, effort, sweat, and tears into making these movies. But when you put that movie up for the first time in a dark room, it doesn't matter how many films you've made or how many billions of dollars your pictures have grossed. The audience is just reacting to what they see on the screen, and it doesn't matter what I think anymore. It matters what the audience thinks. And it's either the best night of your life, an okay night of your life, or a terrible night of your life. Fortunately—or unfortunately—I've tasted all three."

Fortunately, or unfortunately, for my friend Neal, I've often been the person serving those best, okay, and terrible meals. I like to think of myself as an advocate for a film's intended audience, someone who can interpret their needs and desires for studio executives and filmmakers. That's why you will find me sitting in movie theaters more than half the nights of the year—but never in a theater seat. For more than thirty-five years, I've preferred a folding chair, strategically positioned in the aisle off to the side.

Our test audiences are there to watch a movie, but I'm there to watch them. I know from experience that what they say in a postscreening questionnaire doesn't always match up with what I observe them doing while the movie is on the screen. While the film plays, I'm watching for any cues about how they're feeling. How hard are they laughing? Are they fidgeting? I even keep track of when and how often people leave the theater. Do they run and come right back? Walk slowly and take their time to return? Do some people never come back at all? I get massages every week to help work out the neck pains I get from all the twisting and turning I do during a screening.

At the end of each preview, the studio and the filmmakers learn what did or didn't work about their film. Our findings are ultimately informed by many things: survey results, the depth and intensity of the comments we receive, and my own and my analysts' experiences reading the implicit responses of test audiences—body language, the tone they use to share feedback, how quickly and enthusiastically they raise their hands, for example.

The type of feedback that resonates most differs from person to person. "What I love about what you do and how you put these together is that it's not about words on a card or ticking boxes. It's about atmosphere," producer Graham King said. "You can tell in the room of 250 people whether they are enjoying this or not enjoying it. You can tell if there are slow parts, if there's levity. It all comes through the atmosphere." King recalled testing one movie that had a massive atmospheric shift in the third act. "People were entertained and enjoying it for two acts. But in the third act, the director changed genres on the audience, and the movie fell flat. You could feel the energy just leave the room."

Director, writer, and producer Will Gluck, who has worked on projects like *Anyone But You*, *Peter Rabbit*, *Annie* (2014), and *Easy A* relies less on atmosphere and more on the cards audience members fill out after a research screening. But he only looks at the negatives. "I go through all the questionnaires, and I never look at the positives. I throw them in the garbage. It's not helpful when someone says to you, 'This is good.' What's only helpful is what the audience didn't like."

I understand why Gluck takes that approach. On a similar note, I encourage filmmakers to read the "very good" and "good" cards—and to not pay attention to the "excellent," "fair," or "poor" cards. Why? You already have the excellents. You don't need to worry about them. In my experience, the fairs and the poors are almost never going to change their opinions—so it's not worth making a bunch of changes or compromises trying to chase after them. Instead, I recommend diving into the very good and good cards to figure out what changes can be made to boost them up into "excellent." There's almost always a correlation between the number of people who rate a movie excellent and the number of people who will definitely recommend it—the factor that is most critical to the positive word of mouth that will determine a film's success.

"Test screenings are incredibly important," producer Jason Blum told me. His studio, Blumhouse, has earned its reputation as a purveyor of smart horror with hit films like *Paranormal Activity*, *Get Out*, *The Purge*, and *M3GAN*. "Getting the scores is great, but the most important thing of all is reading the individual surveys that audience members fill out. If something comes up two or three times—no big deal. But if sixty people say the same thing—and it's not what you want them to be taking away—you've got to keep working on it, because the movie isn't doing what you want it to do."

Feedback from previews helped Blum get 2014's *Ouija* on track. "All sorts of problems were in the first cut of the movie. So the movie's writer and director, Mike Flanagan, studied the audience research to help outline reshoots." Blum was at the beginning of his relationship with Universal Pictures, which was planning to distribute the film. The pressure was on to deliver a project that worked without breaking the bank. Blum says, "I remember Donna Langley, who was then the head of Universal Movie Group, saying, 'Honey, are you sure these reshoots are going to save this movie? I'm not so sure.' I told her yes, then immediately called Mike and said, 'This is a lot of money. You're sure this is going to work?'" Thankfully, it did. *Ouija* ended up earning more than $100 million worldwide on a reported budget of only $5 million.

Horror movies like *Ouija* can be surprisingly tricky to nail for audiences. You want them to feel familiar but also deliver something that hasn't been seen before. You want to build suspense but not wait too long for the payoff. You want to scare and thrill but not disgust people. I talked to Eli Roth, the director of horror classics like *Cabin Fever*, *Hostel*, and *Thanksgiving*, about how audience testing helps him achieve the right balance.

"It's a calibration when you're making an audience movie," Roth said. "If you're making your million-dollar auteur film for festivals and awards, do whatever you want and stay true to your vision. But if you're making a popcorn movie for broad genre fan appeal, especially if it's new IP, you better listen to those test audiences or at least understand what's keeping them from saying, 'Wow, I love it.'

"At the same time, you must know how to read the data, because you could look at the first test scores, which may not be where they need to be, and think, 'Whoa, we're in trouble. People don't like the movie.' And you should never take that approach." Instead, Roth tells himself, "I'm seeing in the data that they want to like it. They're with the film. You're just taking too long to get to the next kill, and they're getting ahead of the story."

Thanksgiving, Roth's 2023 horror film about a Thanksgiving-inspired killer terrorizing Plymouth, Massachusetts, was largely shaped by what he learned in test previews. Right from the start, it was clear the movie had a more campy, humorous tone than the sadistic *Hostel*. "The first kills of the movie, they're so fun. The one in the apartment, feeding the cat? Gleefully fun," Roth said.

He's referring, of course, to what became one of the favorite scenes in the movie where the killer offs his victim before turning around and feeding the pet cat living in the apartment. The moment was born out of one of Roth's own preoccupations during slasher flicks. "I always worry when I watch a horror movie, if someone who gets killed has a pet. I can't enjoy what I'm watching until I know the pet is okay. Who's gonna feed the cute little critter? That's all I think about. So I wanted to finally address that. We've never before seen a brutal kill in a slasher film where the killer's like, 'I got no problem with the cat, I gotta feed the cat.' That was a fresh idea, and it worked!"

In the initial cut of the movie, the cat scene *killed* with the test audience. But it was quickly followed up by a brutal murder. "You could feel the air get sucked out of the room," Roth said. "People were having fun and then they felt like they got punched in the gut. The movie did not recover from that. It went suddenly to a place of sadism that nobody was there for, and nobody wanted."

Of particular issue was a scene where the killer roasts a woman like a turkey. "We had fifteen shots of a woman roasting in an oven. People were like, 'It's not fun anymore. It's just awful,'" Roth said. "You think, 'Oh, I did *Hostel*, and my fans want that kind of stuff.'" But the *Hostel* approach didn't work on the more humorous and campy *Thanksgiving*. "It was too much of a bait and switch."

"You always learn something at a test screening—whether you want to or not," Roth said. "Thank God we got our asses handed to us. What I do to those characters, the test audiences did to me. And I'm so happy they did, because otherwise I would've gone out on three thousand screens and humiliated myself." *Thanksgiving* did well enough at the box office that Roth is now working on a sequel.

Roth isn't alone in finding test screenings both stressful and revelatory. Antoine Fuqua, the director of films like *Training Day*, *Olympus Has Fallen*, *The Magnificent Seven* (2016), and *The Equalizer* franchise, said, "I'm tortured when I've got to do test screenings. It's one of the most painful processes in making a film. As a director, I become obsessed with my work. I'm like a painter painting, or a chef cooking, and I believe I know every single element that goes into the movie I'm making. Then you do a test, and the audience goes, 'Nah, we don't really care about that—we care about this.' And you go, 'I didn't even think about that, that wasn't even on my mind.' So I suck it up, and I sit there."

He acknowledges that this process is part and parcel of making a film. "A movie is made over and over and over. It's made during development. It's made in preproduction. It's made when you're filming it. And then, when you put it in front of an audience, you finally really see the movie you made."

That doesn't mean Fuqua takes what audiences say as gospel right from the start. "There are times where I sit back and go, 'Are they just being harsh because the movie is not done yet? Or is there truly an issue that needs some addressing?' And I don't really know what to think until I get back into the editing bay and consider what happened during the preview. Maybe this or that scene doesn't pay off. Maybe I'm making a promise that they're expecting to be delivered on, but it never happens. And by the end, I go, 'Thank God we're doing this, because I didn't see it. I didn't know they felt that way.' Because with a real audience talking to you, you have to accept what you hear from them."

Test audiences have even helped Fuqua resolve arguments he was having with himself. "I remember a moment in the first *Equalizer* movie, where this guy comes in, robs a store, and steals a ring from the young woman who is a cashier. Toward the end of the movie, the cash drawer is opened, and the ring is in there. I was like, 'Ah, that's cheesy. I don't want to do that.' But I kept it in. And what do you know, the test audience absolutely loved it. It was one of their favorite moments in the whole movie—and suddenly, I'm a genius. Lesson learned. Sometimes you just need to get out of your own way."

The testing process also helped improve the playability of *The Equalizer 3*—the third installment in Denzel Washington's popular action franchise about a former Special Forces operative dispensing vigilante justice. "We had a storyline in the film about Denzel's character, Robert McCall, getting another opportunity at love," Jason Blumenthal, one of the producers on the project, said. "It was beautiful, and we spent so much time developing it and trying to figure out the right way to tell McCall's love story. Finally, we thought we nailed it—and Denzel was thrilled with it. It really worked."

There was just one problem: when the filmmakers tested it, the audience fully rejected the storyline. "This was the third movie in the franchise. In the first two films, the audience had become deeply connected to Robert McCall. And apparently, they didn't want to share him with anybody," Blumenthal said. "There was a deep, negative, visceral reaction to the idea that McCall was going to settle down with this woman and maybe not be there for them as the 'voice to the voiceless.'"

I remember that Chicago screening. It was crystal clear that the love story was holding back the audience's enthusiasm. I could see that even the women in the audience weren't embracing the romance, and when that happens, it's a big problem. But I knew the movie could be fixed.

"Because of that screening, we went in, we recut, we reshaped, and we took out most of the love story," Blumenthal said. "When we next screened the film, it was clear we had made the right choices. The audience embraced it as strongly as they had the previous two." *The Equalizer 3* went on to gross $185 million worldwide, just a hair off the $192 million gross of *The Equalizer* and the $190 million gross of *The Equalizer 2*—remarkably consistent for a franchise.

In the case of *The Equalizer 3*, it was easy to figure out why the audience wasn't fully embracing the picture. But sometimes it's not so clear-cut—and filmmakers have to be careful about reading the tea leaves in the right way.

I spoke with Kathy Nelson, one of the most influential music supervisors in the business, about her own experiences with testing. She once worked on a project where the composer was bearing the brunt of the criticism after a screening gone wrong. "The studio knew something was off with the movie, and they thought it was the music. They said, 'We should fire the composer, right?' But I wasn't so sure."

Nelson was familiar with the composer's work—they came from a songwriting background, so their composition structures usually included telltale choruses and hooks. "I wasn't hearing any of that in the film's score, so I asked to hear the demos the composer originally submitted," she said. The demos revealed what she suspected: the issue wasn't the music, it was the *mix*. "The sound editors had added too many sound effects to try to fix the movie—that's what the studio executives were reacting to. I told them to go talk to their editor." She ended up saving the composer's job.

AUDIENCES MAY HAVE OPINIONS about movies as an art form, but should market research drive the artistic aspects of what ends up on the screen? Let me be loud and clear: no way. Many films have artistic merits that aren't easily captured in Capability Tests or even in audience test screenings. In fact, some of our most celebrated movies—including Oscar winners—have scored horribly in testing, only to go on to find critical and commercial success.

How does this happen? I wanted to get some perspective from Nancy Utley, the former head of Fox Searchlight Pictures, a studio known for making artistic, critically acclaimed films. She told me she focused first on working with filmmakers who had fresh visions and unique voices. "I have championed movies—like *Birdman*, *The Shape of Water*, and *Black Swan*—where I had no idea what they really would be, but I had complete faith in the talented filmmakers to realize their visions," she said. "For me, a Searchlight movie was a movie that turned the familiar on its ear. I never felt that any Searchlight movie was conventional. We made smart and special films."

But these are the exact kind of movies that can struggle with test audiences. "Most of the Searchlight movies didn't test all that well, but that was with unprepared audiences," Utley said. "Once you add context through marketing, festivals, and publicity, and explain to them why they'll like it, then they usually like it."

This was the case with *Black Swan*, a 2010 film starring Natalie Portman as a ballerina striving for perfection and Mila Kunis as a rival dancer who befriends her. "*Black Swan* was one of the lowest-testing movies I ever worked on, and yet it went on to earn $330 million in global box office," Utley said. It was also a hit with critics and on the awards circuit, with Natalie Portman winning an Academy Award for Best Actress and the film receiving nominations for Best Picture and Best Director.

Here's how Utley summed up the Searchlight alchemy: "With the importance we placed on a movie's core idea and the filmmakers who are making the movie—combined with the quality of the marketing and buzz we put behind our films—we had the capacity to succeed where others might not have."

It's hard to overstate the importance of the "buzz" Utley talks about. Consider this interesting test case: *Men in Black*, the 1997 film where Will Smith and Tommy Lee Jones play secret agents tasked with monitoring alien life on Earth, was a massive hit in the US, grossing $250 million during its domestic run. But when the film was tested in Japan in advance of its planned release there, it was a total flop. The first research screening in Tokyo scored so poorly, in fact, there was a serious discussion about whether the movie should even have a major release there. But then a plan was hatched to host a second test screening—only this time, the audience would be told in advance that the movie had been a huge success in the US and would be shown positive media quotes about it. The assumption was that Japanese moviegoers would be more interested in the film if they knew it was popular in the US. The experiment worked: following that introduction, the test audience scores soared. The studio committed to a strong marketing campaign to support the movie's launch, which ultimately led to a massive opening in Japan.

Buzz can turn a hit like *Men in Black* into an even bigger hit. But buzz is even more critical to smaller movies that are difficult to market. When you have a feathered fish that's hard to describe, or a plot that covers challenging material, or unknown talent in front of or behind the camera, you need to build such positive word of mouth that audiences can't ignore it.

Movies that studios or filmmakers anticipate having the potential for critical acclaim will sometimes debut at one of the "Big Five" film festivals—Venice, Cannes, Berlin, Toronto, or Sundance—to capture the interest of distributors and critics alike. These festivals, to which film aficionados around the globe pay close attention, often provide a film's first opportunity to start building buzz that will ultimately lead to box office success.

This was the story with *Napoleon Dynamite*, which debuted at the Sundance Film Festival in 2004. The comedy, about an oddball teen who decides to run for class president with the help of his best friend, was made on a shoestring budget of $400,000. But it was a hit with festivalgoers and ended up being acquired by Fox Searchlight. With the positive word of mouth from its Sundance debut, its theatrical release went on to gross $46 million worldwide—a box office haul at a whopping 114 times its budget. It's now considered a cult classic, one that returned to the Sundance Film Festival stage to celebrate its twentieth anniversary in January 2024.

Other films have found their audience only after being strongly embraced by critics, who are especially important when it comes to teach-

BALANCING THE ART AND THE AUDIENCE

ing or informing viewers about movies with challenging or dark subjects. *Leaving Las Vegas*, the 1995 film starring Nicolas Cage as an alcoholic who moves to Vegas to drink himself to death, was one of the lowest-testing movies I've ever worked on. It debuted in just seven theaters, to $70,000, in October 1995. But as buzz began to build among critics about revelatory performances from both Cage and Elisabeth Shue, the film slowly found a broader audience. By the time Cage and Shue were nominated for Best Actor and Best Actress at the Academy Awards in February 1996 (with Cage eventually going on to win), the film had expanded to more than 1,300 theaters. All told, it earned $32 million worldwide—a huge success, given its reported $4 million budget.

Another example is 1996's *Fargo*—one of the lowest-testing films Russell Schwartz, then the president of Gramercy Pictures, had ever worked on. *Fargo*, a black comedy about a bungling criminal and the police chief trying to catch him, was the brainchild of Joel and Ethan Coen. "The Coen Brothers had never had a movie tested, ever. No one had ever asked them to do it," Schwartz said. But Polygram Filmed Entertainment, Gramercy's distribution partner, wanted to hold a research screening, which Schwartz facilitated. "We screened the movie, and this thing got single digits in 'definite' recommends. That was the news. Of course, that didn't mean anything to Joel and Ethan."

Despite the terrible test results, both Polygram and Schwartz still loved the film and decided to roll the dice on a release. "We just went for it. It became all about screenings and the critics, and the whole thing completely turned. It did a total 180," Schwartz said. *Fargo* was a massive hit with critics and went on to be an awards darling, with seven total nominations, and wins for Best Actress (Frances McDormand) and Best Original Screenplay at the Academy Awards. It was also a commercial success, grossing $60 million worldwide against a reported $7 million budget.

There's a very human instinct that comes into play with critically acclaimed films like *Leaving Las Vegas*, *Fargo*, and countless others—2002's *About Schmidt*, 2008's *The Hurt Locker*, 2016's *Manchester by the Sea*, and 2022's *The Whale*, to name a few. When people start hearing something is "just *so good*," FOMO—the fear of missing out—kicks in. They have to see it for themselves. They have to be in the know. Once again proving that you don't have to sacrifice art to find an audience.

EPILOGUE

Every Movie Should Make Money

IF I HAVEN'T BEEN CLEAR ENOUGH BY NOW, the question that has nagged me since my earliest days working with studios and filmmakers is: Shouldn't every movie make money? I mean after all, why not? Why would anyone want to risk millions of dollars on making and marketing a movie without a clear understanding of how likely it would be to make money? When the decisions are made about how much will be budgeted to make and market a film, gauging its appeal to an intended audience is critically important in assessing risk. That determination of the right price and the right budget will lead to the best opportunity for that movie to make money. Some executives do use this type of research, while others commission different methods, such as marketing positioning studies—particularly useful in anticipating how a new film might perform in different territories around the world. And yet such measurement of audience appeal is not undertaken nearly as much as it should be.

Maybe there's some ego that stands in the way. The executives at the top take home hefty paychecks because they have "a golden gut" for what will and will not work. And don't get me wrong—they do have many years of experience, expertise, and success that support that idea. But even still, they can't score *every* time at bat. Why not let it be known that quality audience-based research is a very valuable assist in making those critical decisions?

Sometimes when I'm feeling more conspiracy minded I've wondered if executives shun audience research since it could be used as evidence that they simply don't want to have in the files. They go ahead and greenlight a movie that financially fails—and right there in the drawer is the research that informed them of the high risk associated with the project. The execs don't want to have to defend their decision to proceed after having received early warning of the risks associated at the outset.

But I can't say this approach appeals to me. I've been an entrepreneur since I was nine years old, starting a lemonade stand in East Brunswick, New Jersey, where I grew up. And even then, I was focused on making sure I'd turn a profit. I thought about where I'd set up my stand to guarantee foot traffic. I added up what the lemons, sugar, and cups cost my mom and dad, and then figured out what I wanted to charge for a cup. I remember to this day: it was twenty-five cents a cup, and the first day I made close to twenty sales and a profit of two bucks. The early lesson learned? *Every lemonade stand that goes into business at the right price should make money.*

The entrepreneurial spirit was with me once again when at seventeen, after doing my homework, I opened and ran Jazz Arts Studio, a small but profitable dance and acting school in my hometown. It operated after school and on weekends. It may seem a bit unbelievable that I accomplished this in my late teens, so some background will help lay the foundation. By age seventeen, I had already started working as an actor in and around New York. I could be heard on the radio and had appeared in a few TV commercials.

From an early age, I'd been traveling back and forth from New York City to take dance classes with some truly great teachers, and I began to work professionally in high school; I'd become sort of a local celebrity. Friends and neighbors would question me about how their kids could do what I had done, and I began to realize that there might be an opportunity

EPILOGUE: EVERY MOVIE SHOULD MAKE MONEY

for me to make money teaching other kids to dance and act. Maybe I could offer performing arts instruction right in East Brunswick! It might seem surprising that a kid my age would even think about opening a school, but there were several things about me that were true then and are still true now. I was good at what I did, and I was self-confident. But I was also disciplined; I wasn't going to go into any business if the risks of not making money were too great. Even at seventeen, I understood that concept.

I'm not entirely sure how I got that confidence, as I really didn't have very much support at home. My parents both worked full-time jobs—my mom managed an industrial packaging office, and my dad worked in middle management on Wall Street. Looking back, I think they tried to be supportive but just didn't know how. They weren't *unsupportive*, exactly—they just weren't actively involved in helping me fulfill my dreams. I honestly think they didn't quite know what to do with a kid who had such determination and ambition.

My work as a performer had allowed me to save a little bit of money. If I could make the numbers work, I'd be ready to invest those funds in myself. I began to more deeply explore the true level of interest people would have in attending a performing arts school for kids, with me as one of the four instructors. So of course I did some research, and the feedback was very positive. I had a good understanding of how many students I was likely to initially enroll and felt, with a fair degree of confidence, I could get them as paying customers. Knowing that, I went out to find a space I could rent, as I knew rent would be the most significant financial expense in opening the school. I was able to get a short-term lease with an option on a space I liked at a local preschool. As far as paying the instructors, I cut them in on a revenue-sharing system. I also needed adequate liability insurance. I then researched different pricing and pricing schemes, including subscription plans. The research gave me what I needed to figure out how many students to admit—and how much to charge—to make the business work. With limited risk I opened the doors. And I made money.

Am I out of line when I say I think of myself as a born entrepreneur? I mean, why shouldn't *every dance and acting school that goes into business at the right price make money*? Even if the proprietor and principal teacher is just seventeen years old.

PRODUCER DAVID PERMUT was a young entrepreneur, too. He tells the story of what he learned when he decided to start selling his own Hollywood Star Maps—paper maps that pinpoint where various stars live—at a hefty profit.

"I was twelve years old when our family moved to Los Angeles," Permut says. "We had made earlier trips to LA searching for a home to buy, and on one of those trips we bought a map to stars' homes that was being sold along the road. I didn't read comic books, but I was awestruck by this star map. Once enrolled in school, I found myself making friends with a lot of kids whose parents were big Hollywood stars, and I came to the realization that I knew where celebrities lived who weren't even on the map.

"I started thinking that I could make and sell an even better version. And I had a secret weapon—a friend in my seventh-grade class whose father was a bigshot agent at William Morris. He agreed to get me a copy of the agency's client list, which included home addresses, in exchange for me giving him a cut on a little piece of my sales. The cost of the maps would literally be just the cost of the paper, which I could print for free on my dad's office copy machine.

"With my costs almost nothing, the next most important and critical business decision was location. I staked out a prime spot on the corner of Ladera Drive and Sunset. One side of the street was the City of Beverly

EPILOGUE: EVERY MOVIE SHOULD MAKE MONEY

Hills, and the other was the City of Los Angeles. There was, and is today, absolutely no street soliciting in Beverly Hills, so naturally I stationed my operation on the LA side. I sat on that corner in a canvas chair with a yellow-and-black-painted sign simply reading MOVIE MAPS HERE. During the summer tourist season, I wanted to get as much attention as I could from the cars whizzing by my corner on Sunset. That's when I had my brother's girlfriend on my corner in a bikini, dancing to music blasting from my boom box, the words MOVIE MAPS HERE! emblazoned in body paint on her belly. It got the attention of speeding motorists, and increased the volume of business, until the cops told me I couldn't do that because I'd cause a massive pileup.

"If you thought the stars were angry about me selling these maps, the opposite was actually the case. Many big stars would stop at the stop sign at my corner and say hello. Elvis lived around the corner and used to ask me, 'How's business?' Katharine Hepburn always came by in her '57 T-bird; Fred Astaire; Joey Bishop; you name it—the who's who of Hollywood. Randolph Scott's wife thought I was getting too much sun and brought me a big umbrella. And if one of the stars came by while I was selling a map and yelled hello to me, I would get an extra buck or two from the wide-eyed tourists!

"Business was seasonal. I was out there seven days a week in the summer. On a good day I would pull in about thirty dollars, and on one memorable weekend day I stayed until seven p.m. and made a record one hundred dollars! My investment was so low that I would make money if I only sold one three-dollar map during a day.

"The bottom line is whether you're selling a star map or selling a movie, the goal is the same, to satisfy the customer, and in both cases, you are offering an opportunity to peer through the keyhole of another world."

An entrepreneur like me, Permut would probably say *Every star map business that is set up at the right price should make money.*

HOW TO SCORE IN HOLLYWOOD

YEARS LATER, when I began working in the movie industry, I observed how decisions were being made about how much to spend on making and marketing a film. I came to the same conclusion about the financial risk in movies that I had made in opening my lemonade stand and dance and acting school: there had to be a better way to calculate the probability of a movie financially failing or succeeding. And I knew that this calculation would be most valuable if it took place *before* the time that major financial commitments were locked.

What I set out to do was to say with confidence that I could support my claim that *every* movie, if made and marketed for the right price, should make money. Not surprisingly, I soon found that not everyone agreed with that statement. Tom Rothman modified it to, "Every *good* movie, if made and marketed for the right price, should make money." By adding the word "good," Rothman focused on how poor word of mouth can destroy a movie's odds of box office success.

Producer Nancy Utley almost agrees with Rothman. For her it's more comfortably stated as, "*Most* movies, *if made well* and marketed at the right price, should make money." She thinks about cases where a movie's execution is dreadful, doesn't achieve critical acclaim, and consequently spells financial doom.

Former studio chief Rob Friedman also stresses that movies must be made well to make money. "Audiences today are smart and well equipped with social media," he says. "You can't get past one week of release before the bad word gets out. The audience at the six p.m. show on opening day will already be telling everybody how shitty it is. That word travels fast."

"I can't agree that *every* movie should make money," Adam Fogelson says. "But I would say *most* should. I always set out to find a way to marry the artistic integrity of a proposition with the business realities of what it

EPILOGUE: EVERY MOVIE SHOULD MAKE MONEY

needs to cost, both in terms of being made and sold, to get to a rational price. In my experience, we made many movies where we established a meaningful partnership with the filmmaking team to identify a creatively satisfying path to make a movie we all could be proud of, and that we thought an audience would love. One that I could responsibly represent to the people whose money I'm using. And one in which we were not trying to thread an impossible needle."

"Decisions can be made as a movie moves into production that change its opportunity to make money," says executive Elizabeth Gabler. "Casting Russell Crowe in 2006's *A Good Year*, after a highly publicized incident of Russell losing control and throwing a phone at a front desk hotel clerk, is a good example. The director, Ridley Scott, wanted Russell, but I was against that casting as I thought at that moment women didn't want to see him in a romantic role. Russell was good in the movie, but after the hotel incident, it was doomed. That movie should have made money, but once it was cast, no chance."

In some cases, the right talent in the right movie can provide a rationale that a movie will make money. "When it comes to talent and its impact on the green-light process, I want talent to be doing what they do best," said Dwight Caines, Universal's president of domestic marketing shares. "When I look at the campaign for Sony's *Bullet Train*, I go, 'Yeah, that's Brad Pitt doing what I like him to be doing.'" *Bullet Train* grossed close to $240 million globally.

Terry Press wonders if my claim of "every movie, if made and marketed for the right price" takes into account the sheer volume of content competing for attention. "Yes, you can make it, but still, will anyone know it's there?" That's a fair point. Though I contend that anyone deciding to make a movie should know the interest the intended audience has in that movie's core idea and its elements before they say yes to producing it. Only then will they will know if they have what it takes to compete for attention.

HOW TO SCORE IN HOLLYWOOD

Ben Feingold, CEO of Samuel Goldwyn Films and former head of home entertainment at Sony Pictures, does give me pause in my absolute belief that every movie made and marketed at the right price should make money. Among many examples, Feingold pointed to the 2003 movie *Gigli*, which had such a black cloud over it before it was released that it was destined to flop—which it did, earning only $7 million globally. Extremely bad press, as happened with *Gigli*, can kill a picture. Feingold sees how unforeseen events can also dramatically alter a movie's box office potential. September 11 and the 2020 pandemic both dramatically and negatively affected movie theater attendance and individual box office performance. Feingold also points to how scandal can take a film's box office potential off track. *Aloha* (2015) was heavily criticized for the casting of Emma Stone in a role portraying a person of color and earned only $25 million globally. *I Love You, Daddy* (2017) spectacularly failed when its creator and star, Louis C.K., was caught up in sexual misconduct allegations, and the movie was pulled from distribution.

Given these and other similar comments, I put more thinking into the word "should," as in *should make money*. Can I just leave it at "should," or do I need to refine it? Inherent in that word is the notion of probability. I have to legitimately consider assigning a "probability" to the chances of a movie—if made and marketed for the right price—making money.

Reexamining my thesis, and putting a stake in the ground based on decades of experience and thousands of films that I've tested, here's how I would rephrase it with a probability measure:

> Every movie, if made and marketed for the right price, has a 75 percent or greater probability of making money.

EPILOGUE: EVERY MOVIE SHOULD MAKE MONEY

WHAT MAKES A PRICE THE *RIGHT* PRICE? First, the answer will be different for movies produced to play on a streaming platform and those intended for theatrical release. The streamers are still navigating their production budget spends, and as the former head of original films at Netflix, Tendo Nagenda, explained, viewing hours are one of the current measures being used to gauge investment. Entertainment industry financial and valuation expert Dr. Roy Salter weighed in as well. "We're in an evolutionary moment," Salter said. "Those who work outside the streaming sector might wonder how movies made for those platforms are budgeted, which makes pre-greenlight modeling and measures of financial success that much more challenging. The truth is, for the past six or seven years, it didn't matter, because the streamers were offering as much programming as possible in an attempt to build audience and buy relevance. They were rolling the dice to determine whether a business model of any sort could be established. But the mechanisms used to price a film for a streaming platform have now shifted, a change that has coincided with much greater selectivity in funding productions and acquisitions and shocking many in the industry."

Salter continued: "At the same time, we've all seen the retraction of the content going into theaters, obviously driven by the pandemic, but also by the fact that the acceleration, availability, and infinite nature of programming coming into our homes has drawn us away from theaters. The streamers have come to the realization that they have to start matching the amount that is being spent producing and acquiring movies to the audience size, both in terms of adding new subscribers and retaining the ones they have. They—as well as producers, studios, conventional TV broadcasters and cable channels, emerging video-on-demand platforms, and independent financiers—now appear to be more focused on the ability to achieve favorable economics than at any time in my experience. And as a result, the industry has finally reached a place of practice behavior that provides a solid foundation for real growth."

Years of my own experience with this question always point to the right price being one that leaves little risk of not generating a return on all the out-of-pocket costs of a project. Here's an example of this hard-earned wisdom in action. Years ago, I was able to produce several television movies that premiered on the Lifetime network with little to no risk, because I made them at the right price.

I had a partner, and he self-financed the movies we ultimately licensed to Lifetime through their acquisition department. At that time, that division was paying something like $250,000 to license the rights to air a movie in the US for a five-year term. We retained the international sales rights and knew between the Lifetime license and international sales revenue potential—estimated to conservatively pull in $300,000 in its first cycle—we had to make the movie for no more than $500,000 to have the greatest chance of making any money.

At that time, Lifetime's focus was primarily on acquiring suspense thrillers featuring strong female protagonists. Films that fit that bill generated high enough ratings to drive robust ad sales revenue for the network. I met with their head of acquisitions and pitched her a number of suspense thrillers that we had developed at the idea stage. All we had were concepts and no finished scripts. We based our presentation on solid information I had collected about what would work best, specifically on their network. Of course, I used Capability Testing to gather this information.

I conducted this research with nine different suspense thriller ideas put in front of Lifetime viewers and collected their responses to a series of survey questions. I sat in that pitch meeting and told the Lifetime exec that out of the nine movie ideas I tested, there were three they should definitely acquire when produced, three that—with some changes—might work, and three that were losers and not worth any further attention. The

EPILOGUE: EVERY MOVIE SHOULD MAKE MONEY

executive was stunned as I laid out in detail facts about their audience that they themselves didn't even know, and what that audience would be most interested in seeing. My partner and I ended up paying for and producing those three top-testing concepts, which Lifetime eventually licensed. We knew we would make money if we kept to the plan and produced them for the right price, no more than $500,000 each. With the $250,000 first license to Lifetime, state government tax rebates and incentives, and $350,000 in international sales, we made a better-than-expected return on our production investments. On top of that, we also owned the movies, which would generate a decent amount of money in the future.

Sounds like a no-brainer, but after several further successes, I recently breached my very own business model. During Covid, I heard an interesting pitch for a rather contained thriller creature movie, meaning it primarily took place in one location, a garage. A bunch of special effects people were available to work on it at hugely discounted rates just to stay busy during the lockdown. We went nonunion and didn't have any stars—except one, who was working Fi-Core (Financial Core Status) from SAG-AFTRA. Fi-Core status is a special classification that allows actors to opt out of the standard minimums and residuals arrangements negotiated by their union by withdrawing from the union temporarily.

I set out to make the movie for $250,000, which became $285,000 and then $300,000 right before we started shooting. When I saw the first cut, though, it wasn't very good. No, let me be honest—it was pretty bad. It just didn't work, and the effects were super cheesy. I knew from the start that this was never going to be a great movie, so I should have said, "Fuck it, I'm going to see what I can get for it. We'll hope for somewhere around $400,000 worldwide (which was the low- to midrange comp on which I based my original projections) and we'll walk away with a little profit."

Instead, I defied my own philosophy and made a bad decision that led me to make that movie at the wrong price. I funded reshoots that I hoped would make a material difference. Those reshoots raised the budget by almost $200,000. The movie improved after all this, but if I had just stuck with it as it was and not spent more on it, if I had just said, "Well, I screwed up," it likely would've still sold for the same amount. Now a movie that I set out to make for $250,000 cost me around $500,000, and that pretty much decreased the odds of making any profit and significantly raised the risk of not recouping my initial investment. What kind of business is that? I didn't follow my own advice, but the experience taught me a great lesson. It taught me that my hubris, along with drinking my own Kool-Aid, got the best of me. I rolled the dice when the risk was raised too high. I wound up making the movie for the wrong price.

My bad decision isn't unlike similar decisions I often see after a movie is tested in front of an audience. When a movie gets an audience response that's less enthusiastic than what was anticipated, it can lead to costly decisions—to reshoots; to add additional scenes, new endings, or new music; or to make other adjustments to "fix" what isn't working. There's an assumption that things that need to be fixed can be taken care of with enough time and money. In other words, by doubling down. And yet each time I see a movie going that route, I know the essential elements that determine financial risk and the potential for the commercial success of the movie could have been objectively measured before it was ever made. Quite simply, repair before execution.

WHO BETTER TO VALIDATE my thesis that *every movie, if made and marketed for the right price, has a 75 percent or greater probability of making money* than the people who run The Asylum? They have a different budgeting model that has always intrigued me. In fact, this specialty movie and television production company has a 100 percent track record. Literally, *every* movie they make has turned a profit. The Asylum (the seller) only

EPILOGUE: EVERY MOVIE SHOULD MAKE MONEY

makes the movies they know their studio and channel partners (the buyers) want, crafting the content based on market demand. Instead of trying to gauge how a movie premise might resonate with consumers across the globe, they reverse engineer the process. The studio and channel outlets know what appeals to their audiences and where there is opportunity to create fresh content. They provide that input to The Asylum. Then, based on the idea and what their buyers are willing to pay in each individual territory, The Asylum nails down the financial deal *before* anything is produced. Consequently, everything they make is budgeted at the right price.

David Latt, one of three partners at The Asylum, explained that after they establish the premise, they know going into that project how much the domestic outlet will pay for it. Then they have a team that contacts buyers around the world to determine its appeal and what the international territories are willing to cough up. "If Japan is willing to pay this amount, and Turkey is willing to pay that amount, and France is willing to pay some other amount, then I know at the end of the day, before the film is made, how much to spend making it. If I make it for one dollar more than that, I'm screwed," Latt said.

The origins of The Asylum are interesting. David Latt and one of his partners, David Rimawi, were introduced to each other in college, and both set their sights on careers in the movie industry. Rimawi wanted to produce, and after finishing his education, got a job at Raedon Home Video, which in the mid-1980s and early 1990s made low-budget, low-quality, straight-to-video films shot with Super 8 cameras. Latt said, "David was selling these crappy genre films to the networks, including to USA Network for their *Up All Night* series hosted by Gilbert Gottfried." USA was buying horror and cult B movies with no stars, and an opportunity occurred to Rimawi. Comfortable with his client relationship, he asked how much the network would be willing to pay if he made a "no-name" film. The answer was $30,000. Then Rimawi smartly thought to ask about the kind of films they were looking to buy. USA gave him a cheat sheet of exactly what they were looking for—sexy comedies, beach comedies, and sorority comedies. With that information, Rimawi turned to his friend David Latt and said, "Let's go make a sexy sorority comedy."

Latt said, "We made *Sorority House Party* for $25,000, all nonunion. We did what we had to do. We sold it domestically to USA for $35,000, then sold it to Twentieth Century Fox internationally for a lot more money. It was enough to cover the costs for our next movie. More important, it was the guiding philosophy for how we've made every single movie from that point forward. Every single time we enter a deal to make a film, we always presell it, even if it's just a handshake deal. We find out just how much the world is willing to pay for it before production starts."

I think this formula is so intelligent. To date, The Asylum has made more than 350 films, as many as four a month, mostly in the $200,000 range, shot in six to twelve days. Their titles include *Megaboa*, *Nazi Overload*, *Sunday School Musical*, *Christmas Belles*, *Sinister Minister*, and *Izzie's Way Home*. Haven't heard of them? They all turned a nice profit. What about *Sharknado*? That's their film as well, and probably their biggest success to date. I asked Latt what it was about *Sharknado* that made it such a home run for Syfy, which aired it, and for his company. He said, "Well, the president of Syfy didn't like B movies. He wanted more intelligent sci-fi. So they tried to bury it. They took *Sharknado* off Saturday night, which was for years their 'drive-in B movie night.' They put it on a Wednesday night and it got a new audience, including Patton Oswalt and Mia Farrow and all these celebrities who started tweeting about it. That got Syfy's fan base tweeting in a very aggressive way, and it hit the news cycle pretty hard, and not just for fifteen minutes of fame. It was a four-day news cycle. Plus, the title was really unique."

Eleven years later, there are now six movies in the *Sharknado* series. I wondered why The Asylum didn't up its game after that big hit by transitioning into bigger, more expensive films with greater upside potential. "This is how I explain it," said Latt, offering an analogy. "You have a big buffet, with caviar and prime rib and great food being brought in. A lot of producers will want it all. They're waiting for those big food items to hit the buffet—the grand meal, the big deal. But to my partner's credit, he says, 'This food is fine. It is all I'm going to eat. This is all I need, the portion that's right for me.' Other producers are waiting for the big stuff and they're going to end up starving to death."

Latt and Rimawi aren't seduced by the prospect of a bigger deal, and I find that admirable. They move forward when they have the terms that will work within their model. "The most exciting thing about *Sharknado*," Latt said, "was that we were offered a television series with Syfy as a thank-you. We got *Z Nation* green-lit for a full five seasons.

"We get to play in a cool sandbox," he continued. "We have a team that goes out and asks our buyers what they want. We push the witness. It takes some massaging to make sure everyone is happy. If one buyer wants a tsunami film and Japan is all in on a disaster premise but rejects a tsunami because it's 'too soon' after the island nation was struck by one, we go back and massage it. Our development team creates a few concepts, and then I work on the scripts. We want our films to be fun, exciting, and entertaining. We're filmmakers. We're creative. We're still hopeful that we're going to make films that people will really enjoy."

WHILE PASSION DRIVES SOME MOVIES INTO PRODUCTION, it is not uncommon to see projects rise or fall based upon rational business reasons behind the green-light process, if not to the same extent as The Asylum approach. Peter Schlessel sees these decisions from multiple viewpoints. "I've been a producer, a seller, and I've been a studio head, a buyer," Schlessel said. "And I think what a lot of producers don't do well is make a rigorous case for why their movie should be made. They come in and make an emotional case for why they want to do it. They don't think of it from the buyer's perspective.

"Here's an example," Schlessel continued. "The owners of the hit animated TV series *Paw Patrol* wanted to make a *Paw Patrol* movie. They came to me for advice. I gave it to them, and they didn't like it. A month later they called me back and said, 'Tell us again, what would you want to do?' I told them that in my opinion they have a TV show that appeals primarily to three- to six-year-olds, and it's a huge TV show for that age range. But if I'm a theatrical movie distributor and you come to me to make a *Paw Patrol* movie, I'm going to get very nervous about spending $60 million or $70 million on production and marketing. It's a very narrow audience, and three- to six-year-olds don't nag the same way that eight- and nine-year-olds nag their parents. I just didn't know if parents were going to feel the need to take their kids to see a *Paw Patrol* movie in an actual theater. We had a very spirited debate, and ultimately I told them to trust me and give me time and money to put together a presentation to get their movie sold.

"Over three or four months, working with studio veterans Alex DeCastro and Josh Goldstine, we put together a presentation that went way beyond simply adapting the series into a *Paw Patrol* film. We reconceived it to reach a much wider audience. I had looked at their business holistically. I worked with Alex to run the numbers a million different ways—different box office predictions, different fees, different marketing spends. I worked with Josh to seek answers to why a buyer would say yes or no. We concluded that better music was needed. The cast needed to be elevated. It had to be no longer than ninety minutes. We needed elements that distinguished it from the TV series and would appeal to kids older than the young fans of the show.

"I stood in front of the owners and demonstrated that I understood their business and showed them that the uptick they were going to see in

EPILOGUE: EVERY MOVIE SHOULD MAKE MONEY

their toys and merchandising sales based on a theatrical release through a major studio was going to far outweigh my recommendation that they put up half the movie's budget. I was pretty sure that if we committed to half the budget, a studio would say yes to the movie, and we'd also get a much better distribution deal. I persuaded them that we had to go to Paramount first, because Paramount owns Nickelodeon, and they had the TV show.

"They balked at first, thinking that they wanted to play the field and see what was out there. But playing the field, I thought, was to their detriment, so we eventually did go to Paramount first," said Schlessel. "Over the years, I've done a lot of work with Paramount's global head of marketing and distribution, Marc Weinstock, so I sort of have a sense of what interests him. Armed with our presentation, we had a meeting at Paramount with thirty people in the room. Jim Gianopulos, the studio's chairman at the time, sat at the head of the table. 'I think it's for young kids. Like, how do you make it older?' Jim asked. It was the exact right question, and we were prepared with the answer. We presented all the things we had worked on to reach an older audience. It ended up reaching an eight-, nine-, and even ten-year-old audience. And when Jim said, 'Well, it's expensive,' I said, 'We'll put up half the budget.' And he looked at me and said, 'All right, we have a deal.' And it was just sort of that easy because we knew how a studio was going to analyze it," said Schlessel.

For me, the important lesson of this story is the preparation Schlessel and his team put into their presentation to make a rational business case to move forward. They anticipated the kinds of questions that would be thrown at them. You cannot get to making a movie and marketing it for the right price unless you do the hard work inherent in being properly prepared.

Good preparation is the key. Before entering a room to ask somebody to invest in *anything*, you need to know your product cold—you need to know your unique selling proposition and have an answer to any potential question or concern. As mentioned earlier, there are four "abilities" in the life cycle of movie research: Capability, Playability, Marketability, and Buzzability. Once you've made the film, Capability is gone. You can't do anything about that ability. So your next move is to conduct research to show the strengths of your movie's Playability, with empirical evidence, by conducting a test screening. And if you can't afford to pay an outside company for that research, you can always find creative ways to put your film in front of different audiences whose reactions can be gauged without having to spend big bucks. Before entering that room, you can also cut a trailer, or cut a couple of strategically different thirty-second television ads and test those in order to prove that you have Marketability potential. You could even test your movie with a group of film critics, to assess their reactions to it and its Buzzability potential.

So, for example, if you go into Searchlight Pictures and their first reaction is to say, "Well, the movie would have to play incredibly well for us to consider it," you reach into your pocket and present your screening scores and show that you are significantly above the normative benchmarks. The next obstacle out of the executive's mouth will most likely be, "Marketing is so difficult now; we have to be sure we can sell it." And out of your other pocket come your Marketability scores, showing how well your trailers and television spots have tested. The executive who so wants to say no and usher you out of the room then says, "Well, if you don't have critical support, none of it will mean anything." And then, out of yet another pocket (note to self: wear a jacket with *lots* of pockets) come your critics' scores showing that your film is likely to be a four-star movie. What you've now done is given the execs very little room to say no. Unless they were totally leading you on about their initial interest in the project, there's no reason they shouldn't now seriously consider acquiring your film.

Along the way, you'll probably want to detail for Searchlight why you chose to test two strategically created TV spots—purposely taking two to-

EPILOGUE: EVERY MOVIE SHOULD MAKE MONEY

tally different angles—both of which showed similarly promising results. They'll undoubtedly say something like, "We would never sell the movie like *that*." And you counter, "Of course. We could never presume to tell you how to do your jobs; clearly you could do it better than we could ever do it. We just wanted to show you a proof of concept, that the film has potential. We're sure *you* can get these scores even higher, and they're already really high."

Conversely, if you spend the money to test your movie and don't get good Playability, Marketability, or Buzzability scores, you never have to show them the research. Granted, you shelled out beaucoup bucks to create the trailers and TV spots to conduct all these tests, but the upside could be enormous. Once again, if the scores aren't there, it's still important you be aware that you're going to have problems selling your movie to anyone, not just to Searchlight Pictures. This is why I stress just how important it is to test at the Capability stage, to mitigate risk and to make and market your film for the right price at the outset.

WHEN I CONSTRUCTED MY MANTRA that *every movie, if made and marketed for the right price, should make money*, I knew that the single most important element to prove the validity of that statement was the foundation on which I built it: the voice of the audience. I've spent decades listening to audiences talk about the thousands of different movies I've invited them to see. I've read the results from countless numbers of questionnaires that audience members have filled out after seeing these pictures. I've gathered and organized millions of data points against which the performance of a movie can be measured. All this information is derived by respecting and listening to the voice of the audience.

But I found that the voice of the audience isn't often asked for or listened to when early and critical decisions are being made. I wondered how anyone could decide to make a movie without knowing the breadth and intensity of interest that an audience will have in it. Basically, how can you create a financial plan for a movie without knowing the strength of its potential consumer demand? I want to know what specifics in an idea add to and detract from audience enthusiasm. Imagine having a science fiction film that has a romantic subplot, but you discover that while the potential audience is all in on the sci-fi elements, they could not care less about the romance. I would scale back or even eliminate the romantic subplot and beef up the sci-fi. Wouldn't you?

The way I see it, the amount you budget to make a movie for should be based on the intensity of its audience appeal and the breadth and depth of that audience. Again, I've heard story after story confirming that the decisions concerning a movie's budget don't involve considerations of the audience for that film. Production budgets are put together, often too arbitrarily for my comfort level. I'll be told a movie is going to cost $45 million, and if I push back and ask "Based on what?" the likely answer I'll get is that $45 million is the amount it will take for that script, cast and crew, number of shooting days, and all the other estimated costs to bring in a finished movie ready to be released. Or you'll hear, "That's what the comps said!"

That's a crazy way to go about deciding the right price. After all, $45 million may be what a line producer says the movie should be made for, but will that price lead to the picture making money? I know that there's usually a review of a proforma business plan for a project. It normally includes worst-, mid-, and best-case scenarios for revenue performance with comparisons to selected comparable movies, with budgets not only for production but for marketing and distribution. All well and good, but not good enough—because it leaves out the audience and their interest in that specific movie. It leaves out what that specific movie *should* be made for in comparison to what the movie *can* or *will* be made for.

EPILOGUE: EVERY MOVIE SHOULD MAKE MONEY

I've never run a studio. I don't really know what that's like. But I do know that when the approval to make a movie is given, no one really knows how that movie is going to turn out. If you follow Tom Rothman's or Nancy Utley's lead, you make that decision based on whether or not the price is justified against how much money the movie *should* make by hedging with "*every good movie*," or "*most movies, if well made.*" To them, for a movie to reach the hurdle of "should make money" it has to be good, and it has to be well made. They're going to put all the resources they can into buying "insurance" that the movie will turn out *well made* and *good*. They will work on a budget, and against that budget they will secure the best on-screen and off-screen talent the production can afford.

My fear is that apportioning all risk to the actual performance of the movie raises your risk level too high. The fact is that research audiences give most movies they watch a C grade, and that grade represents only an average performance. We have normative data derived from thousands of research screenings conducted throughout the years, representing a statistical average. *Average* doesn't get you very far in almost any endeavor, and it certainly doesn't spell box office success for a film. Knowing everything I know now, I would hope all my movies would get better than an average grade. But I wouldn't green-light movies based on budgets built on expectations that I'm going to get an A or A-plus grade. That strategy is just too undependable.

The people who are in this book are those who are, or have been, on the top rung of the ladder. They rose that high because they recognize average and certainly don't ever set out to say "Yes, let's make an average movie." Be it big ideas, passion, themes, stories, characters, or always looking for unique and bold choices, they are driven to deliver successful financial results. However, if I were sitting where they sit, I would definitely add to my decision-making intelligence the gathering of information from the audience that would benefit me in mitigating the risk of choosing to make a movie at the wrong price.

Here's a bizarre hypothetical example to help understand the demand for a movie and the right price to make that movie for.

Let's say someone comes to me and pitches me their movie idea titled *DIRT!* Here's the pitch: outside of polite society there is a quirky group of people who have a passion for all things dirt. I want this meeting to end as quickly as possible. But hey, I'm open-minded, and just maybe there's an unexplored opportunity here—if there really is a big enough audience for such a movie.

So I do what I do and conduct some research, and I find that there's actually an online community of fellow dirt lovers and a YouTube channel that is geared to them. The channel will pay $15,000 for worldwide rights to this movie in perpetuity and they don't even care about its quality. Make the movie, and you're all but guaranteed $15K. That's it, that's all you'll make. I look at the alternative of self-distributing the movie, but that risk is too high, and unless there would be a big payoff, self-distributing would be a time suck. Selling to the channel is really my only opportunity. But the filmmakers tell me they can't figure out how to make the movie for any less than $20,000. That's an easy "No, I'm not interested." After all, why would I make a movie for a price that has almost no chance of making money?

Weird example, I know, but I hope it drives my point home. I use it because it speaks to the fact that you must be aware of your audience, in terms of both who they are and how many of them there are.

Here's a more realistic example. The logline: a mute cleaning woman leads a life of isolation in 1960s Baltimore until she bonds with an amphibious creature held in the research lab where she works as a janitor.

Okay, I might listen, but the people making the movie want $18 million for production and I'm skeptical that there are enough moviegoers who will pay to see this film in a theater. At best, it seems like a heartwarming little message movie for a single quadrant of older women, a demographic that rarely turns out to see a film on its opening weekend.

EPILOGUE: EVERY MOVIE SHOULD MAKE MONEY

So I'm thinking, based on what I know from the logline, that it has limited appeal and limited potential to build early word of mouth. I'll do some research to see if my hunch is correct. Let's say I conduct Capability Testing on the concept, and in gathering the two-hundred- to three-hundred-word description to be tested, I find there's much more complexity to the storyline. The amphibious creature is highly intelligent, the mute cleaning woman teaches it sign language, and Soviet spies are trying to thwart the American scientists from conducting experiments on it that could give them the edge in the space race. The Soviets are out to kill the creature, and the Americans want to harvest its body parts to advance their knowledge of its origins, a distant planet.

Now I'm seeing broader appeal—a highly intelligent creature from another planet that can communicate with humans, villains out to harm it or kill it, and Cold War–era espionage. Maybe men will be on board. I'm feeling a little more open to the idea.

The results of the Capability Test come back (this is all theoretical; I never tested the concept) and the data confirms that two quadrants are solidly on board—older men and older women—and there may be some interest from women under forty as well. Meanwhile, I learn that the $18 million production budget has Guillermo del Toro attached as writer and director, covers the stunning creature design and water visuals, and includes a magnificent original score by award-winning French composer Alexandre Desplat, performed by the London Symphony Orchestra. Now we're talking!

The movie gets green-lit—not by me, of course, but by Fox Searchlight. At the end of the day, the budget comes in at $19.4 million and it tests through the roof when we conduct an early audience screening (this part is true). It wins the Golden Lion for best film at the August 2017 Venice International Film Festival, signaling that the critics are behind it, and goes on to earn a 92 percent on Rotten Tomatoes (also true). The investment is more than justified. *The Shape of Water* earned $195 million worldwide. It was nominated for thirteen Oscars and won four, including Best Picture, Best Director for Guillermo del Toro, Best Production Design, and Best Original Score for Alexandre Desplat, who also took home a Grammy for the soundtrack.

It's a hierarchy of interest, and as the audience appeal of a movie intensifies and expands with word of mouth and critical support, the revenue potential similarly expands. Likewise, the narrower the audience appeal from the get-go, the narrower the revenue potential.

To put my own spin on an old proverb: If you don't know what you have, shame on you. If you don't know who your audience is, or the size of that audience, shame on you. But then shame on me if I don't recognize that there are great movies that likely wouldn't have gotten made if you'd asked consumers about their interest in them. Such movies are made at a high risk because they are all execution-driven and must get As or even A-pluses from audiences to make money.

The Full Monty, Slumdog Millionaire, and *Juno* were all gambles that paid off. But for every one of those movies, there are hundreds of others that you've never heard of because they didn't get an A or B and were either never released or failed to gain any traction if they were.

When I discuss my mantra—*every movie, if made and marketed for the right price, should make money*—with producers who have some credits to their name but are not yet seasoned pros, at first they nod and say, "That's great to know." But then they almost immediately ask, "But what do I need to know for a movie I'm setting out to develop so I don't get a lot of work done only to find out too late that the audience isn't very interested?"

I tell them right up front that they need to be honest with themselves. They need to know what they have, and not automatically think their project is surely *the exception* and is for *everybody*. A movie for *everybody*

EPILOGUE: EVERY MOVIE SHOULD MAKE MONEY

is one that, by definition, attracts young and old, parents and their kids, and all genders. But many more movies are made for *somebody* and are not intended for *everybody*. You can be very successful making movies for *somebody* if you make them for the right price.

When I was in Cannes one year participating as a guest speaker on an international moviegoing panel, one of the attendees came up afterward with a question. She said she was developing a movie about Muhammad Yunus, the man who created the concept of microcredit, giving disenfranchised people loans to start businesses in developing countries. I told her I loved the idea and asked about what she envisioned for the project. Who was the audience? What would the budget be? She said that she saw it as a drama with a $40 million budget, one that should appeal to everybody. It was like hearing a tire screech in my head. I gently responded with, "A drama about a Nobel Peace Prize winner working on microfinance, even if it's a great story, is not a movie for everybody." As a documentary? Perhaps it has a chance to succeed with a specific audience, but certainly nowhere near her budgeted number—anything over, say, a million dollars, which might still be too much.

I wish conversations like this didn't happen so often, but they do. I'm often asked to speak at the major film schools—schools like USC, NYU, UCLA, Chapman, and AFI. When I do, I'll ask a brave soul or two to pitch me a story about a movie they want to make. Then I ask them what the budget will be. They'll say something like, "Well, it's five million dollars." I'll ask, "Based on what?" And it's always an answer like, "My buddy, who's a line producer, budgeted it for me." I ask, "And who's the audience?" And they say, "Everyone." I put it to the test in the room, asking the whole class to vote anonymously on the pitch that they just heard from their fellow student. Would you want to see it? The choices are: definitely, probably, probably not, or definitely not. In the real world, we only care about "definitely." "Probably" means you're *probably not* going to see it. Out of a class of fifty, I may get two students who say definitely, but everyone else is below that rating.

It's a tough exercise, but it's a necessary one. And it's an especially valuable lesson to learn early in your Hollywood career. Above all else, you have to keep it real. You must be honest with yourself in measuring the box office potential for your intended movie against the performance of movies that have already been released. Select realistic comparisons rather than aspirational ones. Then, don't believe your movie can be some kind of outlier and plan for it to generate a box office gross that is not aligned to the comps you selected. It's like when you sell a house—you must be honest with yourself on your asking price. Yes, you may have done a whole lot of improvements to the home since you bought it, but when a buyer comes along, they are going to compare your asking price with what comparable homes in the neighborhood have been selling for. You may think your house is worth more, but comps don't lie. They set a price range. It's the same with movies. The comps don't lie. Filmmakers will say they have a better movie than the comps ("We have the nicest house on the block"), so their movie is going to bring in more box office dollars than the comps, and they should therefore get more money to make it. Bad idea. Trust the comps! And if there aren't any reliable comps, which can happen at times, that alone should also tell you about the risk you are taking, as you are venturing into uncharted waters.

IF YOU AGREE WITH ME that feedback from an audience has value when they watch a movie, then I hope you agree that feedback from an audience has value in mitigating risk when green-light decisions are being made. We ask a lot of filmmakers when they agree to sit in a theater as their movie unspools for three hundred strangers. It's an angst-filled couple of hours, and I have enormous respect for the courage it takes to face those strangers' unfiltered reactions and opinions. I yearn to see similar courage evidenced by those empowered to give the green light, and have them listen to consumers' unfiltered reactions and opinions as they decide what movies get made. This would better ensure Playability, but would also allow better financial decisions based on just how large or limited the audience potential is.

Here's how I see these jobs: the green-lighter's job is to set up a movie to succeed financially; the filmmaker's job is to make a playable movie; the marketer's job is to build a campaign to make the movie a "want to see." I hope you are nodding in agreement with me that green-lighters can improve their chances to succeed if they have the courage to listen to the audience before the decision to make a movie is ever finalized.

I bring the voice of the audience to filmmakers through Capability Testing as described in chapter 3, and Capability Testing is an apt term for this specific sort of research. While I don't make any claims that such testing can predict final achievement, I do know that it can most definitely help mitigate risk. And that leads to a stronger opportunity to make money. Capability Testing reveals whether the movie has the qualities to succeed financially.

"I always ask, where is the idea?" says marketing executive Josh Goldstine. "What does a movie have working for it and what's working against it?"

"I think clarity of concept is essentially the elevator pitch," Universal Pictures marketing executive Dwight Caines explains. "If in less than two minutes or so I can't tell you what a movie is about, who it is for, who the protagonist is and what his/her obstacle is, and what the promise of that moviegoing experience is going to be, then that's a challenge for marketing. I favor ideas that are clear, interesting, and experiential. A clear concept is one that is easily communicated, remembered, and passed on to others."

I think it's hard for some executives and producers to face the possibility that certain audiences just aren't interested in their project. Yes, it takes courage, but I think that getting the very best information you can is part of being a responsible player. Because the marketing of a poorly testing movie will be a challenge, the film's execution must absolutely succeed. The Capability research responses identify pink flags, and sometimes even red flags, that you should be aware of in terms of the level of financial risk you're willing to take. Plan to make and market the movie at a price—the right price—and you should then make money. Ignore such research and you might be risking more than you should. "I place most of my emphasis on how well a movie works (Playability)," Elizabeth Gabler says. "And can it attract the intended audience (Marketability). While a movie I would want to make might not have the strongest concept, I look to see if it has what I call the complete package."

I'm not saying that Capability Testing is the ultimate and singular path to success; absolutely not. But it is without a doubt undeniable information that helps to inform. Early on, it gives insight into possibilities. It provides directional insight before expensive decisions are made.

Of course, when you greenlight a movie with an expectation of how it will be executed, things can go wrong when it isn't executed in that expected manner. This was exactly what occurred with Jim Gianopulos and 2002's *Solaris*. "I thought, 'Look what I got—Cameron, Soderbergh, Clooney. It doesn't get better than that,'" Gianopulos recalls. "I didn't think it was all that risky at a $40 million budget. As happens at times, though, once Soderbergh started to make the movie, he went down a different path than we had expected, taking it in a very independent, arty direction on the theme of what is reality and what is truth.

"Ultimately it was likely too cerebral for the intended audience. We spent a good deal on marketing it, thinking Clooney would bring in the audience, but despite mostly positive critical support, it only did $30 mil-

EPILOGUE: EVERY MOVIE SHOULD MAKE MONEY

lion total global box office. With all the best of intentions, things can go off the rails. Filmmakers often discover paths once they start making a movie and go off in a different direction than expected, and midstream it is hard for a studio to do anything. In the dailies you see pieces, so you don't really understand where it's all going. When you first see an assembly, it really is the first time you understand what the filmmaker made. I sometimes feel like someone financing a long-ago explorer, who I provision with all the equipment they need, put it on their ship. But once they leave the dock, all you hope for is that they come back with the spices you sought. My guess is that if I had Capability Tested *Solaris*, it would have worked and scored highly. It just wasn't *that* movie that was ultimately made."

In this case, if what was produced had been Capability Tested pre-approval, it would likely have demonstrated strong audience appeal, and that the studio was taking minimal risk in going forward with the projected production and marketing budget. But as Gianopulos points out, a strongly positive Capability Test is no guarantee. If the movie made is different from the elements promised in the test, it changes the risk dynamics, and thus changes the right price to make and market the movie.

As I've repeated often, I don't suggest that the audience should be the ultimate determinants of whether to green-light a picture. But I do strongly recommend that it is at least listened to and heard. Those whose careers go up and down on the decisions they make will be better served if they do so. Caution: Avoid the audience at your own peril.

I can say without question that in the last several decades, I've spoken to more moviegoers than anyone else in the movie industry. And I don't think whoever comes in second to me is even close in comparison. Through all these interactions, I have developed a profound respect for the moviegoing audience. I understand what films mean to boys and girls as young as five and to men and women up to ninety-five. I understand the generational, cultural, socioeconomic, and geographical similarities, differences, and nuances that shape three hundred people sitting in seats and watching a movie that they all find entertaining.

Every one of us has a different set of movie experiences that provide our personal education as to what we ask of a film. Our watched and want-to-watch lists can be quite different, and yet also many times quite similar. This book provides a peek behind the scenes at many of the important processes that lead to what the public is offered to watch. It has one and only one hero: the person watching a movie in a theater or at home. A hero who is ready to offer their voice when asked. I have listened to that voice almost every day for nearly forty years. I respect that voice, and I urge others in the industry to listen to it eagerly and often. The voice of the moviegoing public has no agenda and doesn't expect to gain favor or fortune. It simply wants to be entertained.

Just invite the voice in and listen.

ACKNOWLEDGMENTS

To Samantha Weiner, my executive editor at Simon Element, who believed in this book and championed it, and to Gina Navaroli, who assisted Samantha and ushered it through to the finish line.

A big shout-out to Kari Campano, my chief of staff at Screen Engine, who read the early manuscript and the subsequent iterations and who has worked tirelessly to raise awareness of the book through events, social media, marketing, and publicity. She is a true force of nature.

To Darlene Hayman, my coauthor for *Audience-ology* and a major contributor to *How to Score in Hollywood*. I truly could not have made my deadline for this book had Darlene not stepped up as she did. Her dedication, undying loyalty, and friendship mean the world to me.

To Justine Adelizzi, one of the most gifted writers I know and speechwriter extraordinaire, who was an invaluable contributor to *How to Score in Hollywood*, and to the equally talented David Meadvin for his guidance along the way and for bringing Justine into my orbit.

To Kathy Manabat, who exemplifies the very best qualities that anyone could ask for in an executive assistant. She organizes my life, juggles my calendar—even when there aren't enough hours in the day—and keeps me sane. (Plus, she knows all my secrets, and keeps them!)

To Siena Viencek-Walsh, my second assistant and sounding board, for her keen instincts and good taste whenever it comes to the written word.

To Hilda Wynn, a dear friend and the wife of my coauthor, Bob Levin, who stood by his side through countless revamps and rewrites and put up with my late-night and weekend phone calls.

ACKNOWLEDGMENTS

To Howie Preiser, for his eagle editorial eye, who made creative suggestions and flagged every typo and extra space from the first to the final drafts.

To Clarissa Sendor, for wrangling all the legal clearances, a huge job that required sign-off from all who contributed stories and commentary within these pages.

To Rachel Parness, for being my sounding board day in and day out, and my last phone call every night.

To Theresa DiMasi, my first editor at Simon & Schuster, who continues to provide moral support and wise guidance in navigating the publishing world, which even after two books I'm still learning how to do.

To grammarian Anna Scotti, the living embodiment of the *Oxford English Dictionary* and the best expert on language I know. Whenever in doubt about where to place a comma or whether an ellipsis or a semicolon is the better choice, I can always depend on Anna for the right answer.

To my social media team, Ashton Bracket, Veronica Farias, Daniel Gamino, Adam Ritz, and Dax Ross, who handle writing, video, and still photography support.

To Robbie Davis and DJ Entertainment, for working with Kari and me to produce the lion's share of my audiovisual marketing materials. A professional to his core, Robbie and his team—especially Mike Johnson and Gary Forbes—came through for me time and time again, upholding their quality standards even under the tightest deadlines.

To my team at Lobeline Communications, Tim Williams, Solange Sinclair, Alessandra Fusar Poli, and Mason Bissada, for their PR strategy and execution supporting the launch of *How to Score in Hollywood*.

To the world-renowned Greg Gorman, for shooting my photograph for the book jacket.

To the entire team at Simon Element who contributed their talents to the book, including publisher Richard Rhorer and editor in chief Doris Cooper, and especially Carah Gedeon in publicity, designer Madelyn

ACKNOWLEDGMENTS

Rodriguez and art director Jenny Carrow for the cover art, and designer Laura Levatino for the interiors; senior production editor Benjamin Holmes, senior managing editor Shayna Holmes, and Jesse Harris in production and editorial management; and Ali Kochik and Elizabeth Breeden in marketing.

To the friends and colleagues who read early drafts of the manuscript and offered their intelligent, thoughtful feedback: Caellum Allan, Peter Bart, Nancy Bishop, Steve Buck, Anet Carlin, Andrea Garfield, Judith Hathaway, Rick Nicita, Lyle Snow, and Paula Wagner.

To all the entertainment industry leaders who contributed to *How to Score in Hollywood*, generously taking time from their jam-packed schedules to be interviewed for the book or to participate in episodes of my podcast, *Don't Kill the Messenger*. This book would not exist without the following: Amy Baer, Sean Bailey, Todd Black, Bill Block, Jason Blum, Jason Blumenthal, Cale Boyter, Robbie Brenner, Nicole Brown, Dwight Caines, Mark Canton, Toby Emmerich, Marc Evans, Erik Feig, Ben Feingold, Adam Fogelson, Andrew Form, DeVon Franklin, Rob Friedman, Antoine Fuqua, Elizabeth Gabler, Jim Gianopulos, Will Gluck, Josh Goldstine, Mark Gordon, Brian Grazer, Jordan Harmon, Ron Howard, Broderick Johnson, Graham King, Nancy Kirhoffer, Andrew Kosove, David Latt, Monica Levinson, Gary Lucchesi, Chris Meledandri, Neal Moritz, Tendo Nagenda, Kathy Nelson, Sanford Panitch, Amy Pascal, David Permut, Terry Press, Eli Roth, Tom Rothman, Roy Salter, Couper Samuelson, Peter Schlessel, Cathy Schulman, Russell Schwartz, Tony Sella, William Sherak, Nick Stoller, George Tillman Jr., and Nancy Utley.

To my entire family, especially my late mom, Rhoda, and my dad, Lou, whom I lost while writing this book, and to Lisa, Pete, Nikki, and Riley, as well as my chosen family for their bottomless love and support. And to my little guy (who's not such a little guy), Kasha, the best furry friend a guy could ever ask for.

NOTES

SCAN THIS QR CODE FOR FOOTNOTE CITATIONS
REFERENCED THROUGHOUT THE BOOK.

INDEX OF FILM TITLES

A Beautiful Mind, 185, 199–201
A Family Affair, 16
A Good Year, 219
A Quiet Place, xii, 10
A Quiet Place: Day One, 173
A Wrinkle in Time, 65
About Schmidt, 212
Abraham Lincoln: Vampire Hunter, 110, 150
Aladdin (1992), 47, 131
Alexander, 11
Alice in Wonderland (2010), 117
Alien, 139, 148
Aliens, 148–49
Allegiant, 194–95
Aloha, 220
American Hustle, 138
Anchorman, 139
Annie (2014), 202
Anyone But You, 80–81, 202
Apollo 13, 199–200
Arrival, 72, 130
Ascendent, 194–95
Avatar, xii, 56–57, 150
Avatar: The Way of Water, 72
Avengers, 22
Avengers franchise, 22

Babylon, 64–65
Back to Black, 77
Backdraft, 185
Bambi (1942), 47
Barbie, 8–10, 56, 110

Battleship, 72
Beaches, 129
Beauty and the Beast (1991), 47
Beauty and the Beast (2017), 21, 117
Beetlejuice, 91
Beetlejuice Beetlejuice, 91–93
Being the Ricardos, 180
Beverly Hills Cop, 80
Big Daddy, 116
Big Fish, 186
Bird Box, 22
Birdman, 22, 103, 208
Black Panther, 112, 161
Black Swan, 90, 208–9
Blade Runner 2049, 72, 130
Blockers, 180
Blue Jasmine, 139
Bohemian Rhapsody, 77–78, 198
Booksmart, 180
Borat, 179
Borat Subsequent Moviefilm, 179
Braveheart, 161, 200
Brian Banks, 61
Bridesmaids, 188
Brokeback Mountain, 163
Bros, 187–88
Brüno, 179
Bullet Train, 219

Cabin Fever, 204
Captain America, 22
Captain Phillips, 138
Catch-22, 114

INDEX OF FILM TITLES

Challengers, 59
Chicken Little, 131
Christmas Belles, 226
Cinderella (2015), 21
Cinderella Man, 185
Civil War, 90
Cleopatra (in development), 186
Cloudy with a Chance of Meatballs, 138
Crash, 162–64
Crazy Rich Asians, 10
Creed, 112
Cutthroat Island, 72

Da 5 Bloods, 21
Dallas Buyers Club, 6
Darfur Now, 163
Dark Places, 90
Dawn of the Dead, 12
Dead Again, 168–69
Dead Poets Society, 118
Deadpool, xii
Deadpool & Wolverine, 44, 56
Delivery Man, 87
De-Lovely, 77
Despicable Me, 10, 35, 37–40, 56
Despicable Me 2, 39
Diary of a Wimpy Kid, 23
Die Hard, 16
Divergent, 194–95
Doctor Strange, 151
Dolphin Tale, 130
Dragnet, 15–16
Dumb and Dumber, 193
Dumb and Dumberer: When Harry Met Lloyd, 193
Dumbo (1941), 47
Dumbo (2019), 21
Dune, 72–73
Dune: Part Two, 72–73
Dunkirk, 77

E.T. the Extra-Terrestrial, 17
Easy A, 202
Earth to Echo, 17
Eat Drink Man Woman, 166
Ed Wood, 64
Eden, 199
Elvis, 10, 114
Everything Everywhere All at Once, 90, 102–3
Exit to Eden, 128
Extraction, 22

Fantastic Beasts, 8
Farce of the Penguins, 66–67
Fargo, 211–12
Fast X, 110
Finding Neverland, 24
For Love or Money, 185
Forgetting Sarah Marshall, 33, 187
Forrest Gump, 186
Fried Green Tomatoes, 183
Fruitvale Station, 112
Fun with Dick and Jane (2005), 33
Furious 7, 74–75
Fury, 88

Get Him to The Greek, 33
Get On Up, 77
Get Out, 28–29, 146, 203
Ghostbusters, 79
Ghostbusters: Afterlife, 79
Gigli, 220
Give 'em Hell, Harry!, 14
Gladiator, 86, 161
Glass Onion: A Knives Out Mystery, 21
Gods and Monsters, 64
Gone with the Wind, 85
Good Night, and Good Luck, 164
Goodbye, Mr. Chips, 119
Gravity, 8

INDEX OF FILM TITLES

Gretel & Hansel, 117
Guardians of the Galaxy Vol. 3, 110

Hacksaw Ridge, 67
Halloween, 83
Halloween (2018), 84, 143–44
Hamlet (1964), 14
Harry Potter, 8, 125, 139, 194
Haunted Mansion, 101
Heaven's Gate, 71
Hereditary, 90
Hidden Figures, 23
Hollywoodland, 64
Hope Floats, 139
Horton Hears a Who!, 35–36, 40
Hostel, 204–5
Hustlers, 113

I Feel Pretty, 180
I Love Trouble, 105
I Love You, Daddy, 220
I, Tonya, 139
Ice Age, xii, 35–37, 150
Immortals, 6
Inception, 172
Insurgent, 194
It Ends with Us, 44
Izzie's Way Home, 226

Jack the Giant Slayer, 116
Jaws, 45, 69
Jerry Maguire, 118, 120
John Carter, 72
Joker, 139, 119
Joker: Folie à Deux, 191
Juno, 87, 90, 236

Kingdom of Heaven, 86–87
Kingsman: The Secret Service, xii
Knocked Up, 88

La La Land, 64
Lady Bird, 7–8, 90
Last Vegas, 60
Lawrence of Arabia, 72
Leaving Las Vegas, 211–12
Legally Blonde, 122
Les Miserables, 123–25
Life of Pi, 23–25, 90
Little Miss Sunshine, 149
Little Nicky, 116
Little Women (2019), 7
Longlegs, 59
Lord of the Rings, 72
Love & Basketball, 160
Luca, 50

M3GAN, 203
Madame Web, 193
Magic 8 Ball, 7
Maleficent, 117
Manchester by the Sea, 212
March of the Penguins, 65–66
Marley & Me, 23
Meet Me in St. Louis, 125
Megaboa, 226
Megalopolis, 191
Men in Black, 209–10
Men of Honor, 165
Midsommar, 90
Million Dollar Baby, 168
Minions, 40
Miracle on 34th Street, 16
Mirror Mirror, 6
Mission: Impossible, 22, 72, 176–77
Mission: Impossible—Dead Reckoning Part One, 72
Mission: Impossible—Fallout, xii
Mission: Impossible—Ghost Protocol, 72
Mission: Impossible—Rogue Nation, 72
Moana 2, 44

INDEX OF FILM TITLES

Molly's Game, 180
Moneyball, 138
Monster, 139
Morbius, 193
Mr. and Mrs. Smith, 150
Mulan (2020), 21
My Sister's Keeper, 180

Napoleon (2023), 59
Napoleon Dynamite, 210
Nazi Overload, 226
Neighbors, 33–35, 181, 187
Neighbors 2: Sorority Rising, 181–82
New Year's Eve, 129
Night at the Museum, xii, 150
Night Shift, 199
Nope, 29
Notorious, 165
Nutty Professor II: The Klumps, 80

Ocean's Eleven, 81
Old Dads, 179
Olympus Has Fallen, 205
Once Upon a Time . . . In Hollywood, 8
Oppenheimer, 77, 110
Ouija, 203–4

Paddington, 8
Paranormal Activity, 203
Parenthood, 185, 199
Paw Patrol: The Movie, 228
Peter Rabbit, 202
Pete's Dragon, 59
Pinocchio (1940), 117
Pinocchio (2019), 117
Pirates of the Caribbean, 101
Planet of the Apes, xii, 150
Poor Things, 103
Postcards from the Edge, 114
Pretty Woman, 108–9, 128–29
Primal Fear, 168

Prisoners, 130
Project Hail Mary, 186
Project X, 16
Promising Young Woman, 171
P.S. I Love You, 130
Pushing Tin, 64

Ransom, 199–200
Ravenous, 64
Red Notice, 22
Red Riding Hood, 177
Respect, 77
Ricki and the Flash, 87
Robin Hood, 114
RoboCop 2, 11
RoboCop 3, 11
Robots, 35
Rocketman, xii
Romeo + Juliet, 11
Romeo and Juliet, 111
Runaway Bride, 129
Rush, 199

Safe Haven, 6
Saltburn, 171
Saving Private Ryan, 75–76, 122
Scream, 82–93
Scream 7, 83
Scream VI, 83
Selma, 65
Sharknado, 226–27
Sin City, 11
Sing, 35
Singin' in the Rain, 125
Sinister, 151
Sinister Minister, 226
Sinners, 112–13
Sleeping Beauty, 117
Slumdog Millionaire, 90, 236
Solaris (2002), 240–41
Son of the Mask, 193

INDEX OF FILM TITLES

Sonic the Hedgehog, xii, 136–37
Sonic the Hedgehog 2, 137
Sonic the Hedgehog 3, 137
Sorority House Party, 226
Soul Food, 166
Sound of Freedom, 62–63
Speed, 27–28, 76, 193
Speed 2: Cruise Control, 27–28, 193
Spider-Man, 56, 138, 193
Stand by Me, 17–18
Star Trek, 176
Steal Big, Steal Little, 129
Steel Magnolias, 184
Stop the World: I Want to Get Off, 14
Sunday School Musical, 226
Superbad, 16

Taken, 150
Taylor Swift: The Eras Tour, 10
Thanksgiving, 204–5
The Adam Project, 22
The Age of Adaline, 168
The Aviator, 198
The Beguiled, 51–52
The Big Year, 64
The Birdcage, 114
The Black Cauldron, 117–18
The Black Phone, 151–52
The Blind Side, 106, 130
The Bourne Identity, 22
The Circle, 106
The Da Vinci Code, 138
The Dark Knight, 77
The Day the Earth Stood Still, 151
The Devil Wears Prada, 23
The Disaster Artist, 64
The Emperor's New Groove, 131
The Equalizer, 138, 205, 207
The Equalizer 2, 207
The Equalizer 3, 207
The Exorcism of Emily Rose, 151

The Fast and the Furious, 73
The Fault in Our Stars, 58
The Flash, 69–71
The 40-Year-Old Virgin, 10, 35
The Fugitive, 129
The Full Monty, 236
The Garfield Movie, 131, 133–35
The Girl with the Dragon Tattoo, 52–53
The Goonies, 17–18
The Graduate, 39
The Gray Man, 21–22
The Great Train Robbery, 48
The Grinch (2018), 40
The Guilt Trip, 59
The Hate U Give, 165
The Hunger Games, 16, 194
The Hunger Games: Mockingjay, 194
The Hurt Locker, 212
The Idea of You, 50
The Invisible Man, 151
The Irishman, 50
The Journey of Natty Gann, 197
The Last King of Scotland, 139
The Last Mimzy, 18–20
The Lion King (1994), 47
The Little Mermaid (1989), 47, 118, 124, 131
The Lone Ranger, 57–58, 72
The Lorax, 40
The Magnificent Seven (2016), 138, 205
The Marrying Man, 153–54, 156
The Martian, xii
The Mask, 193
The Maze Runner, 16
The Natural, 149
The Nutty Professor (1963), 79
The Nutty Professor (1996), 80
The Old Guard, 21, 160
The Prestige, 180
The Princess Diaries, 129
The Princess Diaries 2, 129

INDEX OF FILM TITLES

The Purge, 30, 203
The Pursuit of Happyness, 138
The Remains of the Day, 114
The Revenant, xii
The Secret Life of Bees, 160
The Secret Life of Pets, 35, 40–41
The Shape of Water, 22, 208, 236
The Social Network, 138
The Star, 101
The Super Mario Bros. Movie, 40, 110
The Taking of Pelham 123, 138
The Town, 198
The Trial of the Chicago 7, 180
The Unbearable Weight of Massive Talent, 64
The Usual Suspects, 177
The Whale, 212
The Wizard of Oz, 125
The Wolf of Wall Street, 114
The Woman King, 160, 162
Theater Camp, 63
There Will Be Blood, 198
Thirteen Lives, 199
13th, 65
30 Minutes or Less, 179
300, 11–14, 72, 80
tick, tick . . . BOOM!, 141–42
Ticket to Paradise, 80–81
Titanic, xii, 57
Top Gun: Maverick, 26, 81
Training Day, 205

Trainwreck, 188
Transformers, 176–77
Tusk, 90
Twilight, 111–12

Uncut Gems, 90
Underworld, 168
Us, 29

Valentine's Day, 129
Venom, 138, 193
Venom: Let There Be Carnage, 193

Wedding Crashers, 10
West Side Story (2021), 123, 125
What Planet Are You From?, 114–15
Where the Crawdads Sing, 25–26, 58, 167
Whitney Houston: I Wanna Dance with Somebody, 77
Wicked: Part One, 124–25
Wild Iris, 183–84, 191
Windtalkers, 118, 121–22
Wolfs, 50
Wolverine, 150
Wonka, 8
World War Z, 176

X-Men, 150

Zero Dark Thirty, 138
Zoolander, 179

INDEX OF NAMES

Ackerley, Tom, 7–9
Alexander, Jason, 66
Apatow, Judd, 32, 178, 188
Arndt, Michael, 149
Arquette, David, 82
Astaire, Fred, 217
Ayer, David, 89
Aykroyd, Dan, 15, 79

Baer, Amy, 60–61, 245
Bailey, Sean, 89, 245
Baker, Rick, 80
Baldwin, Alec, 91, 154–55
Barrera, Melissa, 83
Barry, Dave, 31
Barrymore, Drew, 80–82
Basinger, Kim, 155
Baum, L. Frank, 125
Baumbach, Noah, 8–9
Bay, Michael, 96–97, 177
Bello, Maria, 160
Belushi, John, 66
Benigni, Roberto, 117
Bening, Annette, 114
Benny, Jack, 44
Bishop, Joey, 217
Black, Jack, 64
Black, Todd, 138, 245
Blanchett, Cate, 139
Block, Bill, 83, 88, 245
Blum, Jason, 7, 9, 28–29, 83, 203, 207, 245
Blumenthal, Jason, 139, 207, 245

Blunt, Emily, 173
Bowles, Camilla Parker, 171
Boyter, Cale, 72–73, 245
Bragman, Howard, 163
Branagh, Kenneth, 168
Brenner, Robbie, 6–9, 71, 245
Brillstein, Bernie, 15
Broadhurst, Kent, 191
Brown, James, 77
Brown, Nicole, 88, 160, 186, 245
Bullock, Sandra, 106, 139–40, 193
Burton, Richard, 14
Burton, Tim, 91–92, 186
Bush, George W., 122
Butler, Austin, 10
Byrne, Rose, 33, 181

Cage, Nicolas, 59, 121–22, 211
Caines, Dwight, 80–81, 219, 239, 245
Calley, John, 114–15
Cameron, James, 57, 148, 240
Campbell, Neve, 82–83
Canton, Mark, 11–12, 14, 80, 245
Carell, Steve, 33
Carey, Mariah, 101
Carrey, Jim, 136
Caviezel, Jim, 62
Chalamet, Timothée, 73
Chazelle, Damien, 64–65
C.K., Louis, 220
Clarkson, Kelly, 101
Clooney, George, 81, 164, 240

INDEX OF NAMES

Cody, Diablo, 87
Coen, Ethan, 211
Coen, Joel, 211
Coffin, Pierre, 36–37
Cohen, Andrew, 33, 181
Cohen, Sacha Baron, 178–79
Connelly, Jennifer, 201
Coogler, Ryan, 112–13
Cooper, Bradley, 80
Cooper, Kim, 27–28
Coppola, Francis Ford, 191–92
Coppola, Sofia, 51
Cox, Courteney, 82
Crowe, Russell, 201, 219
Cruise, Tom, 72, 120
Curtis, Jamie Lee, 83–84, 143

Daurio, Ken, 36, 41
Davis, Andy, 129
Davis, Geena, 91
Davis, Jim, 130–31
Davis, Viola, 160
De Niro, Robert, 60
DeCastro, Alex, 228
del Toro, Guillermo, 235–36
Demme, Jonathan, 87
Depp, Johnny, 58
Derrickson, Scott, 151–52
Desplat, Alexandre, 235–36
Diesel, Vin, 74
Dindal, Mark, 131, 134
Disney, Walt, 35, 46, 56, 89, 195
Dorman, Michael, 152
Douglas, Michael, 60
Duncan, Michael Clark, 19
DuVernay, Ava, 65

Ebert, Roger, 105, 115, 117, 121
Efron, Zac, 16, 33, 187
Eichner, Billy, 187–88

Eisenberg, Lee, 133
Eisner, Michael, 195
Elordi, Jacob, 171
Emmerich, Toby, 91, 245
Evans, Chris, 22
Evans, Marc, 176–77, 245

Farrow, Mia, 226
Feig, Erik, 63, 111, 245
Feingold, Ben, 220, 245
Fennell, Emerald, 171–72
Fincher, David, 52
Flanagan, Mike, 203
Fogelson, Adam, 114, 123–24, 218, 245
Ford, Harrison, 129
Form, Andrew, 174, 245
Franklin, Aretha, 77
Franklin, DeVon, 245
Freeman, Morgan, 60
Friedman, Rob, 111–12, 218, 245
Fuqua, Antoine, 205–6, 245

Gabler, Elizabeth, 23–26, 219, 240, 245
Gallup, George, 85
Garfield, Andrew, 67, 141–42
Garland, Judy, 125
Geisel, Theodor Seuss, 40
Gere, Richard, 108
Gerwig, Greta, 1, 7–9
Gianopulos, Jim, xii, 57, 64, 229, 240–41, 245
Gibson, Mel, 67, 200–201
Gluck, Will, 202–3, 245
Godsick, Jeffrey, 79
Goldberg, Evan, 33, 34, 181–82
Goldberg, Whoopi, 66
Goldsman, Akiva, 201
Goldstine, Josh, 52, 228, 239, 245
Gooding, Cuba Jr., 120
Gordon, Mark, 75–76, 245

INDEX OF NAMES

Gosling, Ryan, 22, 80, 186
Gottfried, Gilbert, 225
Grazer, Brian, 79–80, 141, 185, 199, 245
Greer, Judy, 143, 146
Guillon, Eric, 37

Haggis, Paul, 163
Hahn, Kathryn, 19
Hammer, Armie, 58
Hancock, John Lee, 106
Hanks, Tom, 16, 76, 80, 106
Harmon, Jordan, 62–63, 245
Harrison, Gail, 39
Harrison, George, 14–15
Hathaway, Anne, 6
Hawke, Ethan, 151
Hepburn, Katharine, 217
Herbert, Frank, 72
Heyman, David, 8–9
Hirsch, Emile, 184
Hoffman, Brent, 38
Hooper, Tom, 123
Hoult, Nicholas, 134
Hounsou, Djimon, 173, 176
Howard, Ron, 141, 198, 199–201, 245
Hudson, Ernie, 79
Hutton, Timothy, 19

Iñárritu, Alejandro, xii

Jackson, Samuel L., 66, 134
Jobs, Steve, 89
Johnson, Broderick, 130–34, 245
Johnson, Dakota, 193
Johnson, Dwayne, 74
Jones, Caleb Landry, 148
Jones, Jeffrey, 9
Jones, Tommy Lee, 129, 209
Jordan, Michael B., 112–13
Jupe, Noah, 173

Kaling, Mindy, 65
Kaluuya, Daniel, 28, 147
Karl, Harry, 154
Katzenberg, Jeffrey, 47, 56, 108–9, 153, 195–97
Keaton, Michael, 92
Keener, Catherine, 147
Keoghan, Barry, 171
Key, Keegan-Michael, 29, 101
King, Alan, 154
King, Graham, 77, 198, 202, 245
King, Joey, 16
Kingsley, Ben, 114
Kinnear, Greg, 61, 114
Kirhoffer, Nancy, 180–82, 245
Kline, Kevin, 60
Kosove, Andrew, 130–35, 245
Krasinski, John, 173, 175
Kreiz, Ynon, 7
Kunis, Mila, 209
Kwan, Daniel, 102–3

Laden, Osama bin, 87
Langley, Donna, 203
Larson, Brie, 66
Larson, Jonathan, 141–42
Latt, David, 225–26, 245
Lawrence, Jennifer, 80
Lawton, J. F., 109
Lee, Ang, 23–24
Leto, Jared, 193
Levi, Zachary, 101
Levin, Bob, 51, 84, 105, 109, 117–22, 196–97, 243
Levinson, Monica, 179, 245
Lewis, Jerry, 79
Lincoln, Abraham, 110, 150
Lindelof, Damon, 177
Linney, Laura, 184
Lois, George, 190

INDEX OF NAMES

Lopez, Jennifer, 114
Lourd, Bryan, 88
Lucchesi, Gary, 168–69, 245
Luhrmann, Baz, 10–11

Macfarlane, Luke, 187
Macintosh, Cameron, 123
Magee, David, 24
Malek, Rami, 78
Marsden, James, 136
Marshall, Garry, 108, 128–29
Martel, Yann, 24
Matichak, Andi, 143
McDonald, Marie, 154
McDormand, Frances, 211
McQuarrie, Chris, 177
Meledandri, Chris, 35–41, 192, 245
Mercury, Freddie, 77–78
Mestres, Ricardo, 153
Meyer, Stephenie, 111–12
Miller, Ezra, 70
Miller, Frank, 11–12
Miranda, Lin-Manuel, 142
Mitchell, Elvis, 114
Momoa, Jason, 74
Moore, Julianne, 129
Morgan, Chris, 74
Moritz, Neal, 73–74, 136–37, 201, 245
Moss, Elizabeth, 151
Murphy, Eddie, 79
Murray, Bill, 79

Nagenda, Tendo, 21–22, 221, 245
Nelson, Kathy, 39, 208, 245
Neustadter, Lauren Levy, 25
Nichols, Mike, 114–15
Nicholson, Jack, 163
Nolan, Christopher, 1, 76–77, 172
Nolte, Nick, 105
Nunnari, Gianni, 12
Nyong'o, Lupita, 173

O'Brien, Brendan, 33–34, 181
O'Hara, Catherine, 91
Orbison, Roy, 109
Ortega, Jenna, 83
Oswalt, Patton, 226
Owens, Delia, 25

Pablos, Sergio, 35
Panay, Andrew, 18
Panitch, Sanford, 53, 79, 245
Pascal, Amy, 89, 127, 138, 185, 192, 195, 245
Pascal, Pedro, 96–97
Paul, Cinco, 36, 41
Peele, Jordan, 29
Permut, David, 14–16, 65–67, 153–56, 216–17, 245
Perry, Tyler, 101
Phillips, Todd, 191–92
Phoenix, Joaquin, 59, 139
Pitt, Brad, 64, 88–89, 92, 176–77, 219
Plummer, Christopher, 101
Pollack, Sydney, 168
Porter, Cole, 77
Portman, Natalie, 209
Powell, Glen, 81
Pratt, Chris, 134
Presley, Elvis, 10, 217
Press, Terry, 93, 219, 245
Price, Frank, 15
Prince-Bythewood, Gina, 160–62

Quinn, Joseph, 173

Ramsay, Clark, 45
Redford, Robert, 145
Reeves, Keanu, 193
Reitman, Jason, 79
Renaud, Chris, 36–37, 41
Reynolds, David, 131
Reynolds, Debbie, 154

INDEX OF NAMES

Rhames, Ving, 101, 134
Rhys, Paul, 171
Rice, Anne, 128
Richardson, Joely, 19
Rimawi, David, 225–27
Robbie, Margot, 6–9, 64, 139
Robbins, Jerome, 123
Roberts, Julia, 81, 105, 108–9
Rodat, Bob, 75–76
Rodriguez, Michelle, 74, 245
Rogen, Seth, 32–34, 59, 181–82, 187
Rogers, Fred, 46, 56
Ronan, Saoirse, 8
Rosenfelt, Karen, 111
Roth, Eli, 204, 245
Rothman, Tom, 24, 26–28, 44, 47, 71, 79, 133, 218, 233, 245
Rowlands, Gena, 140, 184
Rubin, Rick, 189–90
Rushfield, Richard, 191–92
Russo, Anthony, 22, 103
Russo, Joe, 22, 103
Ryan, Meg, 80
Ryder, Winona, 91–92

Saget, Bob, 65–66
Saldaña, Zoë, 96–97
Salter, Roy, 221, 245
Samuelson, Couper, 7, 143–49, 151–52, 245
Sandler, Adam, 80, 116
Sargent, Bill, 14–15
Scheider, Roy, 45
Scheinert, Daniel, 102–3
Schlessel, Peter, 186, 227–29, 245
Schulman, Cathy, 160, 162–64, 173, 245
Schumer, Amy, 6
Schwartz, Russell, 17–19, 211, 245
Scorsese, Martin, 1, 198
Scott, Randolph, 217
Scott, Ridley, 86, 148, 219

Segel, Jason, 32–33, 187
Sella, Tony, 108, 110, 150–51, 245
Shandling, Garry, 114–15
Shaye, Bob, 18–19
Sherak, William, 82–83, 245
Shropshire, Terilyn, 161
Shue, Elisabeth, 211
Shulman, Tom, 118
Siegel, Bugsy, 155
Simmonds, Millicent, 173
Simon, Neil, 153–55
Smith, Will, 209
Snyder, Zack, 12, 80
Soderbergh, Steven, 11, 240
Spielberg, Steven, 45, 76, 93, 108, 123
Stoller, Nick, 31–34, 181–82, 187–88, 245
Stone, Emma, 80, 220
Streep, Meryl, 87
Streisand, Barbra, 59
Strong, Cecily, 134
Stupnitsky, Gene, 133
Sweeney, Sydney, 81
Swift, Taylor, 10, 54

Tarantino, Quentin, 1
Thames, Mason, 151
Theron, Charlize, 74, 139
Thompson, Anne, 106
Thompson, Emma, 168
Tillman, George Jr., 165–66, 245
Truman, Harry S., 14

Utley, Nancy, 22–23, 208–9, 218, 233, 245

Valenti, Jack, 46, 129
Vaughn, Vince, 87
Villeneuve, Denis, 72–73, 186

Waddingham, Hannah, 134
Walker, Paul, 74–75

INDEX OF NAMES

Wallace, Christopher (the Notorious B.I.G.), 165
Wang, Jonathan, 103
Ward, Sela, 129
Washington, Denzel, 207
Watson, Emma, 106
Wayans, Damon, 66
Weaver, Sigourney, 148
Weinstein, Steve, 155
Weinstock, Marc, 229
Weir, Andy, 186
Weir, Peter, 118–19
Wells, Frank, 195
Whannell, Leigh, 152
Whitaker, Forest, 139–40
Whitmore, James, 14
Williams, Allison, 28
Williams, John, 45
Williams, Marsha, 119
Williams, Pharrell, 39
Williams, Robin, 118–19
Wilson, Owen, 64
Wilson, Rainn, 19
Winehouse, Amy, 77
Winfrey, Oprah, 65, 101
Wise, Robert, 123
Witherspoon, Reese, 25, 65, 122

Yeun, Steven, 101
Yunus, Muhammad, 237

Zaslav, David, 70
Zeffirelli, Franco, 11
Zendaya, 59, 73
Ziskin, Laura, 166
Zwick, Ed, 54